Probability for Finance

Students and instructors alike will benefit from this rigorous, unfussy text, which keeps a clear focus on the basic probabilistic concepts required for an understanding of financial market models, including independence and conditioning. Assuming only some calculus and linear algebra, the text applies key results of measure and integration to probability spaces and random variables, culminating in Central Limit Theory. Consequently it provides essential pre-requisites to graduate-level study of modern finance and, more generally, to the study of stochastic processes.

Results are proved carefully and the key concepts are motivated by concrete examples drawn from financial market models. Students can test their understanding through the large number of exercises that are integral to the text.

EKKEHARD KOPP is Emeritus Professor of Mathematics at the University of Hull. He has published over 50 research papers and five books, on measure and probability, stochastic analysis and mathematical finance. He has taught in the UK, Canada and South Africa, and he serves on the editorial board of the AIMS Library Series.

JAN MALCZAK has published over 20 research papers and taught courses in analysis, differential equations, measure and probability, and the theory of stochastic differential processes. He is currently Professor of Mathematics at AGH University of Science and Technology in Kraków, Poland.

TOMASZ ZASTAWNIAK holds the Chair of Mathematical Finance at the University of York. He has authored about 50 research publications and four books. He has supervised four PhD dissertations and around 80 MSc dissertations in mathematical finance.

Mastering Mathematical Finance

Mastering Mathematical Finance is a series of short books that cover all core topics and the most common electives offered in Master's programmes in mathematical or quantitative finance. The books are closely coordinated and largely self-contained, and can be used efficiently in combination but also individually.

The MMF books start financially from scratch and mathematically assume only undergraduate calculus, linear algebra and elementary probability theory. The necessary mathematics is developed rigorously, with emphasis on a natural development of mathematical ideas and financial intuition, and the readers quickly see real-life financial applications, both for motivation and as the ultimate end for the theory. All books are written for both teaching and self-study, with worked examples, exercises and solutions.

[DMFM] *Discrete Models of Financial Markets,*
        Marek Capiński, Ekkehard Kopp

[PF]   *Probability for Finance,*
        Ekkehard Kopp, Jan Malczak, Tomasz Zastawniak

[SCF]   *Stochastic Calculus for Finance,*
        Marek Capiński, Ekkehard Kopp, Janusz Traple

[BSM]   *The Black–Scholes Model,*
        Marek Capiński, Ekkehard Kopp

[PTRM] *Portfolio Theory and Risk Management,*
        Maciej J. Capiński, Ekkehard Kopp

[NMFC] *Numerical Methods in Finance with C++,*
        Maciej J. Capiński, Tomasz Zastawniak

[SIR]   *Stochastic Interest Rates,*
        Daragh McInerney, Tomasz Zastawniak

[CR]   *Credit Risk,*
        Marek Capiński, Tomasz Zastawniak

[FE]   *Financial Econometrics,*
        Marek Capiński

[SCAF] *Stochastic Control Applied to Finance,*
        Szymon Peszat, Tomasz Zastawniak

Series editors Marek Capiński, *AGH University of Science and Technology, Kraków*; Ekkehard Kopp, *University of Hull*; Tomasz Zastawniak, *University of York*

Probability for Finance

EKKEHARD KOPP
University of Hull, Hull, UK

JAN MALCZAK
AGH University of Science and Technology, Kraków, Poland

TOMASZ ZASTAWNIAK
University of York, York, UK

CAMBRIDGE
UNIVERSITY PRESS

University Printing House, Cambridge CB2 8BS, United Kingdom

One Liberty Plaza, 20th Floor, New York, NY 10006, USA

477 Williamstown Road, Port Melbourne, VIC 3207, Australia

314-321, 3rd Floor, Plot 3, Splendor Forum, Jasola District Centre, New Delhi - 110025, India

79 Anson Road, #06-04/06, Singapore 079906

Cambridge University Press is part of the University of Cambridge.

It furthers the University's mission by disseminating knowledge in the pursuit of
education, learning and research at the highest international levels of excellence.

www.cambridge.org
Information on this title: www.cambridge.org/9780521175579

© Ekkehard Kopp, Jan Malczak and Tomasz Zastawniak 2014

First published 2014

A catalogue record for this publication is available from the British Library

ISBN 978-1-107-00249-4 Hardback
ISBN 978-0-521-17557-9 Paperback

Additional resources for this publication at www.cambridge.org/9780521175579

Contents

Preface

Mathematical models of financial markets rely in fundamental ways on the concepts and tools of modern probability theory. This book provides a concise but rigorous account of the probabilistic ideas and techniques most commonly used in such models. The treatment is self-contained, requiring only calculus and linear algebra as pre-requisites, and complete proofs are given – some longer constructions and proofs are deferred to the ends of chapters to ensure the smooth flow of key ideas.

New concepts are motivated through examples drawn from finance. The selection and ordering of the material are strongly guided by the applications we have in mind. Many of these applications appear more fully in later volumes of the 'Mastering Mathematical Finance' series, including [SCF], [BSM] and [NMFC]. This volume provides the essential mathematical background of the financial models described in detail there.

In adding to the extensive literature on probability theory we have not sought to provide a comprehensive treatment of the mathematical theory and its manifold applications. We focus instead on the more limited objective of writing a fully rigorous, yet concise and accessible, account of the basic concepts underlying widely used market models. The book should be read in conjunction with its partner volume [SCF], which describes the properties of stochastic processes used in these models.

In the first two chapters we introduce probability spaces, distributions and random variables from scratch. We assume a basic level of mathematical maturity in our description of the principal aspects of measures and integrals, including the construction of the Lebesgue integral and the important convergence results for integrals. Beginning with discrete examples familiar to readers of [DMFM], we motivate each construction by means of specific distributions used in financial modelling. Chapter 3 introduces product measures and random vectors, and highlights the key concept of independence, while Chapter 4 is devoted to a thorough discussion of conditioning, moving from the familiar discrete setting via the properties of inner product spaces and the Radon–Nikodym theorem to the construction of general conditional expectations for integrable random variables. The final chapter explores key limit theorems for sequences of random variables, beginning with orthonormal sequences of square-integrable functions, followed by a discussion of the relationships between various modes of convergence, and concluding with an introduction to weak convergence and the Central Limit Theorem for independent identically distributed random variables of finite mean and variance.

Concrete examples and the large number of exercises form an integral part of this text. Solutions to the exercises and further material can be found at www.cambridge.org/9781107002494.

1

Probability spaces

In all spheres of life we make decisions based upon incomplete information. Frameworks for predicting the uncertain outcomes of future events have been around for centuries, notably in the age-old pastime of gambling. Much of modern finance draws on this experience. Probabilistic models have become an essential feature of financial market practice.

We begin at the beginning: this chapter is an introduction to basic concepts in probability, motivated by simple models for the evolution of stock prices. Emphasis is placed on the collection of events whose probability we need to study, together with the probability function defined on these events. For this we use the machinery of measure theory, including the construction of Lebesgue measure on $\mathbb{R}$. We introduce and study integration with respect to a measure, with emphasis on powerful limit theorems. In particular, we specialise to the case of Lebesgue integral and compare it with the Riemann integral familiar to students of basic calculus.

1.1   Discrete examples

The crucial feature of financial markets is uncertainty related to the future prices of various quantities, like stock prices, interest rates, foreign exchange rates, market indices, or commodity prices. Our goal is to build a mathematical model capturing this aspect of reality.

Example 1.1

Consider how we could model stock prices. The current stock price (the **spot price**) is usually known, say 10. We may be interested in the price at some fixed future time. This future price involves some uncertainty. Suppose first that in this period of time the stock price jumps a number of times, going either up or down by 0.50 (such a price change is called a **tick**). After two such jumps there will be three possible prices: $9, 10, 11$. After 20 jumps there will be a wider range of possible prices: $0, 1, 2, \ldots, 19, 20$.

The set of all possible outcomes will be denoted by Ω and called the **sample space**. The elements of Ω will be denoted by ω. For now we assume that Ω is a finite set.

Example 1.2

If we are interested in the prices after two jumps, we could take $\Omega = \{9, 10, 11\}$. If we want to describe the prices after 20 jumps, we would take $\Omega = \{0, 1, 2, \ldots, 19, 20\}$.

The next step in building a model is to answer to the following question: for a subset $A \subset \Omega$, called an **event**, what is the probability that the outcome lies in A? The number representing the answer will be denoted by $P(A)$, and the convention is to require $P(A) \in [0, 1]$ with $P(\Omega) = 1$ and $P(\varnothing) = 0$. We shall write $p_\omega = P(\{\omega\})$ for any $\omega \in \Omega$. Given p_ω for all $\omega \in \Omega$, the function P is then constructed for any $A \subset \Omega$ by adding the values attached to the elements of A,

$$P(A) = \sum_{\omega \in A} p_\omega.$$

This immediately implies an important property of P, called **additivity**,

$$P(A \cup B) = P(A) + P(B) \quad \text{for any disjoint events } A, B.$$

By induction, it readily extends to

$$P\left(\bigcup_{i=1}^{m} A_i\right) = \sum_{i=1}^{m} P(A_i) \quad \text{for any pairwise disjoint events } A_1, \ldots, A_m.$$

Example 1.3
Consider $\Omega = \{9, 10, 11\}$. The simplest choice is to assign equal probabilities $p_9 = p_{10} = p_{11} = \frac{1}{3}$ to all single-element subsets of Ω.

Example 1.4
In the case of $\Omega = \{0, 1, 2, \ldots, 19, 20\}$ we could, once again, try equal probabilities for all single-element subsets of Ω, namely, $p_0 = p_1 = \cdots = p_{20} = \frac{1}{21}$.

The **uniform probability** on a finite Ω assigns equal probabilities $p_\omega = \frac{1}{N}$ for each $\omega \in \Omega$, where N is the number of elements in Ω.

Example 1.5
Uniform probability does not appear to be consistent with the scheme in Example 1.1, where the stock prices result from consecutive jumps by ±0.50 from an initial price 10. In the case of two consecutive jumps one might argue that the middle price 10 should carry more weight since it can be arrived at in two ways (up–down or down–up), while either of the other two values can occur in just one way (down–down for 9, up–up for 11). Hence, price 10 would be twice as likely as 9 or 11.
To reflect these considerations on $\Omega = \{9, 10, 11\}$ we can take $p_9 = \frac{1}{4}$, $p_{10} = \frac{1}{2}$, $p_{11} = \frac{1}{4}$.

Example 1.6
Similarly, for $\Omega = \{0, 1, 2, \ldots, 19, 20\}$ we can take $p_n = \binom{20}{n}\frac{1}{2^{20}}$, where $\binom{20}{n} = \frac{20!}{n!(20-n)!}$ is the number of scenarios consisting of n upwards and $20-n$ downwards price jumps of 0.50 from the initial price 10, with each scenario equally likely. This is illustrated in Figure 1.1.

In general, when for an N-element Ω we have $p_n = \binom{N}{n}\frac{1}{2^N}$, we call this the **symmetric binomial probability**. Clearly, $\sum_{n=0}^{N} p_n = 1$.

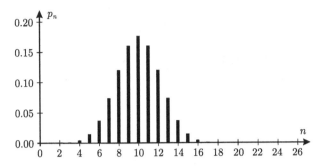

Figure 1.1 Binomial probability and additive jumps.

The mechanism of price jumps by constant additive ticks is not entirely satisfactory as a model for stock prices. After sufficiently many jumps, the range of possible prices will include negative values. To have a more realistic model we need to adjust this mechanism of price jumps.

Example 1.7
The first price jump of ±0.50 means that the price changes by ±5%. In subsequent steps we shall now allow the prices to go up or down by 5% rather than by a constant tick of 0.50. The possible prices will then be $\Omega = \{\omega_n : n = 0, 1, 2, \ldots, 19, 20\}$ after 20 jumps, with $\omega_n = 10 \times 1.05^n \times 0.95^{20-n}$. The prices will remain positive for any number of jumps. We choose the probabilities in a similar manner as before, $p_{\omega_n} = \binom{20}{n} \frac{1}{2^{20}}$. Compare Figure 1.2 with Figure 1.1 to observe a subtle but crucial shift in the distribution of stock prices.

The above examples restrict the possible stock prices to a finite set. In an attempt to extend the model we might want to allow an infinite sequence of possible prices, that is, a countable set Ω.

Example 1.8
Suppose that the number of stock price jumps occurring within a fixed time period is not prescribed, but can be an arbitrary integer N. To be specific, suppose that the probability of N jumps is

$$q_N = \frac{\lambda^N e^{-\lambda}}{N!}$$

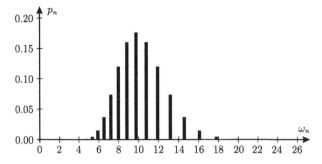

Figure 1.2 Binomial probability and multiplicative jumps.

with $N = 0, 1, 2, \ldots$ for some parameter $\lambda > 0$. The probability of large N is small, but there is no upper bound on N, allowing for some hectic trading. Clearly,

$$\sum_{N=0}^{\infty} q_N = \sum_{N=0}^{\infty} \frac{\lambda^N e^{-\lambda}}{N!} = e^{-\lambda} \sum_{N=0}^{\infty} \frac{\lambda^N}{N!} = e^{-\lambda} e^{\lambda} = 1.$$

This is called the **Poisson probability** with parameter λ.

Furthermore, conditioned on there being N jumps, the possible final stock prices will be described by means of the binomial probability and multiplicative jumps. We assume, like in Example 1.7, that each jump incerases/reduces the stock price by 5% with probability $\frac{1}{2}$. The stock price at time T will become

$$S(T) = 10 \times 1.05^n \times 0.95^{N-n}$$

with probability

$$p_{N,n} = q_N \binom{N}{n} \frac{1}{2^N},$$

that is, the probability q_N of $N = 0, 1, 2, \ldots$ jumps multiplied by the probability $\binom{N}{n} \frac{1}{2^N}$ of n upwards price movements among those N jumps, where $0 \leq n \leq N$. We take Ω to be the set of such pairs of integers N, n. The formula $P(A) = \sum_{\omega \in A} p_\omega$ defining the probability of an event now includes infinite sets $A \subset \Omega$.

This example shows that it is natural to consider a stronger version of the additivity property:

$$P\left(\bigcup_{i=1}^{\infty} A_i\right) = \sum_{i=1}^{\infty} P(A_i)$$

for any sequence of pairwise disjoint events $A_1, A_2, \ldots \subset \Omega$. This is known as **countable additivity**.

Example 1.9
Another example where a countable set emerges in a natural way is related to modelling the instant when something unpredictable may happen. Time is measured by the number of discrete steps (of some fixed but unspecified length). At each step there is an upward/downward price jump with probabilities $p, 1 - p \in (0, 1)$, respectively. The probability that an upward jump occurs for the first time at the nth step can be expressed as $p_n = (1 - p)^{n-1} p$. It is easy to check that $\sum_{n=1}^{\infty} p_n = 1$, which gives a probability on $\Omega = \{1, 2, \ldots\}$. This defines the **geometric probability**.

1.2 Probability spaces

Countable additivity turns out to be the perfect condition for probability theory. The actual construction of a probability measure can present difficulties. In particular, it is sometimes impossible to define P for all subsets of Ω. The domain of P has to be specified, and it is natural to impose some restrictions on that domain ensuring that countable additivity can be formulated.

Definition 1.10
A **probability space** is a triple $(\Omega, \mathcal{F}, P)$ as follows.
   (i) Ω is a non-empty set (called the **sample space**, or set of scenarios).
   (ii) $\mathcal{F}$ is a family of subsets of Ω (called **events**) satisfying the following conditions:
   - $\Omega \in \mathcal{F}$;
   - if $A_i \in \mathcal{F}$ for $i = 1, 2, \ldots$, then $\bigcup_{i=1}^{\infty} A_i \in \mathcal{F}$ (we say that $\mathcal{F}$ is **closed under countable unions**);
   - if $A \in \mathcal{F}$, then $\Omega \setminus A \in \mathcal{F}$ (we say that $\mathcal{F}$ is **closed under complements**).
   Such a family of sets $\mathcal{F}$ is called a σ-**field** on Ω.

(iii) P assigns numbers to events,

$$P : \mathcal{F} \to [0,1],$$

and we assume that
- $P(\Omega) = 1$;
- for all sequences of events $A_i \in \mathcal{F}$, $i = 1, 2, 3, \ldots$ that are pairwise disjoint ($A_i \cap A_j = \varnothing$ for $i \neq j$) we have

$$P\left(\bigcup_{i=1}^{\infty} A_i\right) = \sum_{i=1}^{\infty} P(A_i).$$

This property is called **countable additivity**.

A function P satisfying these conditions is called a **probability measure** (or simply a **probability**).

Exercise 1.1 Let $\mathcal{F}$ be a σ-field and $A_1, A_2, \ldots \in \mathcal{F}$. Show that $\bigcap_{i=1}^{n} A_i \in \mathcal{F}$ for each $n = 1, 2, \ldots$ and that $\bigcap_{i=1}^{\infty} A_i \in \mathcal{F}$.

Exercise 1.2 Suppose that $\mathcal{F}$ is a σ-field containing all open intervals in $[0, 1]$ with rational endpoints. Show that $\mathcal{F}$ contains all open intervals in $[0, 1]$.

Before proceeding further we note some basic properties of probability measures.

Theorem 1.11

If P is a probability measure, then:

 (i) $P(\bigcup_{i=1}^{n} A_i) = \sum_{i=1}^{n} P(A_i)$ *for any pairwise disjoint events $A_i \in \mathcal{F}$, $i = 1, 2, \ldots, n$* (**finite additivity**)*;*

 (ii) $P(\Omega \setminus A) = 1 - P(A)$ *for any $A \in \mathcal{F}$; in particular, $P(\varnothing) = 0$;*

 (iii) $A \subset B$ *implies $P(A) \leq P(B)$ for any $A, B \in \mathcal{F}$* (**monotonicity**)*;*

 (iv) $P(\bigcup_{i=1}^{n} A_i) \leq \sum_{i=1}^{n} P(A_i)$ *for any $A_i \in \mathcal{F}$, $i = 1, 2, \ldots, n$* (**finite sub-additivity**)*;*

 (v) *if $A_{n+1} \supset A_n \in \mathcal{F}$ for all $n \geq 1$, then $P(\bigcup_{n=1}^{\infty} A_n) = \lim_{m \to \infty} P(A_m)$;*

 (vi) $P(\bigcup_{i=1}^{\infty} A_i) \leq \sum_{i=1}^{\infty} P(A_i)$ *for any $A_i \in \mathcal{F}$, $i = 1, 2, \ldots$* (**countable subadditivity**)*;*

 (vii) *if $A_{n+1} \subset A_n \in \mathcal{F}$ for all $n \geq 1$, then $P(\bigcap_{n=1}^{\infty} A_n) = \lim_{m \to \infty} P(A_m)$.*

Proof   (i) Let $A_{n+1} = A_{n+2} = \cdots = \varnothing$ and apply countable additivity.

(ii) Use (i) with $n = 2$, $A_1 = A$, $A_2 = \Omega \setminus A$.

(iii) Since $B = A \cup (B \setminus A)$ and we have disjoint components, we can apply (i), so

$$P(B) = P(A) + P(B \setminus A) \geq P(A).$$

(iv) For $n = 2$,

$$P(A_1 \cup A_2) = P(A_1 \cup (A_2 \setminus A_1)) = P(A_1) + P(A_2 \setminus A_1) \leq P(A_1) + P(A_2)$$

and then use induction to complete the proof for arbitrary n, where the induction step will be the same as the above argument.

(v) Using the above properties, we have (with $A_0 = \varnothing$)

$$P\left(\bigcup_{n=1}^{\infty} A_n\right) = P\left(\bigcup_{n=0}^{\infty}(A_{n+1} \setminus A_n)\right) = \sum_{n=0}^{\infty} P(A_{n+1} \setminus A_n)$$

$$= \lim_{m\to\infty} \sum_{n=0}^{m} P(A_{n+1} \setminus A_n) = \lim_{m\to\infty} P\left(\bigcup_{n=0}^{m}(A_{n+1} \setminus A_n)\right)$$

$$= \lim_{m\to\infty} P(A_{m+1}).$$

(vi) We put $B_n = \bigcup_{i=1}^{n} A_i$, so that $B_{n+1} \supset B_n \in \mathcal{F}$ for all $n \geq 1$, and using (v) we pass to the limit in the finite subadditivity relation (iv):

$$P\left(\bigcup_{n=1}^{\infty} A_n\right) = P\left(\bigcup_{n=1}^{\infty} B_n\right) = \lim_{m\to\infty} P(B_m) = \lim_{m\to\infty} P\left(\bigcup_{n=1}^{m} A_n\right)$$

$$\leq \lim_{m\to\infty} \sum_{n=1}^{m} P(A_n) = \sum_{n=1}^{\infty} P(A_n).$$

(vii) Take $A = \bigcap_{n=1}^{\infty} A_n$, note that $P(A) = 1 - P(\Omega \setminus A)$ by (ii), and apply (v):

$$P(A) = 1 - P\left(\bigcup_{n=1}^{\infty}(\Omega \setminus A_n)\right)$$

$$= 1 - \lim_{m\to\infty} P(\Omega \setminus A_m) = \lim_{m\to\infty} P(A_m).$$

$\qquad\qquad\qquad\qquad\qquad\qquad\qquad\qquad\qquad\qquad\qquad\qquad\qquad\qquad\qquad$ □

The construction of interesting probability measures requires some labour, as we shall see. However, a few simple examples can be given immediately.

Example 1.12
Take any non-empty set Ω, fix $\omega \in \Omega$, and define $\delta_\omega(A) = 1$ if $\omega \in A$ and $\delta_\omega(A) = 0$ if $\omega \notin A$, for any $A \subset \Omega$. It is a probability measure, called the **unit mass,** also known as the **Dirac measure,** concentrated at ω. If $\mathcal{F}$ is taken to be the family of all subsets of Ω, then $(\Omega, \mathcal{F}, \delta_\omega)$ is a probability space.

Example 1.13
Let N be a positive integer. On $\Omega = \{0, 1, \ldots, N\}$ define

$$P(A) = \sum_{n=0}^{N} \binom{N}{n} \frac{1}{2^N} \delta_n(A)$$

for any $A \subset \Omega$, where δ_n is the unit mass concentrated at n from Example 1.12. We take $\mathcal{F}$ to be the family of all subsets of Ω. Then $(\Omega, \mathcal{F}, P)$ is a probability space. This is clearly the symmetric binomial probability considered earlier.

More generally for the same Ω and any $p \in (0, 1)$, the **binomial probability** with parameters N, p is defined by setting

$$P(A) = \sum_{n=0}^{N} \binom{N}{n} p^n (1 - p)^{N-n} \delta_n(A).$$

It is immediate from the binomial theorem that $P(\Omega) = 1$.

This example is often described as providing the probabilities of events relating to the repeated tossing of a coin (where successive tosses are assumed not to affect each other, in a sense that will be made precise later): if for any given toss the probability of 'Heads' is p, the probability of finding exactly k 'Heads' in N tosses is $\binom{N}{k} p^k (1 - p)^{N-k}$.

Example 1.14
Fix $\lambda > 0$, let $\Omega = \{0, 1, 2, \ldots\}$ and let $\mathcal{F}$ be the family of all subsets of Ω. For any $A \in \mathcal{F}$ put

$$P(A) = \sum_{n=0}^{\infty} e^{-\lambda} \frac{\lambda^n}{n!} \delta_n(A),$$

where δ_n is the unit mass concentrated at n. Then $(\Omega, \mathcal{F}, P)$ is a probability space. This gives the Poisson probability mentioned in Example 1.8.

In addition to subsets of $\mathbb{R}$, for example the set $[0, \infty)$ of all non-negative real numbers, it often proves convenient to consider sets containing ∞ or $-\infty$ in addition to real numbers. For instance, we write $[-\infty, \infty]$ for the set of all real numbers in $\mathbb{R}$ together with ∞ and $-\infty$, and $[0, \infty]$ to denote the set of all non-negative real numbers together with ∞.

Probability measures belong to a wider class of countably additive set functions taking values in $[0, \infty]$. Let Ω be a non-empty set and let $\mathcal{F}$ be a σ-field of subsets of Ω.

Definition 1.15
We say that $\mu : \mathcal{F} \rightarrow [0, \infty]$ is a **measure** and call $(\Omega, \mathcal{F}, \mu)$ a **measure space** if

(i) $\mu(\varnothing) = 0$;
(ii) for any pairwise disjoint sets $A_i \in \mathcal{F}$, $i = 1, 2, \ldots$

$$\mu\left(\bigcup_{i=1}^{\infty} A_i\right) = \sum_{i=1}^{\infty} \mu(A_i).$$

Note that some of the terms $\mu(A_i)$ in the sum may be infinite, and we use the convention $x + \infty = \infty$ for any $x \in [0, \infty]$.

Moreover, we call μ a **finite measure** if, in addition, $\mu(\Omega) < \infty$.

The properties listed in Theorem 1.11 and their proofs can readily be adapted to the case of an arbitrary measure.

Corollary 1.16
Properties (i) *and* (iii)–(vi) *listed in Theorem 1.11 remain true for any measure μ. If we assume in addition that $\mu(\Omega) < \infty$, then* (ii) *becomes $\mu(\Omega \setminus A) = \mu(\Omega) - \mu(A)$. Moreover, if $\mu(A_1)$ is finite, then* (vii) *still holds.*

Example 1.17
For any non-empty set Ω and any $A \subset \Omega$ let

$$\mu(A) = \sum_{\omega \in A} \delta_\omega(A),$$

where δ_ω is the unit mass concentrated at ω. The sum is equal to the number of elements in A if A is a finite set, and ∞ otherwise. Then μ is a measure, called the **counting measure**, on Ω defined on the family $\mathcal{F}$ consisting of all subsets of Ω. It is not a probability measure, however, unless Ω is a one-element set.

1.3 Lebesgue measure

The discrete stock price models in Section 1.1 admit only a limited range of prices. To remove this restriction it is natural to allow future prices to take any value in some interval in $\mathbb{R}$. Probability spaces capable of capturing this modelling choice require the notion of Lebesgue measure, introduced in this section. In particular, it will facilitate a study of log-normally distributed stock prices and it will prove instrumental in the development of stochastic calculus, which is of fundamental importance in mathematical finance.

To begin with, take any open interval $I = (a, b) \subset \mathbb{R}$, where $a \le b$. We denote the length of the interval by

$$l(I) = b - a.$$

The family of such intervals will be denoted by $\mathcal{I}$. Observe that $\varnothing = (a, a) \in \mathcal{I}$, and that $l(\varnothing) = 0$.

However, $\mathcal{I}$ is not a σ-field, and the length l as a function defined on $\mathcal{I}$ is not a measure. Can this function be extended to a larger domain, a σ-field containing $\mathcal{I}$, on which it will become a measure? The answer to this question is positive, as we shall see in Theorem 1.19, but not immediately obvious.

First of all, we need to identify the σ-field to provide the domain of such a measure. To make the task of extending the length function easier, we want the σ-field to be as small as possible, as long as it contains $\mathcal{I}$. The intersection of all σ-fields containing $\mathcal{I}$, denoted by

$$\mathcal{B}(\mathbb{R}) = \bigcap \{\mathcal{F} : \mathcal{F} \text{ is a } \sigma\text{-field on } \mathbb{R} \text{ and } \mathcal{I} \subset \mathcal{F}\} \tag{1.1}$$

and called the family of **Borel sets** in $\mathbb{R}$, is the smallest σ-field containing $\mathcal{I}$ as shown in the next exercise.

Exercise 1.3 Show that:
(1) $\mathcal{B}(\mathbb{R})$ is a σ-field on $\mathbb{R}$ such that $\mathcal{I} \subset \mathcal{B}(\mathbb{R})$;
(2) if $\mathcal{F}$ is a σ-field on $\mathbb{R}$ such that $\mathcal{I} \subset \mathcal{F}$, then $\mathcal{B}(\mathbb{R}) \subset \mathcal{F}$.

We could equally have begun with closed intervals $[a, b]$ since this class of intervals leads to the same σ-field $\mathcal{B}(\mathbb{R})$. To see this we only need to note that $[a,b] = \bigcap_{n=1}^{\infty}(a - \frac{1}{n}, b + \frac{1}{n})$ and $(a,b) = \bigcup_{n=1}^{\infty}[a + \frac{1}{n}, b - \frac{1}{n}]$.

In particular, singleton sets $\{a\} = [a, a]$ belong to $\mathcal{B}(\mathbb{R})$ for all $a \in \mathbb{R}$, and so do all finite or countable subsets of $\mathbb{R}$. Hence the set $\mathbb{Q}$ of rationals and its complement $\mathbb{R} \setminus \mathbb{Q}$, the set of irrationals, also belong to $\mathcal{B}(\mathbb{R})$.

Definition 1.18
For each $A \in \mathcal{B}(\mathbb{R})$ we put

$$m(A) = \inf\left\{\sum_{k=1}^{\infty} l(J_k) : A \subset \bigcup_{k=1}^{\infty} J_k\right\}, \qquad (1.2)$$

where the infimum is taken over all sequences $(J_k)_{k=1}^{\infty}$ consisting of open intervals. We call m the **Lebesgue measure** defined on $\mathcal{B}(\mathbb{R})$.

When $A \subset \bigcup_{k=1}^{\infty} J_k$ we say that A is **covered** by the sequence of sets $(J_k)_{k=1}^{\infty}$. The idea is to cover A by a sequence of open intervals, consider the total length of these intervals as an overestimate of the measure of A, and take the infimum of the total length over all such coverings.

Theorem 1.19
$m : \mathcal{B}(\mathbb{R}) \to [0, \infty]$ *is a measure such that* $m((a,b)) = b - a$ *for all* $a \leq b$.

The proof can be found in Section 1.5. The details are not needed in the rest of this volume, but any serious student of mathematics applied in modern finance should have seen them at least once!

Remark 1.20
Lebesgue measure can be defined on a σ-field larger than $\mathcal{B}(\mathbb{R})$, but cannot be extended to a measure defined on all subsets of $\mathbb{R}$.[1]

Exercise 1.4 Find $m\left(\left[\frac{1}{2}, 2\right)\right)$ and $m\left([-2, 3] \cup [3, 8]\right)$.

---

[1] See, for example, M. Capiński and E. Kopp, *Measure, Integral and Probability*, 2nd edition, Springer-Verlag 2004.

Exercise 1.5 Compute $m\left(\bigcup_{n=2}^{\infty}\left(\frac{1}{n+1}, \frac{1}{n}\right]\right)$.

Exercise 1.6 Find $m(\mathbb{N})$, $m(\mathbb{Q})$, $m(\mathbb{R}\backslash\mathbb{Q})$, $m(\{x \in \mathbb{R} : \sin x = \cos x\})$.

Exercise 1.7 Show that the **Cantor set** C, constructed below, is uncountable, but that $m(C) = 0$.

The Cantor set is defined to be $C = \bigcap_{n=0}^{\infty} C_n$, where $C_0 = [0, 1]$, C_1 is obtained by removing from C_0 the 'middle third' $(\frac{1}{3}, \frac{2}{3})$ of the interval $[0, 1]$, C_2 is formed by similarly removing from C_1 the 'middle thirds' $(\frac{1}{9}, \frac{2}{9})$, $(\frac{7}{9}, \frac{8}{9})$ of the two intervals $[0, \frac{1}{3}]$, $[\frac{2}{3}, 1]$, and so on. The set C_n consists of 2^n closed intervals, each of length $(\frac{1}{3})^n$.

Exercise 1.8 Show that for any $A \in \mathcal{B}(\mathbb{R})$ and for any $x \in \mathbb{R}$

$$m(A) = m(A + x),$$

where $A + x = \{a + x \in \mathbb{R} : a \in A\}$. This property of Lebesgue measure is called **translation invariance**.

Lebesgue measure allows us to define a probability on any bounded interval $\Omega = [a, b]$ by writing, for any Borel set $A \subset [a, b]$,

$$P(A) = \frac{m(A)}{m(\Omega)}.$$

This is called the **uniform probability** on $[a, b]$.

1.4 Lebesgue integral

As we noticed in the discrete case, uniform probability does not lend itself well to modelling stock prices. Similarly, in the continuous case, we need more than just the uniform probability on an interval. A natural idea is to replace the sum $P(A) = \sum_{\omega \in A} p_{\omega}$, used in the discrete case to express the probability of an event A, by an integral understood in an appropriate sense. The simplest case is that of an integral of a continuous function on $\mathbb{R}$ when

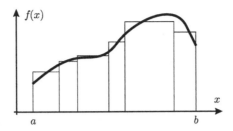

Figure 1.3 Approximating the area under the graph of f by rectangles.

$A = [a, b]$ is an interval. With this in mind, we briefly review some basic facts concerning integrals of continuous functions.

Riemann integral

Let $f : [a, b] \to \mathbb{R}$ be a continuous function. In this case f must be bounded, so the area under the graph of f is finite. To approximate this area we divide it into strips by choosing a sequence of numbers $a = c_0 < c_1 < \cdots < c_n = b$ and approximate each strip by a rectangle. We take the height of such a rectangle with base $[c_{i-1}, c_i]$ to be $f(x_i)$ for some $x_i \in [c_{i-1}, c_i]$, see Figure 1.3. The total area of the rectangles is

$$S_n = \sum_{i=1}^{n} f(x_i)(c_i - c_{i-1}).$$

Let $\delta_n = \max_{i=1,\dots,n} |c_i - c_{i-1}|$. The sequence S_n for $n = 1, 2, \dots$ converges to a limit independent of the way the c_i and x_i are selected, as long as $\lim_{n \to \infty} \delta_n = 0$. We call this limit the **Riemann integral** of f over $[a, b]$ and denote it by

$$\int_a^b f(x)\, dx = \lim_{n \to \infty} S_n.$$

The integral $\int_a^b f(x)\, dx$ exists and is finite for any continuous function f. The same applies to bounded functions having at most a countable number points of discontinuity.

There are, however, some fairly obvious functions for which the Riemann integral cannot be defined.

Example 1.21

Consider the function $f : \mathbb{R} \to [0, \infty)$ defined as

$$f(x) = \begin{cases} 0 & \text{if } x \in \mathbb{Q}, \\ 1 & \text{if } x \in \mathbb{R} \setminus \mathbb{Q}. \end{cases}$$

Fix a sequence $0 = c_0 < c_1 < \cdots < c_n = 1$ of points in the interval $[0, 1]$. Each subinterval $[c_{i-1}, c_i]$ contains both rational and irrational numbers, so taking the x_i to be rationals we get

$$\sum_{i=1}^{n} f(x_i)(c_i - c_{i-1}) = 0,$$

while for irrational x_i we get

$$\sum_{i=1}^{n} f(x_i)(c_i - c_{i-1}) = 1.$$

As n approaches infinity we can get a different limit (or in fact no limit at all), depending on the choice of the x_i, which means that the Riemann integral $\int_0^1 f(x)\,dx$ does not exist.

The following result captures the relationship between derivatives and Riemann integrals.

Theorem 1.22

Let $f : [a, b] \to \mathbb{R}$ be a continuous function. Then we have the following.

(i) *The function defined for any $x \in [a, b]$ by*

$$F(x) = \int_a^x f(y)\,dy$$

is differentiable and its derivative at any $x \in [a, b]$ (at a and b we take right- or left-sided derivatives, respectively) is

$$F'(x) = f(x). \tag{1.3}$$

(ii) *For any function $F : [a, b] \to \mathbb{R}$ satisfying (1.3)*

$$\int_a^b f(x)\,dx = F(b) - F(a).$$

A function F satisfying (1.3) is called an **antiderivative** of f. Such a function is unique up to a constant.

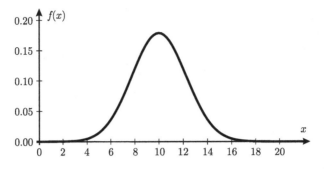

Figure 1.4 Normal density.

Some technicalities are involved to justify these claims about the Riemann integral, of course, but they are not needed in what follows. These elementary techniques of integration form part of any calculus course.

The Riemann integral makes it possible to describe the probability of any event represented by an interval $A = [a, b]$ as the integral

$$P(A) = \int_a^b f(x)\,dx. \tag{1.4}$$

of a continuous (or piecewise continuous) function $f : \mathbb{R} \to [0, \infty)$, as long as

$$\int_{-\infty}^{\infty} f(x)\,dx = 1. \tag{1.5}$$

Here we have used the **indefinite Riemann integral**, defined as $\int_{-\infty}^{\infty} f(x)\,dx = \lim_{c \to \infty} \int_{-c}^{c} f(x)\,dx$.

Example 1.23

Take

$$f(x) = \frac{1}{\sigma\sqrt{2\pi}} e^{-\frac{(x-\mu)^2}{2\sigma^2}}, \tag{1.6}$$

where $\mu \in \mathbb{R}$ and $\sigma > 0$ are parameters. This is called a **normal** (or **Gaussian**) **density**.

In Figure 1.4 we sketch the graph for $\mu = 10$ and $\sigma = 2.236$. As we shall see in Example 5.54, this choice of parameters is related to Example 1.6, where the stock prices change in an additive manner over 20 time steps, which was illustrated in Figure 1.1.

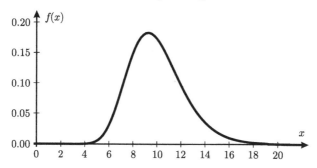

Figure 1.5 Log-normal density.

From the standpoint of modelling stock prices a disadvantage of the normal density is that the probability of negative values is non-zero, which is hardly acceptable when modelling prices even if, as the graph suggests, this probability may be small.

Exercise 1.9 Verify that f given by (1.6) satisfies (1.5).

Example 1.24
An example related to the multiplicative changes of stock prices discussed in Example 1.7 is based on the choice of

$$f(x) = \begin{cases} \frac{1}{x\sigma\sqrt{2\pi}} e^{-\frac{(\ln x - \mu)^2}{2\sigma^2}} & \text{for } x > 0, \\ 0 & \text{for } x \le 0, \end{cases} \tag{1.7}$$

called a **log-normal density**.

The graph for $\mu = 2.2776$ and $\sigma = 0.2238$ is depicted in Figure 1.5. Compare this with Figure 1.2. These values are related to those in Example 1.7, as will be explained in Example 5.55.

Negative prices are excluded. The log-normal density is widely accepted by the financial community as providing a standard model of stock prices.

> **Exercise 1.10**   Verify that f given by (1.7) satisfies (1.5).

Integral with respect to a measure

Difficulties arise when P given by the Riemann integral (1.4) needs to be extended from intervals to a measure on a σ-field. To minimize effort, we take the smallest σ-field containing intervals, that is, the σ-field of Borel sets $\mathcal{B}(\mathbb{R})$, just like we did when introducing Lebesgue measure m.

We outline the constructions involved in this extension, leaving routine verifications as exercises. While we aim primarily to construct an integral on the measure space $(\mathbb{R}, \mathcal{B}(\mathbb{R}), m)$, this is just as easy on an arbitrary measure space $(\Omega, \mathcal{F}, \mu)$, which is what we will now do, thereby achieving greater generality.

First we integrate so-called simple functions. The **indicator function** of any $A \subset \Omega$ will be denoted by

$$\mathbf{1}_A(x) = \begin{cases} 1 & \text{if } x \in A, \\ 0 & \text{if } x \in \Omega \setminus A. \end{cases}$$

Definition 1.25

By definition a (non-negative) **simple function** has the form

$$s = \sum_{i=1}^{n} s_i \mathbf{1}_{A_i},$$

where $A_1, \ldots, A_n \in \mathcal{F}$ are pairwise disjoint sets with $\bigcup_{i=1}^{n} A_i = \Omega$, and where $s_i \geq 0$ for $i = 1, \ldots, n$. We define

$$\int_\Omega s \, d\mu = \sum_{i=1}^{n} s_i \mu(A_i).$$

It may happen that $\mu(A_i) = \infty$ for some i, and then the conventions $0 \cdot \infty = 0$ and $x \cdot \infty = \infty$ for $x > 0$ are used.

> **Exercise 1.11**   Show that if r, s are any non-negative simple functions and $a, b \geq 0$ are any non-negative numbers, then $ar + bs$ is a simple function and
>
> $$\int_\Omega (ar + bs) \, d\mu = a \int_\Omega r \, d\mu + b \int_\Omega s \, d\mu.$$

Exercise 1.12 Show that if r, s are non-negative simple functions such that $r \leq s$, then

$$\int_\Omega r \, d\mu \leq \int_\Omega s \, d\mu.$$

Proposition 1.26

Suppose that s is a non-negative simple function. Then $s\mathbf{1}_B$ is also a non-negative simple function for any $B \in \mathcal{F}$, and

$$\nu(B) = \int_\Omega s\mathbf{1}_B \, d\mu$$

is a measure on Ω defined on the σ-field $\mathcal{F}$.

Proof Take any $B \in \mathcal{F}$, and let $s = \sum_{i=1}^n s_i \mathbf{1}_{A_i}$, where $A_1, \ldots, A_n \in \mathcal{F}$ are pairwise disjoint sets with $\bigcup_{i=1}^n A_i = \Omega$, and $s_i \geq 0$ for $i = 1, \ldots, n$. Then $s\mathbf{1}_B = \sum_{i=1}^{n+1} r_i \mathbf{1}_{C_i}$, where $r_i = s_i$, $C_i = A_i \cap B$ for $i = 1, \ldots, n$ and where $r_{n+1} = 0$, $C_{n+1} = \Omega \setminus B$, is also a simple function. Moreover,

$$\nu(B) = \int_\Omega s\mathbf{1}_B \, d\mu = \sum_{i=1}^{n+1} r_i \mu(C_i) = \sum_{i=1}^n s_i \mu(A_i \cap B).$$

In particular, for $B = \varnothing$

$$\nu(\varnothing) = \sum_{i=1}^n s_i \mu(\varnothing) = 0.$$

Now suppose that $B = \bigcup_{j=1}^\infty B_j$, where $B_j \in \mathcal{F}$ for $j = 1, 2, \ldots$ are pairwise disjoint sets. Then countable additivity of μ gives

$$\nu(B) = \sum_{i=1}^n s_i \mu(A_i \cap B) = \sum_{i=1}^n s_i \sum_{j=1}^\infty \mu(A_i \cap B_j)$$

$$= \sum_{j=1}^\infty \sum_{i=1}^n s_i \mu(A_i \cap B_j) = \sum_{j=1}^\infty \nu(B_j).$$

We have proved that ν is a measure. □

Next, we need to identify the class of functions that will be integrated with respect to a measure. First we introduce some notation. For any $B \subset \mathbb{R}$ we denote by $\{f \in B\}$ or by $f^{-1}(B)$ the **inverse image** of B under f, that is,

$$\{f \in B\} = f^{-1}(B) = \{\omega \in \Omega : f(\omega) \in B\}.$$

The notation extends to the case when the set of values of f is specified in terms of a certain property, for example, $\{f > a\} = \{\omega \in \Omega : f(\omega) > a\}$ is the inverse image of (a, ∞) under f.

Definition 1.27
We say that a function $f : \Omega \to [-\infty, \infty]$ is **measurable** (more precisely, **measurable with respect to $\mathcal{F}$ or $\mathcal{F}$-measurable**) if

$$\{f \in B\} \in \mathcal{F} \qquad \text{for all } B \in \mathcal{B}(\mathbb{R})$$

and

$$\{f = \infty\}, \{f = -\infty\} \in \mathcal{F}.$$

Exercise 1.13 Show that $f : \Omega \to \mathbb{R}$ is measurable if and only if $\{f > a\} \in \mathcal{F}$ for all $a \in \mathbb{R}$.

Exercise 1.14 Show that every simple function is measurable.

Exercise 1.15 Show that the composition $g \circ f$ of a measurable function $f : \Omega \to \mathbb{R}$ with a continuous function $g : \mathbb{R} \to \mathbb{R}$ is measurable.

Exercise 1.16 If f_k are measurable functions for $k = 1, \ldots, n$, show that $\max\{f_1, \ldots, f_n\}$ and $\min\{f_1, \ldots, f_n\}$ are also measurable.

Exercise 1.17 If f_n are measurable functions for $n = 1, 2, \ldots$, show that $\sup_{n \geq 1} f_n$ and $\inf_{n \geq 1} f_n$ are also measurable.

Exercise 1.18 Suppose that f_n are measurable functions for $n = 1, 2, \ldots$. Recall that, by definition,

$$\limsup_{n \to \infty} f_n = \inf_{k \geq 1} \left(\sup_{n \leq k} f_n \right), \quad \liminf_{n \to \infty} f_n = \sup_{k \geq 1} \left(\inf_{n \leq k} f_n \right).$$

Show that $\limsup_{n \to \infty} f_n$ and $\liminf_{n \to \infty} f_n$ are also measurable functions.

Exercise 1.19 For any sequence of measurable functions f_n for $n = 1, 2, \ldots$, show that $\lim_{n \to \infty} f_n$ is also a measurable function.

Proposition 1.28

Let $f : \Omega \to [0, \infty]$. The following conditions are equivalent:
  (i) *f is a measurable function;*
  (ii) *there is a non-decreasing sequence of non-negative simple functions s_n, $n = 1, 2, \ldots$ such that $f = \lim_{n \to \infty} s_n$.*

Proof (i) $\Rightarrow$ (ii) Let $f : \Omega \to [0, \infty]$ be a measurable function. For each $n = 1, 2, \ldots$ we put

$$s_n = \sum_{i=0}^{n2^n} i2^{-n} \mathbf{1}_{A_{i,n}}, \tag{1.8}$$

where $A_{i,n} = \{i2^{-n} \le f < (i + 1)2^{-n}\}$. This defines a non-decreasing sequence of simple functions such that $f = \lim_{n \to \infty} s_n$ (see Exercise 1.20).
  (ii) $\Rightarrow$ (i) This is a consequence of Exercises 1.14 and 1.19. □

Exercise 1.20 Verify that (1.8) defines a non-decreasing sequence of non-negative simple functions such that $f = \lim_{n \to \infty} s_n$.

Exercise 1.21 Show that if f, g are non-negative measurable functions and $a, b \ge 0$, then $af + bg$ is measurable.

Exercise 1.22 Show that if f, g are non-negative measurable functions, then fg is measurable.

The next step is to define the integral of any non-negative measurable function.

Definition 1.29

For any non-negative measurable function $f : \Omega \to [0, \infty]$ the **integral** of f is defined as

$$\int_\Omega f \, d\mu = \sup \left\{ \int_\Omega s \, d\mu : s \text{ is a simple function such that } s \le f \right\}.$$

If the supremum is finite, we say that f is **integrable**.

Exercise 1.23 For any non-negative measurable functions f, g such that $f \le g$ show

$$\int_\Omega f \, d\mu \le \int_\Omega g \, d\mu.$$

Remark 1.30
For any non-negative simple function s, Exercise 1.23 implies that Definitions 1.25 and 1.29 of the integral give the same result, so the same notation $\int_\Omega s \, d\mu$ can be used in both cases.

The monotone convergence theorem, stated here for non-negative measurable functions, is a standard tool for handling limit operations, something that the integral with respect to a measure can tackle with remarkable ease.

Theorem 1.31 (monotone convergence)
If $f : \Omega \to [0, \infty]$ and $f_n : \Omega \to [0, \infty]$ for $n = 1, 2, \ldots$ is a non-decreasing sequence of non-negative measurable functions such that $f = \lim_{n\to\infty} f_n$, then f is a non-negative measurable function and

$$\int_\Omega f \, d\mu = \lim_{n\to\infty} \int_\Omega f_n \, d\mu.$$

Proof That f is measurable follows from Exercise 1.19. We put $L = \lim_{n\to\infty} \int_\Omega f_n \, d\mu$ for brevity. The limit exists (but may be equal to ∞) and satisfies $L \le \int_\Omega f \, d\mu$ because $\int_\Omega f_n \, d\mu$ is an non-decreasing sequence and $\int_\Omega f_n \, d\mu \le \int_\Omega f \, d\mu$ by Exercise 1.23.

To show that, on the other hand, $L \ge \int_\Omega f \, d\mu$ we take any non-negative simple function s such that $s \le f$. We also take any $\alpha \in (0, 1)$ and put $B_n = \{f_n \ge \alpha s\}$. Because $f_n \ge f_n \mathbf{1}_{B_n} \ge \alpha s \mathbf{1}_{B_n}$, using Exercise 1.23 once again, together with Exercise 1.11, we obtain

$$\int_\Omega f_n \, d\mu \ge \int_\Omega \alpha s \mathbf{1}_{B_n} \, d\mu = \alpha \int_\Omega s \mathbf{1}_{B_n} \, d\mu = \alpha \nu(B_n)$$

for each n, where ν is the measure on $\mathcal{F}$ defined in Proposition 1.26. Since f_n is a non-decreasing sequence, it follows that $B_n \subset B_{n+1}$ for each n. Moreover, since $\lim_{n\to\infty} f_n = f \ge s > \alpha s$, we have $\bigcup_{n=1}^\infty B_n = \Omega$. Because ν is a measure, we therefore have

$$L \ge \alpha \lim_{n \to \infty} \nu(B_n) = \alpha \nu(\Omega) = \alpha \int_\Omega s \, d\mu$$

from Theorem 1.11 (v) adapted to the case of a measure in Corollary 1.16. This is so for any $\alpha \in (0, 1)$ and any simple function s such that $s \le f$, which implies that $L \ge \int_\Omega f \, d\mu$, completing the proof. $\qquad \square$

Exercise 1.24 Let f_n for $n = 1, 2, \ldots$ be a sequence of non-negative measurable functions. Show that $\sum_{n=1}^\infty f_n$ is a non-negative measurable function and

$$\int_\Omega \left(\sum_{n=1}^\infty f_n \right) d\mu = \sum_{n=1}^\infty \int_\Omega f_n \, d\mu.$$

Proposition 1.32
Let $f, g : \Omega \to [0, \infty]$ be non-negative measurable functions and take any $a, b \ge 0$. Then $af + bg$ is measurable and

$$\int_\Omega (af + bg) \, d\mu = a \int_\Omega f \, d\mu + b \int_\Omega g \, d\mu,$$

where we use the conventions $x \cdot 0 = 0$, $x \cdot \infty = \infty$ for any $x > 0$, and $x + \infty = \infty$ for any $x \ge 0$.

Proof According to Proposition 1.28, there are non-decreasing sequences r_n and s_n of simple functions such that $f = \lim_{n \to \infty} r_n$ and $g = \lim_{n \to \infty} s_n$. It follows that $ar_n + bs_n$ is a non-decreasing sequence of simple functions and $af + bg = \lim_{n \to \infty} (ar_n + bs_n)$. By the monotone convergence theorem (Theorem 1.31) and Exercise 1.11, it follows that

$$\int_\Omega (af + bg) \, d\mu = \lim_{n \to \infty} \int_\Omega (ar_n + bs_n) \, d\mu$$

$$= a \lim_{n \to \infty} \int_\Omega r_n \, d\mu + b \lim_{n \to \infty} \int_\Omega s_n \, d\mu$$

$$= a \int_\Omega f \, d\mu + b \int_\Omega g \, d\mu.$$

$\qquad \square$

The final step in the construction of the integral with respect to a measure is to extend the definition from non-negative measurable functions to arbitrary ones by integrating their positive and negative parts separately.

Definition 1.33
Let $f : \Omega \to [-\infty, \infty]$ be a measurable function. If both the positive and negative parts

$$f^+ = \max\{f, 0\}, \quad f^- = \max\{-f, 0\} \tag{1.9}$$

are integrable, we say that f itself is **integrable**. When at least one of the functions f^+, f^- is integrable, we define the integral of f as

$$\int_\Omega f \, d\mu = \int_\Omega f^+ \, d\mu - \int_\Omega f^- \, d\mu,$$

where the conventions $x + \infty = \infty$ and $x - \infty = -\infty$ for any $x \in \mathbb{R}$ apply whenever one of the integrals on the right-hand side is equal to ∞. When neither f^+ nor f^- are integrable, then the integral of f will remain undefined.

Exercise 1.25 Let f be a measurable function. Show that f is integrable if and only if $|f|$ is.

Exercise 1.26 For any integrable function f show that

$$\left| \int_\Omega f \, d\mu \right| \le \int_\Omega |f| \, d\mu.$$

Exercise 1.27 Let f, g be integrable functions and let $a, b \in \mathbb{R}$. Show that $af + bg$ is integrable and

$$\int_\Omega (af + bg) \, d\mu = a \int_\Omega f \, d\mu + b \int_\Omega g \, d\mu.$$

Exercise 1.28 For any integrable functions f, g such that $f \le g$ show

$$\int_\Omega f \, d\mu \le \int_\Omega g \, d\mu.$$

Exercise 1.29 Extend the monotone convergence theorem (Theorem 1.31) to the case when f_n for $n = 1, 2, \ldots$ is a non-decreasing sequence of integrable functions and $f = \lim_{n \to \infty} f_n$ is also an integrable function.

It proves convenient to consider the integral over any $B \in \mathcal{F}$ rather than just over Ω.

Definition 1.34
For any $B \in \mathcal{F}$ and any measurable $f : \Omega \to [-\infty, \infty]$ we define the integral of f over B by

$$\int_B f \, d\mu = \int_\Omega f \mathbf{1}_B \, d\mu$$

whenever the integral $\int_\Omega f \mathbf{1}_B \, d\mu$ exists (including the cases when it is ∞ or $-\infty$), and we say that f is integrable over B whenever this integral is finite.

The following result is an extension of Proposition 1.26.

Theorem 1.35
Suppose that $f : \Omega \to [0, \infty]$ is measurable, and

$$\nu(B) = \int_B f \, d\mu$$

for any $B \in \mathcal{F}$. Then ν is a measure on Ω defined on the σ-field $\mathcal{F}$.

Proof Suppose that $B = \bigcup_{j=1}^\infty B_i$, where $B_i \in \mathcal{F}$ for $i = 1, 2, \ldots$ are pairwise disjoint sets. Then

$$g_n = f \mathbf{1}_{\bigcup_{i=1}^n B_i} = \sum_{i=1}^n f \mathbf{1}_{B_i}$$

is a non-decreasing sequence of measurable functions, and $\lim_{n \to \infty} g_n = f \mathbf{1}_B$. It follows by the monotone convergence theorem (Theorem 1.31) that

$$\nu(B) = \int_B f \, d\mu = \int_\Omega f \mathbf{1}_B \, d\mu = \int_\Omega \left(\lim_{n \to \infty} g_n \right) d\mu$$

$$= \lim_{n \to \infty} \int_\Omega g_n \, d\mu = \sum_{i=1}^\infty \int_\Omega f \mathbf{1}_{B_i} \, d\mu = \sum_{i=1}^\infty \nu(B_i).$$

Moreover, for $B = \varnothing$ we have $\mathbf{1}_\varnothing = 0$, so

$$\nu(\varnothing) = \int_\Omega f \mathbf{1}_\varnothing \, d\mu = 0.$$

This completes the proof. □

If a measurable function $f : \Omega \to \mathbb{R}$ has a property everywhere except on some set $B \in \mathcal{F}$ such that $\mu(B) = 0$, we say that it has this property μ-**almost everywhere** (μ-a.e. for short) or, particularly when μ is a probability measure, μ-**almost surely** (μ-a.s. for short). For instance, if $\mu(\{f \neq 0\}) = 0$, we say that $f = 0$, μ-a.e.

Proposition 1.36

Let $f : \Omega \to [0, \infty]$ be a non-negative measurable function. Then $f = 0$, μ-a.e. if and only if $\int_\Omega f \, d\mu = 0$.

Proof Suppose that $f = 0$, μ-a.e., that is, $\mu(B) = 0$ for $B = \{f > 0\}$. For every simple function s such that $s \leq f$ we have $s = 0$ on $\Omega \setminus B$. Writing the simple function as $s = \sum_{i=1}^n s_i \mathbf{1}_{A_i}$, where $A_1, \ldots, A_n \in \mathcal{F}$ and $s_i \geq 0$ for $i = 1, \ldots, n$, we then have $\mu(A_i) = 0$ if $A_i \subset B$, and $s_i = 0$ otherwise. This means that $\int_\Omega s \, d\mu = \sum_{i=1}^n s_i \mu(A_i) = 0$ because $\mu(A_i) = 0$ or $s_i = 0$ for each i. Because $\int_\Omega s \, d\mu = 0$ for every simple function s such that $s \leq f$, it follows that $\int_\Omega f \, d\mu = 0$.

Conversely, if $\int_\Omega f \, d\mu = 0$, then $B = \{f > 0\} = \bigcup_{n=1}^\infty B_n$ where $B_n = \{f \geq \frac{1}{n}\}$. This is an increasing sequence of sets in $\mathcal{F}$, so $\mu(B) = \lim_{n\to\infty} \mu(B_n)$. The simple function $s_n = \frac{1}{n} \mathbf{1}_{B_n}$ satisfies $s_n \leq f$, so

$$\frac{1}{n}\mu(B_n) = \int_\Omega s_n \, d\mu \leq \int_\Omega f \, d\mu = 0,$$

which means that $\mu(B_n) = 0$ for all n, hence $\mu(B) = 0$. Therefore $f = 0$, μ-a.e. □

Exercise 1.30 Let $f : \Omega \to [-\infty, \infty]$ be a measurable function. Show that $\int_B f \, d\mu = 0$ for every $B \in \mathcal{F}$ if and only if $f = 0$, μ-a.e.

The origin of the next proposition is the familiar change of variables formula for transforming Riemann integrals. In the case of integrals with respect to a measure we have the following **change of measure** result.

Proposition 1.37

Suppose that $(\Omega, \mathcal{F}, \mu)$ and $(\tilde{\Omega}, \tilde{\mathcal{F}}, \tilde{\mu})$ are measure spaces, and $\varphi : \Omega \to \tilde{\Omega}$ is a function such that $\varphi^{-1}(A) \in \mathcal{F}$ and $\mu(\varphi^{-1}(A)) = \tilde{\mu}(A)$ for every $A \in \tilde{\mathcal{F}}$. If $g = \tilde{g} \circ \varphi$ is the composition of φ and a measurable function $\tilde{g} : \tilde{\Omega} \to [-\infty, \infty]$, then $g : \Omega \to [-\infty, \infty]$ is a measurable function, the integral $\int_\Omega g\,d\mu$ exists if and only $\int_{\tilde\Omega} \tilde g\,d\tilde\mu$ exists (including the cases when the integrals are equal to ∞ or $-\infty$), and

$$\int_\Omega g\,d\mu = \int_{\tilde\Omega} \tilde g\,d\tilde\mu.$$

Proof Suppose that $\tilde s = \sum_{i=1}^n s_i \mathbf{1}_{A_i}$ is a non-negative simple function on $\tilde\Omega$, where $s_i \in [0,\infty)$ and where $A_i \in \tilde{\mathcal F}$ for $i = 1,\ldots,n$ are disjoint sets such that $\bigcup_{i=1}^n A_i = \tilde\Omega$. Then $\varphi^{-1}(A_i) \in \mathcal F$ for $i = 1,\ldots,n$ are disjoint sets such that $\bigcup_{i=1}^n \varphi^{-1}(A_i) = \Omega$, and $s = \tilde s \circ \varphi = \sum_{i=1}^n s_i \mathbf{1}_{\varphi^{-1}(A_i)}$ is a non-negative simple function on Ω. It follows that

$$\int_\Omega s\,d\mu = \sum_{i=1}^n s_i \mu(\varphi^{-1}(A_i)) = \sum_{i=1}^n s_i \tilde\mu(A_i) = \int_{\tilde\Omega} s\,d\tilde\mu.$$

Now suppose that $\tilde g$ is non-negative measurable function on $\tilde\Omega$. By Proposition 1.28 there is a non-decreasing sequence of non-negative simple functions $\tilde s_k$, $k = 1,2,\ldots$ on $\tilde\Omega$ such that $\tilde g = \lim_{k\to\infty} \tilde s_k$. Then $s_k = \tilde s_k \circ \varphi$ is a non-decreasing sequence of non-negative simple functions on Ω and $g = \lim_{k\to\infty} s_k$ is a measurable function on Ω. It follows by the monotone convergence theorem (Theorem 1.31) that

$$\int_\Omega g\,d\mu = \lim_{k\to\infty} \int_\Omega s_k\,d\mu = \lim_{k\to\infty} \int_{\tilde\Omega} s_k\,d\tilde\mu = \int_{\tilde\Omega} g\,d\tilde\mu.$$

In general, if $\tilde g$ is a measurable function on $\tilde\Omega$, then $g = \tilde g \circ \varphi$ is a measurable function on Ω. We can write $\tilde g = \tilde g^+ - \tilde g^-$ and, correspondingly, $g = g^+ - g^-$, where $\tilde g^+, \tilde g^-$ are non-negative measurable functions on $\tilde\Omega$ and $g^+ = \tilde g^+ \circ \varphi$, $g^- = \tilde g^- \circ \varphi$ are non-negative measurable functions on Ω. From the above argument we know that

$$\int_\Omega g^+\,d\mu = \int_{\tilde\Omega} \tilde g^+\,d\tilde\mu, \qquad \int_\Omega g^-\,d\mu = \int_{\tilde\Omega} \tilde g^-\,d\tilde\mu.$$

It follows that $\int_\Omega g\,d\mu$ exits if and only if $\int_{\tilde\Omega} \tilde g\,d\tilde\mu$ exists, and

$$\int_\Omega g\,d\mu = \int_\Omega g^+\,d\mu - \int_\Omega g^-\,d\mu$$
$$= \int_{\tilde\Omega} \tilde g^+\,d\tilde\mu - \int_{\tilde\Omega} \tilde g^-\,d\tilde\mu = \int_{\tilde\Omega} \tilde g\,d\tilde\mu.$$

$\square$

Lebesgue integral

Our aim when constructing an integral with respect to a measure was to extend the Riemann integral. To achieve this, we now specialise to the measure space $(\mathbb{R}, \mathcal{B}(\mathbb{R}), m)$ with Lebesgue measure m defined on the Borel sets $\mathcal{B}(\mathbb{R})$.

Definition 1.38
Let $f : \mathbb{R} \to [-\infty, \infty]$.
  (i) We say that f is **Borel measurable** whenever it is measurable as a function on the measure space $(\mathbb{R}, \mathcal{B}(\mathbb{R}), m)$.
  (ii) The integral $\int_{\mathbb{R}} f\, dm$, whenever it exists (including the cases when it is equal to ∞ or $-\infty$), is called the Lebesgue integral of f.
  (iii) When the integral $\int_{\mathbb{R}} f\, dm$ is finite, we say that f is **Lebesgue integrable**.

We need to make sure that Lebesgue integral is indeed what we are looking for, that is, it coincides with the Riemann integral of any continuous function over an interval.

Proposition 1.39
For any continuous function $f : \mathbb{R} \to \mathbb{R}$ and any numbers $a \leq b$

$$\int_a^b f(x)\, dx = \int_{[a,b]} f\, dm,$$

with the Riemann integral on the left-hand side and Lebesgue integral on the right-hand side.

Proof It is enough to consider $f \geq 0$. Otherwise we can consider f^+ and f^- separately, and then combine the results.

For any $n = 1, 2, \ldots$, take $c_i = a + (b-a)i2^{-n}$ so that $a = c_0 < c_1 < \cdots < c_{2^n} = b$. For each $i = 1, \ldots, 2^n$, since f is a continuous function, it has a minimum on $[c_{i-1}, c_i]$, which we can write as $f(x_i)$ for some $x_i \in [c_{i-1}, c_i]$. We put $S_n = \sum_{i=1}^{2^n} f(x_i)(c_i - c_{i-1})$. Then, by the definition of the Riemann integral,

$$\int_a^b f(x)\, dx = \lim_{n \to \infty} S_n.$$

On the other hand,

$$s_n = \sum_{i=1}^{2^n} f(x_i)\mathbf{1}_{[c_{i-1}, c_i)} + f(b)\mathbf{1}_{\{b\}}$$

is a non-decreasing sequence of simple functions, and $\lim_{n \to \infty} s_n = f\mathbf{1}_{[a,b]}$.

Moreover, $\int_{\mathbb{R}} s_n \, dm = S_n$. By the monotone convergence theorem (Theorem 1.31),

$$\int_{[a,b]} f \, dm = \int_{\mathbb{R}} f \mathbf{1}_{[a,b]} \, dm = \lim_{n \to \infty} \int_{\mathbb{R}} s_n \, dm = \lim_{n \to \infty} S_n,$$

completing the proof. □

While the Lebesgue integral coincides with the Riemann integral for continuous functions integrated over intervals, it is in fact much more general and covers various other cases. Here are a couple of relatively simple examples.

Example 1.40

In Example 1.21 we saw that the Riemann integral $\int_0^1 f(x) \, dx$ does not exist when the function f is defined as

$$f(x) = \begin{cases} 0 & \text{if } x \in \mathbb{Q}, \\ 1 & \text{if } x \in \mathbb{R} \setminus \mathbb{Q}. \end{cases}$$

However, the Lebesgue integral $\int_{[0,1]} f \, dm$ does exist and equals 1, as the function f is the indicator of the Borel measurable set $[0, 1] \setminus \mathbb{Q}$, which has Lebesgue measure 1.

Exercise 1.31 Recall the Cantor set C (Exercise 1.7). Suppose that $f : [0, 1] \to \mathbb{R}$ is defined by setting $f(x) = 0$ for all x in C, and $f(x) = k$ for all x in each of the 2^{k-1} intervals of length 3^{-k} removed from $[0, 1]$ in forming C_k. Calculate the Lebesgue integral $\int_{[0,1]} f \, dm$ and show that the Riemann integral $\int_0^1 f(x) \, dx$ does not exist.

Exercise 1.32 For any integrable function $f : \mathbb{R} \to [-\infty, \infty]$ and any $a \in \mathbb{R}$ show that the function $g(x) = f(x - a)$ defined for all $x \in \mathbb{R}$ is integrable and

$$\int_{\mathbb{R}} g \, dm = \int_{\mathbb{R}} f \, dm.$$

This is known as **translation invariance** of the Lebesgue integral.

Hint. Refer to Exercise 1.8 concerning translation invariance for the Lebesgue measure *m*.

More convergence results

In addition to the monotone convergence theorem, there are other powerful results concerning limits of integrals. It will be important to have these ready in our toolbox. Once again we work with a general measure space $(\Omega, \mathcal{F}, \mu)$, and begin with the following two inequalities.

Lemma 1.41 (Fatou lemmas)
Let $f_n : \Omega \to [0, \infty]$ be measurable functions for $n = 1, 2, \dots$.
  (i) *The inequality*

$$\int_\Omega \left(\liminf_{n \to \infty} f_n \right) d\mu \le \liminf_{n \to \infty} \int_\Omega f_n \, d\mu$$

  holds.
  (ii) *If, moreover, $f_n \le g$ for all n, where $g : \Omega \to [0, \infty]$ is integrable, then*

$$\limsup_{n \to \infty} \int_\Omega f_n \, d\mu \le \int_\Omega \left(\limsup_{n \to \infty} f_n \right) d\mu.$$

Proof (i) Set $g_k = \inf_{n \ge k} f_n$. Then g_k for $k = 1, 2, \dots$ is a non-decreasing sequence, and

$$\lim_{k \to \infty} g_k = \sup_{k \ge 1} g_k = \sup_{k \ge 1} \inf_{n \ge k} f_n = \liminf_{n \to \infty} f_n.$$

Moreover, $g_k \le f_n$ and so $\int_\Omega g_k \, d\mu \le \int_\Omega f_n \, d\mu$ whenever $k \le n$. Hence, for each $k \ge 1$

$$\int_\Omega g_k \, d\mu \le \inf_{n \ge k} \int_\Omega f_n \, d\mu.$$

Because g_k for $k = 1, 2, \dots$ is a non-decreasing sequence, so is $\int_\Omega g_k \, d\mu$, and it follows by the monotone convergence theorem (Theorem 1.31) that

$$\int_\Omega \left(\liminf_{n \to \infty} f_n \right) d\mu = \int_\Omega \left(\lim_{k \to \infty} g_k \right) d\mu = \lim_{k \to \infty} \int_\Omega g_k \, d\mu = \sup_{k \ge 1} \int_\Omega g_k \, d\mu$$

$$\le \sup_{k \ge 1} \inf_{n \ge k} \int_\Omega f_n \, d\mu = \liminf_{n \to \infty} \int_\Omega f_n \, d\mu.$$

  (ii) Let $h_n = g - f_n$ (where we set $h_n(\omega) = 0$ for any $\omega \in \Omega$ such that $g(\omega) = f_n(\omega) = \infty$). The functions $h_n : \Omega \to [0, \infty]$ are measurable for all

$n = 1, 2, \ldots$, and we can apply (i) to get

$$\int_\Omega \left(\liminf_{n \to \infty} h_n \right) d\mu \le \liminf_{n \to \infty} \int_\Omega h_n \, d\mu.$$

Because g is integrable and $0 \le f_n \le g$ for each n, it follows that f_n is integrable for each n. Moreover, it follows that $0 \le \limsup_{n \to \infty} f_n \le g$, and so $\limsup_{n \to \infty} f_n$ is also integrable. As a result, by Exercise 1.27,

$$\int_\Omega \left(\liminf_{n \to \infty} h_n \right) d\mu = \int_\Omega \left(g - \limsup_{n \to \infty} f_n \right) d\mu = \int_\Omega g \, d\mu - \int_\Omega \left(\limsup_{n \to \infty} f_n \right) d\mu$$

on the left-hand side of the inequality, and

$$\liminf_{n \to \infty} \int_\Omega h_n \, d\mu = \liminf_{n \to \infty} \left(\int_\Omega g \, d\mu - \int_\Omega f_n \, d\mu \right) = \int_\Omega g \, d\mu - \limsup_{n \to \infty} \int_\Omega f_n \, d\mu$$

on the right-hand side, completing the proof. $\qquad\square$

Example 1.42
In general, we cannot expect equality in Lemma 1.41 (i). On the measure space $(\mathbb{R}, \mathcal{B}(\mathbb{R}), m)$ let $f_n = \mathbf{1}_{(n,n+1]}$ for $n = 1, 2, \ldots$. Then $\lim_{n \to \infty} f_n = 0$ because for any fixed real number x we can find $n > x$. Hence $\int_\mathbb{R} (\liminf_{n \to \infty} f_n) \, dm = 0$, while $\liminf_{n \to \infty} \int_\mathbb{R} f_n \, dm = 1$ since $\int_\mathbb{R} f_n \, dm = 1$ for each $n = 1, 2, \ldots$.

Exercise 1.33 Let $(\Omega, \mathcal{F}, P)$ be a probability space. Use Fatou's lemma to show that for any sequence of events $A_n \in \mathcal{F}$, where $n = 1, 2, \ldots$, we have

$$P\left(\bigcup_{n \ge 1} \bigcap_{k \ge n} A_k \right) \le \liminf_{n \to \infty} P(A_n).$$

In situations when we need to integrate the limit of a non-monotone sequence of functions, the following result often comes to the rescue.

Theorem 1.43 (dominated convergence)
Suppose that $f_n : \Omega \to [-\infty, \infty]$ are measurable functions for $n = 1, 2, \ldots$ and there is an integrable function $g : \Omega \to [0, \infty]$ such that $|f_n| \le g$ for

each n. Suppose further that $\lim_{n\to\infty} f_n = f$. *Then* f *and* f_n *for each* n *are integrable, and*

$$\lim_{n\to\infty} \int_\Omega f_n \, d\mu = \int_\Omega f \, d\mu. \tag{1.10}$$

Proof   Since $|f_n| \leq g$ for each n, it follows that $|f| \leq g$, where g is integrable. This means that f and f_n for each n are integrable, and so are $f - f_n$ and $|f - f_n|$ because $|f - f_n| \leq |f| + |f_n| \leq 2g$. The second Fatou lemma (Lemma 1.41 (ii)) gives

$$\limsup_{n\to\infty} \int_\Omega |f_n - f| \, d\mu \leq \int_\Omega \left(\limsup_{n\to\infty} |f_n - f| \right) d\mu = 0$$

since $\limsup_{n\to\infty} |f_n - f| = \lim_{n\to\infty} |f_n - f| = 0$. This completes the proof because

$$\left| \int_\Omega f_n \, d\mu - \int_\Omega f \, d\mu \right| = \left| \int_\Omega (f_n - f) \, d\mu \right| \leq \int_\Omega |f_n - f| \, d\mu,$$

where Exercise 1.26 is used in the last inequality.   □

Example 1.44

For an example with no integrable dominating function, consider the sequence of functions on the measure space $(\mathbb{R}, \mathcal{B}(\mathbb{R}), m)$ defined by $f_n = n\mathbf{1}_{(0,\frac{1}{n}]}$ for $n = 1, 2, \ldots$. Here $g = \sup_{n\geq 1} f_n$ satisfies $g = n$ on the interval $\left(\frac{1}{n+1}, \frac{1}{n}\right]$, so $\int_{\mathbb{R}} g \, dm = \sum_{n=1}^\infty n\left(\frac{1}{n} - \frac{1}{n+1}\right) = \sum_{n=1}^\infty \frac{1}{n+1} = \infty$. We have $\lim_{n\to\infty} f_n = 0$ and $\int_{\mathbb{R}} f_n \, dm = 1$ for each n, which means that (1.10) fails in this case.

Exercise 1.34   Let f_n for $n = 1, 2, \ldots$ be a sequence of integrable functions and suppose that $\sum_{n=1}^\infty \int_\Omega |f_n| \, d\mu$ is finite. Show that the series $\sum_{n=1}^\infty f_n$ converges μ-a.e., that its sum is an integrable function, and that

$$\int_\Omega \left(\sum_{n=1}^\infty f_n \right) d\mu = \sum_{n=1}^\infty \int_\Omega f_n \, d\mu.$$

Exercise 1.35   Use the previous exercise to calculate $\int_0^\infty \frac{x}{e^x - 1} dx$.

Exercise 1.36 Prove the following version of the dominated convergence theorem.

Suppose we are given real numbers $a < b$ and a function $f : \Omega \times [a,b] \to \mathbb{R}$ such that $\omega \mapsto f(\omega, s)$ is measurable for each $s \in [a,b]$. Suppose further that for some fixed $t \in [a,b]$ we have $f(\omega, t) = \lim_{s \to t} f(\omega, s)$ for each $\omega \in \Omega$, and there is an integrable function $g : \Omega \to \mathbb{R}$ such that $|f(\omega, s)| \leq g(\omega)$ for each $\omega \in \Omega$ and each $s \in [a,b]$. Then

$$\int_{\Omega} f(\omega, t) d\mu(\omega) = \lim_{s \to t} \int_{\Omega} f(\omega, s) d\mu(\omega).$$

1.5 Lebesgue outer measure

Definition 1.45
For any $A \subset \mathbb{R}$ we define

$$m^*(A) = \inf \left\{ \sum_{k=1}^{\infty} l(J_k) : A \subset \bigcup_{k=1}^{\infty} J_k \right\},$$

where the infimum is taken over all sequences $(J_k)_{k=1}^{\infty}$ consisting of open intervals. This is called **Lebesgue outer measure**.

The Lebesgue outer measure m^* extends the function m defined on $\mathcal{B}(\mathbb{R})$ by (1.2) to the family of all subsets of $\mathbb{R}$. We have

$$m(A) = m^*(A)$$

for each $A \in \mathcal{B}(\mathbb{R})$. Despite its name, Lebesgue outer measure is not a measure on the subsets of $\mathbb{R}$.

Proposition 1.46
The Lebesgue outer measure m^* has the following properties:
   (i) $m^*(\varnothing) = 0$;
   (ii) $A \subset B$ implies $m^*(A) \leq m^*(B)$ for any $A, B \subset \mathbb{R}$ (monotonicity);
   (iii) $m^*\left(\bigcup_{i=1}^{\infty} A_i\right) \leq \sum_{i=1}^{\infty} m^*(A_i)$ for any $A_i \subset \mathbb{R}$, $i = 1, 2, \ldots$ (countable subadditivity);
   (iv) $m^*([a,b]) = m^*((a,b)) = m^*((a,b]) = m^*([a,b)) = b - a$ for each $a \leq b$.

Proof (i) Take $J_k = (a, a) = \varnothing$ for $k = 1, 2, \ldots$. This sequence covers $\varnothing$
by open intervals with total length 0. It follows that $m^*(\varnothing) = 0$.

(ii) If $A \subset B$ and B is covered by a sequence $(J_k)_{k=1}^{\infty}$ of open intervals, then
A is covered by the same sequence, which implies that $m^*(A) \leq m^*(B)$.

(iii) To prove countable subadditivity, let $\varepsilon > 0$ be given. For each $i = 1, 2, \ldots$ there is a sequence $(J_{i,k})_{k=1}^{\infty}$ covering A_i by open intervals and such
that

$$\sum_{k=1}^{\infty} l(J_{i,k}) < m^*(A_i) + \frac{\varepsilon}{2^i}.$$

Summing over i, we have

$$\sum_{i=1}^{\infty} \sum_{k=1}^{\infty} l(J_{i,k}) < \sum_{i=1}^{\infty} \left(m^*(A_i) + \frac{\varepsilon}{2^i} \right) = \sum_{i=1}^{\infty} m^*(A_i) + \varepsilon.$$

But the double sequence $(J_{i,k})_{i,k=1}^{\infty}$ covers $\bigcup_{i=1}^{\infty} A_i$ by open intervals, so by
the definition of Lebesgue outer measure,

$$m^* \left(\bigcup_{i=1}^{\infty} A_i \right) \leq \sum_{i=1}^{\infty} \sum_{k=1}^{\infty} l(J_{i,k}) < \sum_{i=1}^{\infty} m^*(A_i) + \varepsilon.$$

This argument works for an arbitrary $\varepsilon > 0$, which proves the claim.

(iv) Let $a \leq b$. Take any $\varepsilon > 0$, and put $J_1 = (a - \frac{\varepsilon}{2}, b + \frac{\varepsilon}{2})$ and $J_k = (a, a) = \varnothing$ for $k = 2, 3, \ldots$. This sequence covers $[a, b]$ by open intervals,
so

$$m^*([a, b]) \leq \sum_{k=1}^{\infty} l(J_k) = l(J_1) = b - a + \varepsilon.$$

This is so for every $\varepsilon > 0$, which implies that $m^*([a, b]) \leq b - a$.

To prove that, on the other hand, $m^*([a, b]) \geq b - a$ take any $\varepsilon > 0$ and a
covering $(J_k)_{k=1}^{\infty}$ of $[a, b]$ by open intervals $J_k = (c_k, d_k)$ such that

$$\sum_{k=1}^{\infty} l(J_k) < m^*([a, b]) + \varepsilon.$$

For any $x \geq a$ we say that $[a, x]$ has a finite subcover whenever $[a, x] \subset \bigcup_{k=1}^{K} J_k$ for some positive integer K. We are going to show that $[a, b]$ has a
finite subcover. To this end, define

$$s = \sup \left\{ x \geq a : [a, x] \text{ has a finite subcover} \right\}.$$

Since $a \in J_k$ for some k and J_k is an open interval, we have $[a, a + \varepsilon] \subset J_k$
for some $\varepsilon > 0$, implying that $s > a$. Now suppose that $s \leq b$. Since

$(J_k)_{k=1}^{\infty}$ covers $[a, b]$, we can find i such that $s \in J_i$, and as J_i is open we can find $x_1, x_2 \in J_i$ with $a < x_1 < s < x_2$. Now $[a, x_1]$ has a finite subcover since $x_1 < s$. But that subcover, together with J_i, gives a finite subcover of $[a, x_2]$, and since $x_2 > s$, this contradicts the definition of s. Therefore we cannot have $s \le b$. It means that $s > b$. As a result, we have shown that $[a, b]$ has a finite subcover $(J_k)_{k=1}^{K}$ for some positive integer K.

Let

$$c = \min_{k=1,\dots,K} c_k, \quad d = \max_{k=1,\dots,K} d_k.$$

Because $[a, b] \subset \bigcup_{k=1}^{K}(c_k, d_k)$, we must have $c < a \le b < d$. It follows that

$$b - a < d - c \le \sum_{k=1}^{K}(d_k - c_k) = \sum_{k=1}^{K} l(J_k) \le \sum_{k=1}^{\infty} l(J_k) < m^*([a, b]) + \varepsilon.$$

This must be so for every $\varepsilon > 0$, implying that $b - a \le m^*([a, b])$. We can conclude that $b - a = m^*([a, b])$.

Next, using (ii), (iii), (iv), we have

$$
\begin{aligned}
m^*((a, b)) \le m^*([a, b]) &= m^*([a, a] \cup (a, b) \cup [b, b]) \\
&\le m^*([a, a]) + m^*((a, b)) + m^*([b, b]) \\
&= (a - a) + m^*((a, b)) + (b - b) \\
&= m^*((a, b)),
\end{aligned}
$$

so that $m^*((a, b)) = m^*([a, b])$. A similar argument shows that $m^*((a, b)) = m^*([a, b))$ and $m^*((a, b)) = m^*((a, b])$. □

Definition 1.47
A set $A \subset \mathbb{R}$ is said to be m^*-**measurable** if

$$m^*(E) \ge m^*(E \cap A) + m^*(E \cap (\mathbb{R}\backslash A)) \qquad (1.11)$$

for every $E \subset \mathbb{R}$. The collection of all m^*-measurable sets is denoted by $\mathcal{M}$.

Remarkably, as we shall see, this property will suffice for countable additivity.

Proposition 1.48
The following properties hold:
   (i) *$\mathcal{M}$ is a σ-field on $\mathbb{R}$;*
   (ii) *m^* restricted to $\mathcal{M}$ is a measure;*
   (iii) *every interval (a, b) belongs to $\mathcal{M}$, that is, $\mathcal{I} \subset \mathcal{M}$.*

Proof (i) We already know that $m^*(\varnothing) = 0$, so for every $E \subset \mathbb{R}$

$$m^*(E) = m^*(E) + m^*(\varnothing) = m^*(E \cap \mathbb{R}) + m^*(E \cap (\mathbb{R} \setminus \mathbb{R})),$$

which means that $\mathbb{R} \in \mathcal{M}$. Moreover, because $A = \mathbb{R} \setminus (\mathbb{R} \setminus A)$, it follows from (1.11) that $A \in \mathcal{M}$ implies $\mathbb{R} \setminus A \in \mathcal{M}$.

Now let $A, B \in \mathcal{M}$. For any $E \subset \mathbb{R}$ we have by (1.11)

$$m^*(E) \geq m^*(E \cap A) + m^*(E \cap (\mathbb{R} \setminus A))$$
$$\geq m^*(E \cap A \cap B) + m^*(E \cap A \cap (\mathbb{R} \setminus B))$$
$$+ m^*(E \cap (\mathbb{R} \setminus A) \cap B) + m^*(E \cap (\mathbb{R} \setminus A) \cap (\mathbb{R} \setminus B)),$$

where in the second inequality we use $E \cap A$ and $E \cap (\mathbb{R} \setminus A)$, respectively, in place of E in (1.11). Since $A \cup B \subset (A \cap B) \cup (A \cap (\mathbb{R} \setminus B)) \cup ((\mathbb{R} \setminus A) \cap B)$, by the subadditivity of m^*, the sum of the first three terms is at least $m^*(E \cap (A \cup B))$. In the final term $(\mathbb{R} \setminus A) \cap (\mathbb{R} \setminus B) = \mathbb{R} \setminus (A \cup B)$. As a result,

$$m^*(E) \geq m^*(E \cap (A \cup B)) + m^*(E \cap (\mathbb{R} \setminus (A \cup B))),$$

which shows that $A \cup B \in \mathcal{M}$. We have shown that $A, B \in \mathcal{M}$ implies $A \cup B \in \mathcal{M}$. By induction, this extends to any finite number of sets. If $A_i \in \mathcal{M}$ for $i = 1, \ldots, n$, then $\bigcup_{i=1}^{n} A_i \in \mathcal{M}$.

Finally, take any sequence $A_i \in \mathcal{M}$ for $i = 1, 2, \ldots$, and put $D_n = \bigcup_{i=1}^{n} A_i$ and $D = \bigcup_{i=1}^{\infty} A_i$. It follows that $D_n \in \mathcal{M}$, so for any $E \subset \mathbb{R}$

$$m^*(E) \geq m^*(E \cap D_n) + m^*(E \cap (\mathbb{R} \setminus D_n)).$$

Clearly $D_n \subset D$, so $\mathbb{R} \setminus D_n \supset \mathbb{R} \setminus D$, and by the monotonicity of m^*

$$m^*(E \cap (\mathbb{R} \setminus D_n)) \geq m^*(E \cap (\mathbb{R} \setminus D)).$$

Next put $B_1 = A_1$ and $B_n = A_n \setminus D_{n-1}$ for $n = 2, 3, \ldots$. From what has already been shown it follows that $B_n \in \mathcal{M}$ for all n. Using $E \cap D_n$ in place of E in (1.11), we get

$$m^*(E \cap D_n) \geq m^*(E \cap D_n \cap B_n) + m^*(E \cap D_n \cap (\mathbb{R} \setminus B_n))$$
$$= m^*(E \cap B_n) + m^*(E \cap D_{n-1}).$$

We can repeat this for $m^*(E \cap D_i)$ with $i = n - 1, n - 2, \ldots, 1$ and obtain

$$m^*(E \cap D_n) \geq \sum_{i=1}^{n} m^*(E \cap B_i).$$

It follows that

$$m^*(E) \geq \sum_{i=1}^{n} m^*(E \cap B_i) + m^*(E \cap (\mathbb{R} \setminus D))$$

for each n, and so

$$m^*(E) \geq \sum_{i=1}^{\infty} m^*(E \cap B_i) + m^*(E \cap (\mathbb{R} \setminus D)) \tag{1.12}$$

$$\geq m^*(E \cap \bigcup_{i=1}^{\infty} B_i) + m^*(E \cap (\mathbb{R} \setminus D))$$

$$= m^*(E \cap D) + m^*(E \cap (\mathbb{R} \setminus D)),$$

where the second inequality is due to the countable subadditivity of m^*. We have shown that $D = \bigcup_{i=1}^{\infty} A_i \in \mathcal{M}$, completing the proof that $\mathcal{M}$ is a σ-field.

(ii) We already know that $m^*(\varnothing) = 0$. Let $A_i \in \mathcal{M}$ for $i = 1, 2, \ldots$ be a sequence of pairwise disjoint sets. Then $B_i = A_i$ for each i and (1.12) with $E = D = \bigcup_{i=1}^{\infty} A_i$ gives

$$m^*(D) \geq \sum_{i=1}^{\infty} m^*(A_i).$$

Countable subadditivity, see Proposition 1.46 (iii), gives the reverse inequality, proving that m^* is countably additive, and hence it is a measure on $\mathcal{M}$.

(iii) Let $\varepsilon > 0$ be given. There is a sequence $(J_k)_{k=1}^{\infty}$ of open intervals covering E such that $m^*(E) + \varepsilon \geq \sum_{k=1}^{\infty} m^*(J_k)$. By subadditivity

$$m^*(E \cap (a, b)) + m^*(E \cap (\mathbb{R} \setminus (a, b)))$$

$$\leq m^*(E \cap (a, b)) + m^*(E \cap (-\infty, a]) + m^*(E \cap [b, \infty))$$

$$\leq \sum_{k=1}^{\infty} [m^*(J_k \cap (a, b)) + m^*(J_k \cap (-\infty, a]) + m^*(J_k \cap [b, \infty))].$$

Inside the square brackets we have the lengths of the disjoint intervals $J_k \cap (a, b)$, $J_k \cap (-\infty, a]$, $J_k \cap [b, \infty)$, which add up to give the length $l(J_k)$ of J_k. Hence

$$m^*(E \cap (a, b)) + m^*(E \cap (\mathbb{R} \setminus (a, b))) \leq \sum_{k=1}^{\infty} l(J_k) \leq m^*(E) + \varepsilon.$$

Since this holds for all $\varepsilon > 0$, we have shown that (1.11) with $A = (a, b)$ holds for every $E \subset \mathbb{R}$, which means that $(a, b) \in \mathcal{M}$. It follows that $\mathcal{I} \subset \mathcal{M}$. $\square$

Finally, we are ready to prove Theorem 1.19.

Theorem 1.19

$m : \mathcal{B}(\mathbb{R}) \to [0, \infty]$ *is a measure such that* $m((a,b)) = b - a$ *for all* $a \leq b$.

Proof Because $\mathcal{M}$ is a σ-field and $\mathcal{I} \subset \mathcal{M}$, we know that $\mathcal{B}(\mathbb{R}) \subset \mathcal{M}$ (see Exercise 1.3). Because m^* is a measure on $\mathcal{M}$ and $m(A) = m^*(A)$ for every $A \in \mathcal{B}(\mathbb{R})$, it follows that m is a measure on $\mathcal{B}(\mathbb{R})$. Moreover, for any $a \leq b$, since $(a,b) \in \mathcal{B}(\mathbb{R})$, we have $m((a,b)) = m^*((a,b)) = b - a$. $\square$

2

Probability distributions and random variables

We again motivate our discussion through simple examples of pricing models. In such applications, we often have information about the probability distribution of future prices, so it is natural to begin our analysis with distribution functions and densities. Then we look at measurable functions defined on probability spaces, commonly known as random variables, and the probability distributions associated with them. One often has to infer the structure of the distribution from simpler data, such as the expectation, variance or higher moments, and methods for computing these thus play a major role. Finally, we introduce characteristic functions as a vehicle for analysing distributions and computing the moments of a given random variable. The full power of characteristic functions will become apparent in Chapter 5, where it will be shown that the characteristic function of a random variable determines its distribution.

2.1 Probability distributions

In Chapter 1 we looked at some examples of probabilities. These included the uniform, binomial, Poisson and geometric probabilities in a discrete setting, and the probabilities associated with the normal and log-normal densities in a continuous setting. These examples can be revisited using

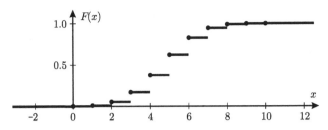

Figure 2.1 Distribution function for the binomial distribution in Example 2.2 with $N = 10$ and $p = 0.5$.

the notions of probability distribution and distribution function, which can also be used to describe a multitude of other useful probabilities in a unified manner.

Definition 2.1

A **probability distribution** is by definition a probability measure P on $\mathbb{R}$ defined on the σ-field of Borel sets $\mathcal{B}(\mathbb{R})$. The function $F : \mathbb{R} \to [0, 1]$ defined as

$$F(x) = P((-\infty, x])$$

for each $x \in \mathbb{R}$ is called the (cumulative) **distribution function**.

Example 2.2

Let $0 < p < 1$ and fix $N = 1, 2, \ldots$. For any $A \in \mathcal{B}(\mathbb{R})$ let

$$P(A) = \sum_{n=0}^{N} \binom{N}{n} p^n (1-p)^{N-n} \mathbf{1}_A(n).$$

This defines a probability measure on $\mathbb{R}$, called the **binomial distribution** with parameters N, p. It corresponds to the binomial probability defined in Example 1.13. The corresponding distribution function is piecewise constant:

$$F(x) = \begin{cases} 0 & \text{for } x < 0, \\ \sum_{n=0}^{k} \binom{N}{n} p^n (1-p)^{N-n} & \text{for } k = 0, 1, \ldots, N-1 \text{ and } k \le x < k+1, \\ 1 & \text{for } N \le x. \end{cases}$$

This function is shown in Figure 2.1. The dots represent the values $F(x)$ at $x = 0, 1, \ldots, 10$, where the distribution function has discontinuities.

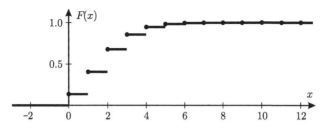

Figure 2.2 Distribution function for the Poisson distribution in Example 2.3 with $\lambda = 2$.

Example 2.3

Let $\lambda > 0$. The probability measure on $\mathbb{R}$ defined by

$$P(A) = \sum_{n=0}^{\infty} \frac{\lambda^n}{n!} e^{-\lambda} \mathbf{1}_A(n)$$

for any $A \in \mathcal{B}(\mathbb{R})$ is called the **Poisson distribution** with parameter λ. Compare this with the Poisson probability in Example 1.8. The corresponding distribution function

$$F(x) = \begin{cases} 0 & \text{for } x < 0, \\ \sum_{n=0}^{k} \frac{\lambda^n}{n!} e^{-\lambda} & \text{for } k = 0, 1, \dots \text{ and } k \le x < k+1 \end{cases}$$

is depicted in Figure 2.2. The dots represent the values $F(x)$ at $x = 0, 1, \dots,$ where the distribution function has discontinuities.

Definition 2.4

We say that a probability distribution P is **discrete** whenever there is a sequence $x_1, x_2, \dots \in \mathbb{R}$ such that $\sum_{n=1}^{\infty} P(\{x_n\}) = 1$.

Example 2.5

The binomial distribution and the Poisson distribution are examples of discrete probability distributions.

According to Theorem 1.35, if $f : \mathbb{R} \to [0, \infty]$ is Borel measurable, then the integral $\int_B f\,dm$, considered as a function of $B \in \mathcal{B}(\mathbb{R})$, is a measure. If, in addition, $\int_{\mathbb{R}} f\,dm = 1$, then this is a probability measure. We have seen

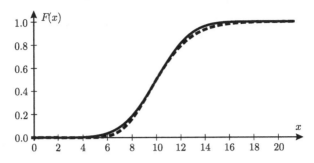

Figure 2.3 Distribution function for the normal distribution in Example 2.8 (solid line) and for the log-normal distribution in Example 2.9 (broken line).

two examples of such functions f, the normal density (Example 1.23) and the log-normal density (Example 1.24).

Definition 2.6
Any Borel measurable function $f : \mathbb{R} \to [0, \infty]$ such that $\int_{\mathbb{R}} f \, dm = 1$ is called a **probability density**.

When f is a probability density, then

$$P(B) = \int_B f \, dm$$

defined for any Borel set $B \in \mathcal{B}(\mathbb{R})$ is a probability distribution with distribution function

$$F(x) = P((-\infty, x]) = \int_{(-\infty,x]} f \, dm.$$

Definition 2.7
We say that a probability distribution P is **continuous** (sometimes referred to as **absolutely continuous**) if there is a density function f such that for each $B \in \mathcal{B}(\mathbb{R})$

$$P(B) = \int_B f \, dm.$$

Example 2.8
The **normal distribution** is the probability distribution corresponding to the normal density specified in Example 1.23. See Figure 2.3 for the distribution function in this case.

Example 2.9
The probability distribution with the log-normal density in Example 1.24 is referred to as the **log-normal distribution**. The corresponding distribution function is shown as a broken line in Figure 2.3.

Example 2.10
The density

$$f(x) = \begin{cases} \lambda e^{-\lambda x} & \text{if } x \geq 0, \\ 0 & \text{if } x < 0, \end{cases} \tag{2.1}$$

yields the so-called **exponential distribution** with parameter $\lambda > 0$. The corresponding distribution function is given by

$$F(x) = \begin{cases} 1 - e^{-\lambda x} & \text{if } x \geq 0, \\ 0 & \text{if } x < 0, \end{cases}$$

and shown in Figure 2.4.

The following proposition lists some properties shared by all distribution functions.

Proposition 2.11
The distribution function F of any probability distribution has the following properties:
  (i) $F(x) \leq F(y)$ *for every $x \leq y$ (F is non-decreasing);*
  (ii) $\lim_{x \searrow a} F(x) = F(a)$ *for each $a \in \mathbb{R}$ (F is right-continuous);*
  (iii) $\lim_{x \to -\infty} F(x) = 0;$
  (iv) $\lim_{x \to \infty} F(x) = 1.$

Proof Let F be the distribution function of a probability distribution P, that is, let $F(x) = P((-\infty, x])$ for each $x \in \mathbb{R}$.
  (i) Note that $x \leq y$ implies $(-\infty, x] \subset (-\infty, y]$, so $P((-\infty, x]) \leq P((-\infty, y])$ by Theorem 1.11 (iii).
  (ii) Take any non-increasing sequence of numbers x_n such that $x_n > a$ and $\lim_{n \to \infty} x_n = a$. Then $(-\infty, a] = \bigcap_{n=1}^{\infty}(-\infty, x_n]$, and $P((-\infty, a]) = P\left(\bigcap_{n=1}^{\infty}(-\infty, x_n]\right) = \lim_{n \to \infty} P((-\infty, a_n])$ by Theorem 1.11 (vii).
  (iii) If x_n is a non-increasing sequence of numbers such that $\lim_{n \to \infty} x_n =$

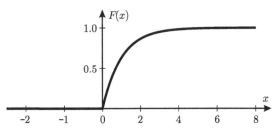

Figure 2.4 Distribution function for the exponential distribution in Example 2.10 with $\lambda = 1$.

$-\infty$, then $\varnothing = \bigcap_{n=1}^{\infty}(-\infty, x_n]$, so $0 = P(\bigcap_{n=1}^{\infty}(-\infty, x_n]) = \lim_{n\to\infty} P((-\infty, x_n])$ once again by Theorem 1.11 (vii).

(iv) Using Theorem 1.11 (v) with $B_n = (-\infty, x_n]$, where x_n is a non-decreasing sequence such that $\lim_{n\to\infty} x_n = \infty$, we have $\mathbb{R} = \bigcup_{n=1}^{\infty}(-\infty, x_n]$, and so $1 = P(\bigcup_{n=1}^{\infty}(-\infty, x_n]) = \lim_{n\to\infty} P((-\infty, x_n])$. $\qquad\square$

In general, F does not have to be continuous. Because F is non-decreasing, the left limit $F(a-) = \lim_{x \nearrow a} F(x)$ exists for each $a \in \mathbb{R}$. We have

$$P(\{a\}) = P\left(\bigcap_{n=1}^{\infty}(a - \tfrac{1}{n}, a]\right) = \lim_{n\to\infty} P\left((a - \tfrac{1}{n}, a]\right)$$
$$= \lim_{n\to\infty}\left(F(a) - F(a - \tfrac{1}{n})\right) = F(a) - F(a-).$$

If F has a discontinuity at a, then $F(a-) < F(a)$, and so $P(\{a\}) > 0$. On the other hand, if F is continuous at a, then $F(a-) = F(a)$ and $P(\{a\}) = 0$.

Exercise 2.1 Suppose F is a distribution function. Show that there are at most countably many $a \in \mathbb{R}$ such that $F(a-) < F(a)$. (We say that F has at most countably many jump discontinuities.)

Example 2.12

Suppose that F is a piecewise constant distribution function with a finite number of jumps at points $a_1 < a_2 < \cdots < a_N$ with $F(a_n) - F(a_n-) = p_n$, where $\sum_{n=1}^{N} p_n = 1$. So

$$F(x) = \begin{cases} 0 & \text{for } x < a_1, \\ \sum_{n=1}^{k} p_k & \text{for } k = 1, \ldots, N-1 \text{ and } a_k \leq x < a_{k+1}, \\ 1 & \text{for } a_N \leq x. \end{cases}$$

The corresponding probability distribution satisfies $P(\{a_n\}) = p_n$ for each n, and $P(\{a_1, \ldots, a_N\}) = 1$. It is a discrete probability distribution concentrated on a finite set. Example 2.2 falls into this category.

Example 2.13

In particular if $N = 1$ and $a_1 = a$ for some $a \in \mathbb{R}$, we have

$$F(x) = \mathbf{1}_{[a,\infty)}(x).$$

The corresponding probability distribution is the unit mass concentrated at a (see Example 1.12),

$$\delta_a(A) = \begin{cases} 1 & \text{if } a \in A, \\ 0 & \text{if } a \notin A, \end{cases}$$

for any Borel set $A \in \mathcal{B}(\mathbb{R})$.

Example 2.14

Let $F_{\text{log-norm}}$ denote the log-normal distribution function from Example 2.9. Fix a number $0 < p < 1$ and write

$$F(x) = \begin{cases} 0 & \text{for } x < 0, \\ p + (1-p)F_{\text{log-norm}}(x) & \text{for } x \geq 0. \end{cases}$$

This is a distribution function, with a jump of size p at 0. The resulting probability distribution is

$$P = p\delta_0 + (1-p)P_{\text{log-norm}},$$

where δ_0 is the unit mass concentrated at 0, and where $P_{\text{log-norm}}$ is the log-

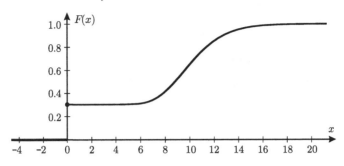

Figure 2.5 Distribution function in Example 2.14 with $p = 0.3$.

normal distribution with density given in Example 1.24. Here we have a
mixture of discrete and continuous distributions. It can be viewed as a
model of the stock price for a company which can suffer bankruptcy with
probability p. The graph of F with $p = 0.3$ is shown in Figure 2.5. The dot
represents the value $F(x)$ at $x = 0$, where the distribution function has a
discontinuity.

Exercise 2.2 Let $P_1, P_2, \ldots$ be probability measures defined on a σ-
field $\mathcal{F}$, and let $a_1, a_2, \ldots > 0$. What condition on the sequence a_n is
needed to ensure that $P = \sum_{n=1}^{\infty} a_n P_n$ is a probability measure?

Remark 2.15
The converse of Proposition 2.11 is also true. If $F : \mathbb{R} \to [0, 1]$ satisfies
conditions (i)–(iv) of this proposition, then F is the distribution function of
some probability distribution P. This provides a simple and convenient way
to describe a probability distribution by specifying its distribution function.

2.2 Random variables

Derivative securities (also called **contingent claims**) play an important
role in finance. They represent financial assets whose present value is determined by some future payoff. In the case of **European derivative securities** the payoff is available at a prescribed future time T and depends on

the value $S(T)$ at that time of a stock or some other risky asset, called the **underlying security**. We can write the payoff as $H = h(S(T))$ for some function h. For example, with $h(x) = (x - K)^+$ we have a (European) **call option**, while $h(x) = (K - x)^+$ gives a **put option**. Here K is called the **strike price**.

An important step in studying derivative securities is to build a model of the future values of $S(T)$. Various such models have been proposed. Suppose that we have chosen a probability space $(\Omega, \mathcal{F}, P)$ where the set Ω represents all possible values of $S(T)$. It is natural to ask for the probability $P(\{H \in B\})$ that the payoff H takes values in some Borel set $B \in \mathcal{B}(\mathbb{R})$, for example in an interval $B = [a, b]$. The set $\{H \in B\}$ should belong to the domain of P (which is $\mathcal{F}$, the σ-field of events). Functions with this property were called measurable in Definition 1.27. When working with probability spaces we call them random variables.

Definition 2.16

A **random variable** is a function $X : \Omega \to R$ such that for each Borel set $B \in \mathcal{B}(\mathbb{R})$

$$\{X \in B\} \in \mathcal{F}.$$

The family of all sets of the form $\{X \in B\}$ for some $B \in \mathcal{B}(\mathbb{R})$ is denoted by $\sigma(X)$ and is called the σ-field **generated** by X. We can see that X is a random variable if and only if $\sigma(X) \subset \mathcal{F}$.

Exercise 2.3   Show that $\sigma(X)$ is indeed a σ-field.

If $h : \mathbb{R} \to \mathbb{R}$ and $X : \Omega \to \mathbb{R}$, we shall often write $h(X)$ to denote the composition $h \circ X$. In fact this has already been done implicitly in the expression $h(S(T))$ above.

If h is a Borel measurable function, then $h(X)$ is measurable with respect to $\sigma(X)$ since $h^{-1}(B)$ is a Borel set for any $B \in \mathcal{B}(\mathbb{R})$, and so

$$\{h(X) \in B\} = \{X \in h^{-1}(B)\} \in \sigma(X).$$

In particular, when X is a random variable, it follows that $h(X)$ is also a random variable.

It turns out that all functions measurable with respect to $\sigma(X)$ are of the form $h(X)$ for some Borel measurable function h.

Exercise 2.4   Show that $Y : \Omega \to \mathbb{R}$ is measurable with respect to $\sigma(X)$ if and only if there is a Borel measurable function $h : \mathbb{R} \to \mathbb{R}$ such that $Y = h(X)$.

Example 2.17

The payoff functions of derivative securities provide many examples of random variables. For European options we can express the payoff in the form $h(S(T))$, so we need only to show that the function h is Borel measurable. Familiar examples are call or put options with strike K, whose payoff functions are $h(x) = (x - K)^+$ and $h(x) = (K - x)^+$ respectively. Other popular options include the following.

(1) A **bottom straddle**, which consists of buying a call and a put with the same strike K, so that the payoff is $h(x) = |x - K|$.

(2) A **strangle**, where we buy a call and a put with different strikes $K_1 < K_2$, so that

$$h(x) = (x - K_1)^+ + (K_2 - x)^+.$$

This reduces to a straddle when $K_1 = K_2$.

(3) A **bull spread**, consisting of two calls, one long and one short, with strikes $K_1 < K_2$, so that

$$h(x) = (x - K_1)^+ - (x - K_2)^+ = \begin{cases} 0 & \text{if } x < K_1, \\ x - K_1 & \text{if } K_1 \le x \le K_2, \\ K_2 - K_1 & \text{if } x > K_2. \end{cases}$$

(4) A **butterfly spread**, where we buy calls at strikes $K_1 < K_3$ and sell two calls at strike $K_2 = \frac{1}{2}(K_1 + K_3)$. You should verify that the payoff is zero outside (K_1, K_3) and equals $x - K_1$ on $[K_1, K_2]$ and $K_3 - x$ on $[K_2, K_3]$.

In all these cases the Borel measurability of h follows at once from the exercises in Chapter 1, so the payoffs are random variables.

Definition 2.18

With every random variable X we can associate a probability distribution P_X, called the **distribution** of X, defined as

$$P_X(B) = P(\{X \in B\})$$

for any Borel set $B \in \mathcal{B}(\mathbb{R})$. The corresponding distribution function

$$F_X(x) = P_X((-\infty, x])$$

defined for each $x \in \mathbb{R}$ is called the (cumulative) **distribution function** of the random variable X.

Since we will frequently work with probabilities of the form $P(\{X \in B\})$, from now on we condense these to $P(X \in B)$ for ease of notation when there is no risk of ambiguity.

Exercise 2.5 Let X be a random variable modelling a single coin toss, with two possible outcomes: 1 (heads) or -1 (tails). For a fair coin, the probabilities are $P(X = 1) = P(X = -1) = \frac{1}{2}$. Sketch the distribution function F_X.

Exercise 2.6 Let X be the number of tosses of a fair coin up to and including the first toss showing heads. Compute and sketch the distribution function F_X.

Exercise 2.7 Suppose that X_n for each $n = 1, 2, \ldots$ is a random variable having the binomial distribution with parameters n, p (see Example 2.2), where $p = \frac{\lambda}{n}$ for some $\lambda > 0$. Find $P_{X_n}(k)$ for $k = 0, 1 \ldots$, and determine $\lim_{n \to \infty} P_{X_n}(k)$.

The two classes of random variables that will mainly concern us can be distinguished by the nature of their distributions.

Definition 2.19
We say that a random variable X is **discrete** if it has a discrete probability distribution P_X, that is, if there is a sequence $x_1, x_2, \ldots \in \mathbb{R}$ such that

$$\sum_{n=1}^{\infty} P_X(\{x_n\}) = 1.$$

Definition 2.20
We say that a random variable X is **continuous** if there exists an integrable

function $f_X : \mathbb{R} \to [0, \infty]$ such that for every Borel set $B \in \mathcal{B}(\mathbb{R})$

$$P_X(B) = \int_B f_X \, dm.$$

We call f_X the **density** of X.

In these cases the distribution function F_X can be expressed as follows: for any $y \in \mathbb{R}$

(i) if X is discrete,

$$F_X(y) = \sum_{x_n \leq y} p_n \,, \text{ where } p_n = P_X(\{x_n\});$$

(ii) if X is continuous,

$$F_X(y) = \int_{(-\infty, y]} f_X \, dm.$$

Example 2.21

In Example 1.9 we saw that $p_n = (1 - p)^{n-1} p$ (where $0 < p < 1$) defines a probability on $\Omega = \{1, 2, \ldots\}$. This gives rise to a random variable $X(n) = n$ for $n = 1, 2, \ldots$ with **geometric distribution** $P_X(\{n\}) = P(X = n) = p_n$. Since $\sum_{n=1}^{\infty} p_n = 1$, it is clear that X is a discrete random variable.

Exercise 2.8   As in Example 1.9, we can think of $1, 2, \ldots$ as trading dates, and regard p and $1 - p$ as the probabilities of upward/downward price moves on any given trading date. Let Y be the number of trading dates needed to record r upward price moves. Show that $P_Y(\{n\}) = \binom{n-1}{r-1} p^r (1-p)^{n-r}$ for $n = r, r+1, \ldots$, and verify that this is a probability distribution. It is called the **negative binomial distribution**.

Example 2.22

We say that a random variable X has **normal distribution** if the probability density takes the form introduced in Example 1.23:

$$f_X(x) = \frac{1}{\sigma \sqrt{2\pi}} e^{-\frac{(x-\mu)^2}{2\sigma^2}},$$

for some $\mu \in \mathbb{R}$ and $\sigma > 0$. In this case we say simply that X has the

$N(\mu, \sigma^2)$ distribution, abbreviated to $X \sim N(\mu, \sigma^2)$. The corresponding distribution function is

$$F_X(x) = \int_{-\infty}^{x} \frac{1}{\sigma \sqrt{2\pi}} e^{-\frac{(y-\mu)^2}{2\sigma^2}} \, dy.$$

Since $f_X(x) > 0$ for all x, it follows that $F_X : \mathbb{R} \to [0, 1]$ is strictly increasing, hence invertible.

In particular, if $\mu = 0$ and $\sigma = 1$ we use the notation $N(x)$ for $F_X(x)$, and say that the random variable $X \sim N(0, 1)$ has the **standard normal distribution.**

Exercise 2.9   Given a random variable X with standard normal distribution $N(0, 1)$, let $Y = \mu + \sigma X$ for some $\mu, \sigma \in \mathbb{R}$ such that $\sigma > 0$. Show that Y has the normal distribution $N(\mu, \sigma^2)$.

Example 2.23
With $X \sim N(\mu, \sigma^2)$, write $Y(x) = F_X^{-1}(x)$. This function is a random variable on the probability space $[0, 1]$ with uniform probability given by the Lebesgue measure m. The random variable Y has the same normal distribution $N(\mu, \sigma^2)$ since

$$F_Y(a) = m(\{x \in [0, 1] : Y(x) \le a\}) = m(\{x \in [0, 1] : F_X^{-1}(x) \le a\})$$
$$= m(\{x \in [0, 1] : x \le F_X(a)\}) = m([0, F_X(a)]) = F_X(a).$$

The distributions (and the densities, when they exist) of simple algebraic functions of X can often be found directly.

Example 2.24
Let X be a random variable and let $Y = aX + b$ for some $a \ne 0$ and $b \in \mathbb{R}$. We find the distribution function F_Y in terms of F_X. For $a > 0$

$$F_Y(x) = P(aX + b \le x) = P\left(X \le \frac{x-b}{a}\right) = F_X\left(\frac{x-b}{a}\right).$$

On the other hand, for $a < 0$

$$F_Y(x) = P(aX + b \leq x) = P\left(X \geq \frac{x-b}{a}\right)$$

$$= 1 - P\left(X < \frac{x-b}{a}\right)$$

$$= 1 - \lim_{y \nearrow \frac{x-b}{a}} F_X(y) = 1 - F_X\left(\frac{x-b}{a}-\right).$$

Exercise 2.10 Suppose that X has continuous distribution with density f_X, and let $Y = aX + b$ for some $a, b \in \mathbb{R}$ such that $a \neq 0$. Show that

$$f_Y(x) = \frac{1}{|a|} f_X\left(\frac{x-b}{a}\right).$$

Exercise 2.11 Suppose that X is a random variable having uniform distribution on the interval $[-1, 1]$, i.e. such that the density of X is $f_X = \frac{1}{2}\mathbf{1}_{[-1,1]}$. Find the distribution function of $Y = \frac{1}{X}$.

Example 2.25
We say that a random variable $Y > 0$ has **log-normal distribution** if $X = \ln Y$ has normal distribution. We shall find the density of Y. Take any $0 < a < b$, which is sufficient because $Y = e^X$ takes only positive values, and employ the normal density f_X:

$$P(a \leq Y \leq b) = P(\ln a \leq X \leq \ln b)$$

$$= \int_{\ln a}^{\ln b} \frac{1}{\sigma\sqrt{2\pi}} e^{-\frac{(x-\mu)^2}{2\sigma^2}} dx = \int_a^b \frac{1}{y\sigma\sqrt{2\pi}} e^{-\frac{(\ln y-\mu)^2}{2\sigma^2}} dy,$$

where we make the substitution $x = \ln y$ in the integral. The probability density of Y has the familiar form of the log-normal density from Example 1.24.

Exercise 2.12 Suppose that X is a random variable with known density f_X. Find the density of $Y = g(X)$ if $g : \mathbb{R} \to \mathbb{R}$ is continuously differentiable and $g'(x) \neq 0$ for all $x \in \mathbb{R}$.

Application to stock prices and option payoffs

If X is a random variable with standard normal distribution $N(0, 1)$ defined on any probability space, then $\mu T + \sigma \sqrt{T} X$ has the normal distribution $N(\mu T, \sigma^2 T)$ (see Exercise 2.9), and

$$S(T) = S(0)e^{\mu T + \sigma \sqrt{T} X} \tag{2.2}$$

can be used as a model of log-normally distributed stock prices.

Example 2.26
If we want to represent the random future stock price $S(T)$ on a concrete probability space, we can for example take $\Omega = \mathbb{R}$ with P given by $P(B) = \int_B f \, dm$, where $f(x) = \frac{1}{\sqrt{2\pi}} e^{-x^2/2}$ is the standard normal density. Then X such that $X(\omega) = \omega$ for each $\omega \in \mathbb{R}$ is random variable on $(\mathbb{R}, \mathcal{B}(\mathbb{R}), P)$ with the standard normal distribution $N(0, 1)$, and $S(T)$ given by (2.2) is a log-normally distributed random variable defined on this probability space.

Various choices of the probability space can lead to the same distribution. There is no single universally accepted probability space, allowing much flexibility in selecting one to suit particular needs.

Example 2.27
Let X be a random variable with standard normal distribution $N(0, 1)$ defined on the unit interval $\Omega = [0, 1]$ with Lebesgue measure m as the uniform probability. Such a random variable was constructed in Example 2.23. Then the log-normally distributed stock price $S(T)$ modelled by (2.2) will also be a random variable on $\Omega = [0, 1]$. This lends itself well to applying a numerical technique known as **Monte Carlo simulation**. An approximation of the log-normal distribution function generated in this way is shown in Figure 2.6. Here $T = 1$, the parameters μ and σ of the log-normal distribution are as in Example 1.24, and a sample of 100 points drawn from

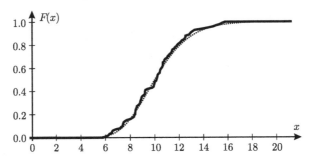

Figure 2.6 Monte Carlo simulation of the log-normal distribution function.

[0, 1] is used. For comparison, the dotted line shows the exact distribution function.

The payoff $H = h(S(T))$ of a European derivative security is a random variable defined on the same probability space as $S(T)$.

Example 2.28
The distribution function F_H of the call option payoff $H = (S(T) - K)^+$ can be written as

$$F_H(x) = P\{(S(T) - K)^+ \leq x\}$$
$$= \begin{cases} 0 & \text{if } x < 0 \\ P\{S(T) \leq K + x\} & \text{if } x \geq 0 \end{cases}$$
$$= \begin{cases} 0 & \text{if } x < 0 \\ F_{S(T)}(K + x) & \text{if } x \geq 0 \end{cases}$$

in terms of the distribution function $F_{S(T)}$ of $S(T)$.

In Figure 2.7 we can see the distribution function F_H for a call option with expiry time $T = 1$ and strike price $K = 8$ written on a log-normally distributed stock given by (2.2) with parameters μ and σ as in Example 1.24. The dot indicates the value $F_H(0) = F_{S(1)}(K)$ at $x = 0$, where F_H has a discontinuity. For comparison, the log-normal distribution function $F_{S(1)}$ is shown as a dotted line.

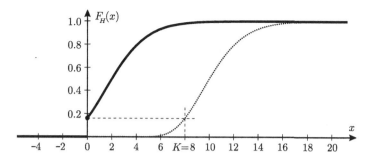

Figure 2.7 Distribution function for the call option payoff in Example 2.28.

Exercise 2.13   Find and sketch the distribution function of the payoff $H = (K - S(T))^+$ of a put option with expiry time $T = 1$ and strike price $K = 8$ written on a stock having a log-normal distribution with parameters μ and σ as in Example 1.24.

As a simple alternative to the log-normal model, we consider discrete stock prices by revisiting and extending Example 1.7. Suppose that the initial stock price is positive, $S(0) > 0$, and assume that there are N multiplicative price changes by a factor $1 + U$ or $1 + D$ (where $-1 < D < U$) with respective probabilities p and $1 - p$ (with $0 < p < 1$), so that at a future time $T > 0$ the stock price $S(T)$ will reach one of the possible values $S(0)(1+U)^n(1+D)^{N-n}$ with probability $\binom{N}{n}p^n(1-p)^{N-n}$ for $n = 0, 1, \ldots, N$; see [DMFM].

Example 2.29
A simple choice of the probability space for such a discrete model is $\Omega = \{0, 1, \ldots, N\}$ equipped with the binomial probability; see Example 1.13. The future stock price can be considered as a random variable on Ω defined by $S(T)(\omega) = S(0)(1 + U)^\omega(1 + D)^{N-\omega}$ for each $\omega \in \{0, 1, \ldots, N\}$. The payoff $H = h(S(T))$ of any European option is a function of the stock price $S(T)$ at expiry time T, so it can also be considered as a random variable on $\Omega = \{0, 1, \ldots, N\}$.

Example 2.30

Next we turn our attention to **path-dependent options**, whose payoff depends not just on the stock price $S(T)$ at expiry time T but also on the stock prices $S(t)$ at intermediate times $0 \le t \le T$. In the discrete model the time interval is divided into N steps $0 < t_1 < \cdots < t_N = T$. An **arithmetic Asian call** with payoff

$$H = \left(\frac{1}{N} \sum_{i=1}^{N} S(t_i) - K \right)^{+}$$

can serve as an example of a path-dependent option. It is a call option on the average of stock prices sampled at times $t_1, \ldots, t_N$.

To describe H as a random variable we need a richer probability space than that in Example 2.29. Let us take Ω to be the set of all sequences of length N consisting of symbols U or D to keep track of up and down stock price moves. To any such sequence $\omega = (\omega_1, \ldots, \omega_N) \in \Omega$ we assign the probability

$$P(\{\omega\}) = p^{k_N}(1 - p)^{N-k_N},$$

where k_N is the number of occurrences of U and $N - k_N$ is the number of occurrences of D in the sequence ω. For any $n = 1, \ldots, N$ we then put

$$S(t_n)(\omega) = S(0)(1 + U)^{k_n}(1 + D)^{n-k_n},$$

where k_n is the number of occurrences of U and $n - k_n$ is the number of occurrences of D among the first n entries in the sequence $\omega = (\omega_1, \ldots, \omega_N) \in \Omega$. This is the **binomial tree model** studied in [DMFM].

2.3 Expectation and variance

The probability distribution provides detailed information about the values of a random variable along with the associated probabilities. Sometimes simplified information is more practical, hence the need for some numerical characteristics of random variables.

For a discrete random variable X such that $\sum_{n=1}^{\infty} p_n = 1$ with $p_n = P(X =$

x_n) for some $x_1, x_2, \ldots \in \mathbb{R}$, the **expectation** of X is the weighted average

$$\mathbb{E}(X) = \sum_{n=1}^{\infty} x_n p_n.$$

In particular, in the case of a finite $\Omega = \{x_1, \ldots, x_N\}$ with uniform probability we obtain the arithmetic average

$$\mathbb{E}(X) = \frac{1}{N} \sum_{n=1}^{N} x_n.$$

Exercise 2.14   Find a discrete random variable X such that the expectation of X is undefined.

Exercise 2.15   A random variable X on $\Omega = \{0, 1, 2, \ldots\}$ has the Poisson distribution with parameter $\lambda > 0$ if $p_n = e^{-\lambda} \frac{\lambda^n}{n!}$ for $n = 0, 1, 2, \ldots$; see Example 2.3. Find $\mathbb{E}(X)$.

The above definition of the expectation is familiar in another context: a non-negative discrete random variable X is nothing other than a **simple function**, as in Definition 1.25, with $A_n = \{X = x_n\}$ and $p_n = P(A_n)$ for $n = 1, \ldots, N$. Its integral can therefore be written as

$$\int_{\Omega} X \, dP = \sum_{n=1}^{N} x_n p_n = \mathbb{E}(X).$$

We use the fact that the expectation and integral coincide in this simple case to motivate the general definition.

Definition 2.31
The **expectation** $\mathbb{E}(X)$ of an integrable random variable X defined on a probability space $(\Omega, \mathcal{F}, P)$ is its integral over Ω, that is,

$$\mathbb{E}(X) = \int_{\Omega} X \, dP.$$

We can immediately deduce the following properties from Exercises 1.27, 1.28 and 1.26, respectively.

Proposition 2.32
If X and Y are integrable random variables on $(\Omega, \mathcal{F}, P)$ and $a, b \in \mathbb{R}$, then:

(i) $\mathbb{E}(aX + bY) = a\mathbb{E}(X) + b\mathbb{E}(Y)$ **(linearity)**;

(ii) *if $X \leq Y$, then $\mathbb{E}(X) \leq \mathbb{E}(Y)$* **(monotonicity)**;

(iii) $|\mathbb{E}(X)| \leq \mathbb{E}(|X|)$.

For a general X it may not be obvious how to calculate the expectation directly from the definition. However, the task becomes more tractable when we examine the relationship between integrals with respect to P and P_X.

Theorem 2.33
If $X : \Omega \to \mathbb{R}$ is a random variable on $(\Omega, \mathcal{F}, P)$ and $g : \mathbb{R} \to \mathbb{R}$ is integrable under P_X, then

$$\mathbb{E}(g(X)) = \int_\Omega g(X)\,dP = \int_\mathbb{R} g\,dP_X.$$

Proof   This follows immediately from Proposition 1.37, in which we take $\left(\tilde{\Omega}, \tilde{\mathcal{F}}, \tilde{\mu}\right) = (\mathbb{R}, \mathcal{B}(\mathbb{R}), P_X)$ and $\varphi = X$.   □

It will sometimes prove helpful to be explicit about the variable of integration, so we allow ourselves the freedom to write

$$\int_\Omega X\,dP = \int_\Omega X(\omega)\,dP(\omega)$$

or

$$\int_\mathbb{R} g\,dP_X = \int_\mathbb{R} g(x)\,dP_X(x),$$

as the need arises. As a special case, for $g(x) = x$ we obtain

$$\mathbb{E}(X) = \int_\mathbb{R} x\,dP_X(x).$$

This formula enables us to compute the expectation when the distribution of X is known.

In particular, if X has continuous distribution with density f_X, then $P_X(B) = \int_B f_X\,dm$, where m is the Lebesgue measure, and we can conclude, with g and X as in Theorem 2.33, that

$$\mathbb{E}(g(X)) = \int_\mathbb{R} g(x)f_X(x)\,dm(x). \tag{2.3}$$

Exercise 2.16   Prove (2.3), first for any simple function g, then using monotone convergence for any non-negative measurable g, and finally for any g integrable under P_X.

In particular, whenever $g(x) = x$ is an integrable function under P_X, we have

$$\mathbb{E}(X) = \int_{\mathbb{R}} x f_X(x)\, dm(x).$$

Example 2.34
If $X \sim N(0,1)$, then $\mathbb{E}(X) = \int_{-\infty}^{\infty} x f_X(x)\, dx$ by Proposition 1.39, since the density $f_X(x) = \frac{1}{\sqrt{2\pi}} e^{-\frac{1}{2}x^2}$ is a continuous function on $\mathbb{R}$. We compute the expectation

$$\mathbb{E}(X) = \int_{-\infty}^{\infty} x f_X(x)\, dx = \frac{1}{\sqrt{2\pi}} \int_{-\infty}^{\infty} x e^{-\frac{1}{2}x^2}\, dx = 0.$$

The result is 0 since the integrand $g(x) = x e^{-\frac{1}{2}x^2}$ is an odd function, that is, $g(-x) = -g(x)$, so that the integrals from $-\infty$ to 0 and from 0 to ∞ cancel each other.

Exercise 2.17 Let $X \sim N(\mu, \sigma^2)$ for some $\mu \in \mathbb{R}$ and $\sigma > 0$. Verify that $\mathbb{E}(X) = \mu$.

Exercise 2.18 Let X have the Cauchy distribution with density

$$f_X(x) = \frac{1}{\pi} \frac{1}{1 + x^2}.$$

Show that the expectation of X is undefined.

Example 2.35
Suppose that $P_X = p\delta_{x_0} + (1-p)P$, where P has density f. Then $\mathbb{E}(X) = px_0 + (1-p)\int_{\mathbb{R}} x f(x)\, dm(x)$. (Compare with Example 2.14.)

Exercise 2.19 Find $\mathbb{E}(X)$ for a random variable X with distribution $P_X = \frac{1}{4}\delta_0 + \frac{3}{4}P$, where P is the exponential distribution with parameter $\lambda = 1$, see Example 2.10.

The expectation can be viewed as a weighted average of the values of a random variable X, with the corresponding probabilities acting as weights. However, this tells us nothing about how widely the values of X are spread around the expectation. Averaging the (positive) distance $|X - \mathbb{E}(X)|$ would be one possible measure of the spread, but the expectation of the squared distance $(X - \mathbb{E}(X))^2$ proves to be much more convenient and has become the standard approach.

Definition 2.36
The **variance** of an integrable random variable X is defined as

$$\text{Var}(X) = \mathbb{E}[(X - \mathbb{E}(X))^2].$$

(Note that the variance may be equal to ∞.) The square root of the variance yields the **standard deviation**

$$\sigma_X = \sqrt{\text{Var}(X)}.$$

When X is discrete with values x_n and corresponding probabilities $p_n = P(X = x_n)$ for $n = 1, 2, \ldots$, the variance becomes

$$\text{Var}(X) = \sum_{n=1}^{\infty} (x_n - \mathbb{E}(X))^2 p_n,$$

revealing its origins as a weighted sum of the squared distances between the x_n and $\mathbb{E}(X)$.

Exercise 2.20 Show that the variance of a random variable with Poisson distribution with parameter λ is equal to λ.

The linearity of expectation implies that

$$\text{Var}(X) = \mathbb{E}((X - \mathbb{E}(X))^2)$$
$$= \mathbb{E}(X^2 - 2X\mathbb{E}(X) + \mathbb{E}(X)^2) = \mathbb{E}(X^2) - \mathbb{E}(X)^2,$$

hence

$$\text{Var}(aX + b) = a^2 \text{Var}(X), \quad \sigma_{aX+b} = |a|\,\sigma_X.$$

By Theorem 2.33 with $g(x) = (x - \mathbb{E}(X))^2$,

$$\text{Var}(X) = \int_{\mathbb{R}} (x - \mathbb{E}(X))^2 \, dP_X(x).$$

If X has a density, we obtain

$$\text{Var}(X) = \int_{\mathbb{R}} (x - \mathbb{E}(X))^2 f_X(x)\, dm(x).$$

Example 2.37
We saw that if X has the standard normal distribution, its expectation is 0.
So $\text{Var}(X) = \int_{-\infty}^{\infty} x^2 f_X(x)\, dx = 1$, as is easily seen using integration by parts.

Exercise 2.21 Compute the variance of $X \sim N(\mu, \sigma^2)$.

This shows that for a normally distributed X the shape of the distribution is fully determined by the expectation and variance.

Exercise 2.22 Compute $\mathbb{E}(X)$ and $\text{Var}(X)$ in the following cases:
  (1) X has the exponential distribution with density (2.1).
  (2) X has the log-normal distribution with density (1.7).

The are several useful inequalities involving expectation and/or variance that enable one to estimate certain probabilities. Here we present just two simple examples.

Proposition 2.38 (Markov inequality)
Let $f : \mathbb{R} \to [0, \infty)$ be an even function, that is, $f(-x) = f(x)$ for any $x \in \mathbb{R}$, and non-decreasing for $x > 0$. If X is a random variable and $c > 0$, then

$$P(|X| \geq c) \leq \frac{\mathbb{E}(f(X))}{f(c)}.$$

Proof Define $A = \{|X| \geq c\}$. It follows that $f(|X|) > f(c)$ on A. Since f is an even function, we have $f(X) = f(|X|)$, so

$$\mathbb{E}(f(X)) = \mathbb{E}(f(|X|)) = \int_{\Omega} f(|X|)\, dP \geq \int_{A} f(|X|)\, dP \geq f(c)P(A).$$

$\square$

In particular, we can apply Proposition 2.38 with $f(x) = x^2$ to obtain the following inequality.

Corollary 2.39 (Chebyshev inequality)

$$P(|X| \geq c) \leq \frac{\mathbb{E}(X^2)}{c^2}.$$

For X with finite mean μ and variance σ^2 we can apply Chebyshev's inequality to $|X - \mu|$ and $c = k\sigma$ to obtain

$$P(|X - \mu| \geq k\sigma) \leq \frac{1}{k^2}.$$

Thus, if X has small variance, it will remain close to its mean with high probability.

2.4   Moments and characteristic functions

Definition 2.40

For any $k \in \mathbb{N}$ we define the kth **moment** of a random variable X as the expectation of X^k, that is,

$$m_k = \mathbb{E}(X^k),$$

and the kth **central moment** as

$$\sigma_k = \mathbb{E}((X - \mathbb{E}(X))^k).$$

Clearly, $m_1 = \mathbb{E}(X)$ is just the expectation of X. Moreover, $\sigma_1 = 0$ and $\sigma_2 = \text{Var}(X)$.

We can ask whether a single function might suffice to identify all the moments of a random variable X. It turns out that the expectation of e^{itX} does the job. To make sense of such an expectation we define the integral of a function $f : \Omega \to \mathbb{C}$ with values among complex numbers by means of the integral of its real and imaginary parts: if $f = \text{Re}f + i\text{Im}f$ and both the (real-valued) functions $\text{Re}f$ and $\text{Im}f$ are integrable, we set

$$\int_\Omega f \, dP = \int_\Omega \text{Re}f \, dP + i \int_\Omega \text{Im}f \, dP.$$

In other words, we set

$$\mathbb{E}(f) = \mathbb{E}(\text{Re}f) + i\mathbb{E}(\text{Im}f).$$

Definition 2.41

Let $X : \Omega \to \mathbb{R}$ be a random variable. Then $\phi_X : \mathbb{R} \to \mathbb{C}$ defined by

$$\phi_X(t) = \mathbb{E}(e^{itX}) = \mathbb{E}(\cos(tX)) + i\mathbb{E}(\sin(tX))$$

for all $t \in \mathbb{R}$ is called the **characteristic function** of X.

To compute ϕ_X it is sufficient to know the probability distribution of X:

$$\phi_X(t) = \int_{\mathbb{R}} e^{itx} \, dP_X(x),$$

and if X has a density, this reduces to

$$\phi_X(t) = \int_{\mathbb{R}} e^{itx} f_X(x) \, dm(x).$$

Vice versa, it turns out (see the inversion formula, Theorem 5.41) that the probability distribution of X is uniquely determined by the characteristic function ϕ_X.

The function ϕ_X has the advantage that it always exists because the random variable e^{itX} is bounded. We begin by stating the simplest properties of ϕ_X and give several examples as exercises.

Exercise 2.23   Show that for any random variable X
(1) $\phi_X(0) = 1$;
(2) $|\phi_X(t)| \le 1$ for all $t \in \mathbb{R}$.

The characteristic function $\phi_X(t)$ is continuous in t. In fact

$$|\phi_X(t + h) - \phi_X(t)| \le \int_{\mathbb{R}} |e^{ihx} - 1| \, dP_X(x),$$

so it follows that $\phi_X(t)$ is uniformly continuous.

Exercise 2.24   Let X have the Poisson distribution with parameter $\lambda > 0$. Find its characteristic function.

Exercise 2.25   Verify that if X is a random variable with the standard normal distribution, then $\phi_X(t) = e^{-\frac{1}{2}t^2}$.

Exercise 2.26   Let $Y = aX + b$, where X, Y are random variables and $a, b \in \mathbb{R}$. Show that for all $t \in \mathbb{R}$

$$\phi_Y(t) = e^{itb} \phi_X(at).$$

Use this relation to find ϕ_Y when Y is normally distributed with mean μ and variance σ^2.

As hinted above, there is a close relationship between the characteristic function and the moments of a random variable.

Theorem 2.42
Let X be a random variable and let n be a non-negative integer such that $\mathbb{E}(|X|^n) < \infty$. *Then*

$$\mathbb{E}(X^n) = \frac{1}{i^n}\phi_X^{(n)}(0).$$

Proof   First observe that for any $x \in \mathbb{R}$

$$e^{ix} - 1 - ix = i\int_0^x \left(e^{is} - 1\right)ds.$$

Estimating the integral gives the inequality

$$\left|e^{ix} - 1 - ix\right| = \left|\int_0^x \left(e^{is} - 1\right)ds\right| \le \int_0^x \left|e^{is} - 1\right|ds \le 2\,|x|. \qquad (2.4)$$

We show by induction that

$$\phi_X^{(n)}(t) = \mathbb{E}((iX)^n e^{itX})$$

for every random variable X such that $\mathbb{E}(|X|^n) < \infty$. For $n = 0$ this is trivially satisfied: $\phi_X^{(0)}(t) = \phi_X(t) = \mathbb{E}(e^{itX})$. Now suppose that the assertion has already been established for some $n = 0, 1, 2, \ldots$, and take any random variable X such that $\mathbb{E}(|X|^{n+1}) < \infty$. It follows that

$$\mathbb{E}(|X|^n) = \mathbb{E}(\mathbf{1}_{\{|X|\le 1\}}\,|X|^n) + \mathbb{E}(\mathbf{1}_{\{|X|>1\}}\,|X|^n)$$
$$\le 1 + \mathbb{E}(\mathbf{1}_{\{|X|>1\}}\,|X|^{n+1}) \le 1 + \mathbb{E}(|X|^{n+1}) < \infty.$$

By the induction hypothesis we therefore have

$$\frac{\phi_X^{(n)}(t+h) - \phi_X^{(n)}(t)}{h} - \mathbb{E}((iX)^{n+1}e^{itX}) = \mathbb{E}\left((iX)^n e^{itX}\frac{e^{ihX} - 1 - ihX}{h}\right). \qquad (2.5)$$

By (2.4) the random variables

$$Y_n(h) = (iX)^n e^{itX}\frac{e^{ihX} - 1 - ihX}{h}$$

are dominated by $2\,|X|^{n+1}$. The derivative of the exponential function gives $\lim_{h\to 0}\frac{e^{ihX}-1}{h} = iX$, hence $\lim_{h\to 0} Y_n(h) = 0$, and by the version of the dominated convergence theorem in Exercise 1.36 it follows that $\lim_{h\to 0} \mathbb{E}(Y_n(h)) = 0$. This shows that

$$\phi_X^{(n+1)}(t) = \mathbb{E}((iX)^{n+1}e^{itX}),$$

completing the induction argument. Putting $t = 0$ proves the theorem. $\quad\square$

Exercise 2.27 Use the formula in Theorem 2.42 to obtain an expression for the variance of X in terms of the characteristic function ϕ_X and its derivatives, evaluated at zero.

Exercise 2.28 Suppose that $X \sim N(0, \sigma^2)$. Show that for any odd n we have $\mathbb{E}(X^n) = 0$, and for any even n,

$$\mathbb{E}(X^n) = 1 \times 3 \times \cdots \times (n-1) \times \sigma^n.$$

In the general case, when $X \sim N(\mu, \sigma^2)$, show that

$$\mathbb{E}(X^2) = \mu^2 + \sigma^2,$$
$$\mathbb{E}(X^3) = \mu^3 + 3\mu\sigma^2,$$
$$\mathbb{E}(X^4) = \mu^4 + 6\mu^2\sigma^2 + 3\sigma^4.$$

Remark 2.43

If X is a random variable with values in $\{1, 2, \ldots\}$, the **probability generating function** $G_X(s) = \mathbb{E}(s^X) = \sum_{n\geq 1} s^n p_n$ allows us (in principle) to reconstruct the sequence $p_n = P(X = n)$. Setting $s = e^t$ turns G_X into the **moment generating function** $m_X(t) = \mathbb{E}[e^{tX}]$ of X.

The moment generating function is not always finite-valued, not even in an open interval around the origin. However, if X has a finite moment generating function m_X on some interval $(-a, a)$, then we can read off the kth moment of X directly as the value of its kth derivative at 0, namely $\mathbb{E}[X^k] = m_X^{(k)}(0)$.

3

Product measure and independence

In a financial market, the price of stocks in one company may well influence those of another: if company A suffers a decline in the market share for their product, its competitor B may have an opportunity to increase their sales, and thus the shares in B may increase in price while those of A decline. On the other hand, if the overall market for a particular product contracts, we may find that the shares of two rival companies will decline simultaneously, though not necessarily at the same rate.

Modelling the relationships between the prices of different shares is therefore of particular interest. We can regard the prices as random variables X, Y defined on a common probability space $(\Omega, \mathcal{F}, P)$, and endeavour to describe their joint behaviour.

In Chapter 2 the distribution of a single random variable X was defined as the probability measure on $\mathbb{R}$ given by

$$P_X(B) = P(X \in B)$$

for all Borel sets $B \subset \mathbb{R}$. In the case of two random variables X, Y a natural extension would be to write the joint distribution as

$$P_{X,Y}(B) = P(X \in B_1, Y \in B_2) \tag{3.1}$$

for any $B \subset \mathbb{R}^2$ of the form $B = B_1 \times B_2$, where $B_1, B_2 \subset \mathbb{R}$ are Borel sets.

However, the family of such sets B is not a σ-field, and we need to extend it further to be able to consider $P_{X,Y}$ as a probability measure. This will lead to the notion of Borel sets in $\mathbb{R}^2$.

Exercise 3.1   Show that the family of sets $B \subset \mathbb{R}^2$ of the form $B = B_1 \times B_2$, where $B_1, B_2 \subset \mathbb{R}$ are Borel sets, is not a σ-field.

In particular, for a continuous random variable X with density $f_X : \mathbb{R} \to [0, \infty)$ the probability distribution P_X can be expressed as

$$P_X(B) = \int_B f_X(x)dm(x),$$

for any Borel set $B \subset \mathbb{R}$, where m is the Lebesgue measure on the real line $\mathbb{R}$. To extend this we need to introduce the notion of joint density $f_{X,Y} : \mathbb{R}^2 \to [0, \infty)$ and define Lebesgue measure m_2 on the plane $\mathbb{R}^2$, so that the joint probability distribution can be written as

$$P_{X,Y}(B) = \int_B f_{X,Y}(x, y)dm_2(x, y)$$

for any Borel set B in $\mathbb{R}^2$.

3.1   Product measure

When constructing Lebesgue measure m on $\mathbb{R}$, we started by taking $m(I) = b - a$ to be the length of any interval $I = (a, b)$, and extended this to a measure defined on all Borel sets in $\mathbb{R}$, that is, on the smallest σ-field containing all intervals. The idea behind the construction of Lebesgue measure m_2 on $\mathbb{R}^2$ is similar. For any rectangle $R = (a, b) \times (c, d)$ we take $m_2(R) = (b - a)(d - c)$ to be the surface area, and would like to extend this to a measure on the family of all Borel sets in $\mathbb{R}^2$ defined as the smallest σ-field containing all rectangles.

Product of finite measures

It is not much more effort to consider measures on arbitrary spaces. This has the advantage of wider applicability. Consider arbitrary measure spaces

$(\Omega_1, \mathcal{F}_1, \mu_1)$ and $(\Omega_2, \mathcal{F}_2, \mu_2)$ with finite measures μ_1, μ_2. We want to construct a measure μ on the Cartesian product $\Omega_1 \times \Omega_2$ such that

$$\mu(A_1 \times A_2) = \mu_1(A_1)\mu_2(A_2) \qquad (3.2)$$

for any $A_1 \in \mathcal{F}_1$ and $A_2 \in \mathcal{F}_2$. The construction has several steps.

In $\Omega_1 \times \Omega_2$ a **measurable rectangle** is a product $A_1 \times A_2$ for which $A_1 \in \mathcal{F}_1$ and $A_2 \in \mathcal{F}_2$. We denote the family of all measurable rectangles by

$$\mathcal{R} = \{A_1 \times A_2 : A_1 \in \mathcal{F}_1, A_2 \in \mathcal{F}_2\}.$$

Then we consider the smallest σ-field containing the family $\mathcal{R}$ of measurable rectangles, which we denote by

$$\mathcal{F}_1 \otimes \mathcal{F}_2 = \bigcap \{\mathcal{F} : \mathcal{F} \text{ is a } \sigma\text{-field on } \Omega_1 \times \Omega_2 \text{ and } \mathcal{R} \subset \mathcal{F}\} \qquad (3.3)$$

and call it the **product σ-field**.

Exercise 3.2 Show that the product σ-field $\mathcal{F}_1 \otimes \mathcal{F}_2$ is the smallest σ-field such that the projections

$$Pr_1 : \Omega_1 \times \Omega_2 \to \Omega_1, \qquad Pr_1(\omega_1, \omega_2) = \omega_1$$
$$Pr_2 : \Omega_1 \times \Omega_2 \to \Omega_2, \qquad Pr_2(\omega_1, \omega_2) = \omega_2$$

are measurable.

Definition 3.1
The family of Borel sets on the plane can be defined as

$$\mathcal{B}(\mathbb{R}^2) = \mathcal{B}(\mathbb{R}) \otimes \mathcal{B}(\mathbb{R}).$$

Exercise 3.3 Show that the smallest σ-field on $\mathbb{R}^2$ containing the family

$$\{I_1 \times I_2 : I_1, I_2 \text{ are intervals in } \mathbb{R}\}$$

is equal to $\mathcal{B}(\mathbb{R}^2)$.

Since the domain of a measure is a σ-field by definition, the construction described in (3.3) is an example of quite a general idea.

Definition 3.2

Let Ω be a non-empty set. For a family $\mathcal{A}$ of subsets of Ω we denote the smallest σ-field on Ω that contains $\mathcal{A}$ by

$$\sigma(\mathcal{A}) = \bigcap \{\mathcal{F} : \mathcal{F} \text{ is a } \sigma\text{-field on } \Omega, \mathcal{A} \subset \mathcal{F}\}.$$

We call $\sigma(\mathcal{A})$ the σ-field **generated by** $\mathcal{A}$.

Example 3.3

The Borel sets in $\mathbb{R}$ form the σ-field generated by the family $\mathcal{I}$ of open intervals in $\mathbb{R}$,

$$\mathcal{B}(\mathbb{R}) = \sigma(\mathcal{I}).$$

Example 3.4

The product σ-field is generated by the family $\mathcal{R}$ of measurable rectangles,

$$\mathcal{F}_1 \otimes \mathcal{F}_2 = \sigma(\mathcal{R}).$$

The next step in constructing a measure μ on $\mathcal{F}_1 \otimes \mathcal{F}_2$ that satisfies (3.2) is to define **sections** of a subset $A \subset \Omega_1 \times \Omega_2$. Namely, for any $\omega_2 \in \Omega_2$ we put

$$A_{\omega_2} = \{\omega_1 \in \Omega_1 : (\omega_1, \omega_2) \in A\},$$

and, similarly, for any $\omega_1 \in \Omega_1$

$$A_{\omega_1} = \{\omega_2 \in \Omega_2 : (\omega_1, \omega_2) \in A\}.$$

Exercise 3.4 Let $A \in \mathcal{F}_1 \otimes \mathcal{F}_2$. Show that $A_{\omega_2} \in \mathcal{F}_1$ and $A_{\omega_1} \in \mathcal{F}_2$ for any $\omega_1 \in \Omega_1$ and $\omega_2 \in \Omega_2$.

In particular, for a measurable rectangle $A = A_1 \times A_2$ with $A_1 \in \mathcal{F}_1$ and $A_2 \in \mathcal{F}_2$, we obtain $A_{\omega_2} = A_1$ if $\omega_2 \in A_2$ and $A_{\omega_2} = \varnothing$ otherwise. So $\omega_2 \mapsto \mu_1(A_{\omega_2}) = \mathbf{1}_{A_2}(\omega_2)\mu_1(A_1)$ is a simple function. Hence, from (3.2)

$$\mu(A_1 \times A_2) = \mu_1(A_1)\mu_2(A_2) = \int_{\Omega_2} \mu_1(A_{\omega_2}) d\mu_2(\omega_2).$$

By symmetry, we can also write

$$\mu(A_1 \times A_2) = \mu_1(A_1)\mu_2(A_2) = \int_{\Omega_1} \mu_2(A_{\omega_1}) d\mu_1(\omega_1).$$

This motivates the general formula defining μ on $\mathcal{F}_1 \otimes \mathcal{F}_2$. Namely, for any $A \in \mathcal{F}_1 \otimes \mathcal{F}_2$ we propose to write

$$\mu(A) = \int_{\Omega_1} \mu_2(A_{\omega_1}) d\mu_1(\omega_1) = \int_{\Omega_2} \mu_1(A_{\omega_2}) d\mu_2(\omega_2),$$

along with the conjecture that the last two integrals are well defined and equal to one another. We already know from Exercise 3.4 that $\mu_1(A_{\omega_2})$ and $\mu_2(A_{\omega_1})$ make sense since $A_{\omega_2} \in \mathcal{F}_1$ and $A_{\omega_1} \in \mathcal{F}_2$. Moreover, for the integrals to make sense we need the function $\omega_1 \mapsto \mu_2(A_{\omega_1})$ to be $\mathcal{F}_1$-measurable and $\omega_2 \mapsto \mu_1(A_{\omega_2})$ to be $\mathcal{F}_2$-measurable. Our objective is therefore to prove the following result.

Theorem 3.5
Suppose that μ_1 and μ_2 are finite measures defined on the σ-fields $\mathcal{F}_1$ and $\mathcal{F}_2$, respectively. Then:
  (i) *for any $A \in \mathcal{F}_1 \otimes \mathcal{F}_2$ the functions*

$$\omega_1 \mapsto \mu_2(A_{\omega_1}), \qquad \omega_2 \mapsto \mu_1(A_{\omega_2})$$

  are measurable, respectively, with respect to $\mathcal{F}_1$ and $\mathcal{F}_2$;
  (ii) *for any $A \in \mathcal{F}_1 \otimes \mathcal{F}_2$ the following integrals are well defined and equal to one another:*

$$\int_{\Omega_1} \mu_2(A_{\omega_1}) d\mu_1(\omega_1) = \int_{\Omega_2} \mu_1(A_{\omega_2}) d\mu_2(\omega_2);$$

  (iii) *the function $\mu : \mathcal{F}_1 \otimes \mathcal{F}_2 \to [0, \infty)$ defined by*

$$\mu(A) = \int_{\Omega_1} \mu_2(A_{\omega_1}) d\mu_1(\omega_1) = \int_{\Omega_2} \mu_1(A_{\omega_2}) d\mu_2(\omega_2) \qquad (3.4)$$

  for each $A \in \mathcal{F}_1 \otimes \mathcal{F}_2$ is a measure on the σ-field $\mathcal{F}_1 \otimes \mathcal{F}_2$;
  (iv) *μ is the only measure on $\mathcal{F}_1 \otimes \mathcal{F}_2$ such that*

$$\mu(A_1 \times A_2) = \mu_1(A_1)\mu_2(A_2)$$

  for each $A_1 \in \mathcal{F}_1$ and $A_2 \in \mathcal{F}_2$.

The proof of this theorem can be found in Section 3.7. It is quite technical and can be omitted on first reading. The theorem shows that the following definition is well posed.

Definition 3.6
Let μ_1 and μ_2 be finite measures defined on the σ-fields $\mathcal{F}_1$ and $\mathcal{F}_2$, respectively. We call μ defined by (3.4) the **product measure** on $\mathcal{F}_1 \otimes \mathcal{F}_2$ and denote it by $\mu_1 \otimes \mu_2$.

Product of σ-finite measures

Observe that Theorem 3.5 and Definition 3.6 do not apply directly to the Lebesgue measure m on $\mathbb{R}$ because $m(\mathbb{R}) = \infty$. However, the definition of product measure can be extended to a large class of measures with the following property, which does include Lebesgue measure.

Definition 3.7
Let $(\Omega, \mathcal{F}, \mu)$ be a measure space. We say that μ is a σ-**finite** measure whenever $\Omega = \bigcup_{n=1}^{\infty} A_n$ for some sequence of events $A_n \in \mathcal{F}$ such that $\mu(A_n) < \infty$ and $A_n \subset A_{n+1}$ for each $n = 1, 2, \dots$.

Example 3.8
Taking for example $A_n = [-n, n]$, we can see that Lebesgue measure m is indeed σ-finite.

Definition 3.9
Let $(\Omega_1, \mathcal{F}_1, \mu_1)$ and $(\Omega_2, \mathcal{F}_2, \mu_2)$ be measure spaces with σ-finite measures μ_1, μ_2. The **product measure** $\mu_1 \otimes \mu_2$ is constructed as follows.
  (i) Take two sequences of events $A_n \in \mathcal{F}_1$ with $\mu_1(A_n) < \infty$ and $A_n \subset A_{n+1}$, and $B_n \in \mathcal{F}_2$ with $\mu_2(B_n) < \infty$ and $B_n \subset B_{n+1}$ for $n = 1, 2, \dots$ such that

$$\Omega_1 = \bigcup_{n=1}^{\infty} A_n, \quad \Omega_2 = \bigcup_{n=1}^{\infty} B_n.$$

 (ii) For each $n = 1, 2, \dots$ denote by $\mu_1^{(n)}$ the **restriction** of μ_1 to A_n defined by

$$\mu_1^{(n)}(A) = \mu_1(A) \quad \text{for each } A \in \mathcal{F}_1 \text{ such that } A \subset A_n,$$

and by $\mu_2^{(n)}$ the restriction of μ_2 to B_n, defined analogously; clearly $\mu_1^{(n)}$ and $\mu_2^{(n)}$ are finite measures.
(iii) Define $\mu_1 \otimes \mu_2$ for any $C \in \mathcal{F}_1 \otimes \mathcal{F}_2$ as

$$(\mu_1 \otimes \mu_2)(C) = \lim_{n \to \infty} (\mu_1^{(n)} \otimes \mu_2^{(n)})(C \cap (A_n \times B_n)).$$

Exercise 3.5   Show that the limit in Definition 3.9 (iii) exists and does not depend on the choice of the sequences A_n, B_n in (i).

Exercise 3.6   Show that $\mu_1 \otimes \mu_2$ from Definition 3.9 (iii) is a σ-finite measure.

Example 3.10

In Example 3.8 we observed that the Lebesgue measure m on $\mathbb{R}$ is σ-finite. The construction in Definition 3.9 therefore applies, and yields the product measure $m \otimes m$ defined on the Borel sets $\mathcal{B}(\mathbb{R}^2) = \mathcal{B}(\mathbb{R}) \otimes \mathcal{B}(\mathbb{R})$ in $\mathbb{R}^2$, which will be denoted by

$$m_2 = m \otimes m$$

and called the **Lebesgue measure on $\mathbb{R}^2$**.

Exercise 3.7   Verify that $m_2(R) = (b - a)(d - c)$ for any rectangle $R = (a, b) \times (c, d)$ in $\mathbb{R}^2$.

Example 3.11

We can extend the construction of Lebesgue measure to $\mathbb{R}^n$ for any $n = 2, 3, \ldots$ by iterating the product of measures.

Thus, we put, for example

$$m_3 = m \otimes m \otimes m$$

for the Lebesgue measure defined on the Borel sets

$$\mathcal{B}(\mathbb{R}^3) = \mathcal{B}(\mathbb{R}) \otimes \mathcal{B}(\mathbb{R}) \otimes \mathcal{B}(\mathbb{R})$$

in $\mathbb{R}^3$. Note that this triple product can be interpreted in two ways: as $m \otimes (m \otimes m)$, a measure on $\mathbb{R} \times \mathbb{R}^2$, or as $(m \otimes m) \otimes m$, a measure on $\mathbb{R}^2 \times \mathbb{R}$. For simplicity, we identify both $\mathbb{R} \times \mathbb{R}^2$ and $\mathbb{R}^2 \times \mathbb{R}$ with $\mathbb{R}^3$ and thus make no distinction between $(m \otimes m) \otimes m$ and $m \otimes (m \otimes m)$.

In a similar manner we define the Lebesgue measure

$$m_n = \underbrace{m \otimes m \otimes \cdots \otimes m}_{n}$$

on the Borel sets

$$\mathcal{B}(\mathbb{R}^n) = \underbrace{\mathcal{B}(\mathbb{R}) \otimes \mathcal{B}(\mathbb{R}) \otimes \cdots \otimes \mathcal{B}(\mathbb{R})}_{n}$$

in $\mathbb{R}^n$.

3.2 Joint distribution

A random variable on a probability space $(\Omega, \mathcal{F}, P)$ is a function $X : \Omega \to \mathbb{R}$ such that $\{X \in B\} \in \mathcal{F}$ for every Borel set $B \in \mathcal{B}(\mathbb{R})$ on the real line $\mathbb{R}$; see Definition 2.16. We extend this to the case of functions with values in $\mathbb{R}^2$.

Definition 3.12
We call $Z : \Omega \to \mathbb{R}^2$ a **random vector** if $\{Z \in B\} \in \mathcal{F}$ for every Borel set $B \in \mathcal{B}(\mathbb{R}^2)$ on the plane $\mathbb{R}^2$.

Exercise 3.8   Show that $X, Y : \Omega \to \mathbb{R}$ are random variables if and only if $(X, Y) : \Omega \to \mathbb{R}^2$ is a random vector.

We are now ready to define the joint distribution for a pair of random variables $X, Y : \Omega \to \mathbb{R}$. Exercise 3.8 ensures that $\{(X, Y) \in B\} \in \mathcal{F}$ so it makes sense to consider the probability $P((X, Y) \in B)$ for any $B \in \mathcal{B}(\mathbb{R}^2)$.

Definition 3.13
The **joint distribution** of the pair X, Y is the probability measure $P_{X,Y}$ on $(\mathbb{R}^2, \mathcal{B}(\mathbb{R}^2))$ given by

$$P_{X,Y}(B) = P((X, Y) \in B)$$

for any $B \in \mathcal{B}(\mathbb{R}^2))$.

In particular, when $B = B_1 \times B_2$ for some Borel sets $B_1, B_2 \subset \mathbb{R}$, then

$$P_{X,Y}(B) = P((X, Y) \in B_1 \times B_2) = P(X \in B_1, Y \in B_2).$$

The distributions P_X and P_Y of the individual random variables X and Y can be reconstructed from the joint distribution $P_{X,Y}$. Namely, for any Borel set $B \in \mathcal{B}(\mathbb{R})$

$$P_X(B) = P(X \in B) = P(X \in B, Y \in \mathbb{R}) = P_{X,Y}(B \times \mathbb{R}),$$
$$P_Y(B) = P(Y \in B) = P(X \in \mathbb{R}, Y \in B) = P_{X,Y}(\mathbb{R} \times B).$$

We call P_X and P_Y the **marginal distributions** of $P_{X,Y}$. On the other hand, as shown in Exercise 3.9, the marginal distributions P_X and P_Y are by no means enough to construct the joint distribution $P_{X,Y}$.

Exercise 3.9   On the two-element probability space $\Omega = \{\omega_1, \omega_2\}$ with uniform probability consider two pairs or random variables X_1, Y_1 and X_2, Y_2 defined in the table below.

	X_1	Y_1	X_2	Y_2
ω_1	110	60	110	40
ω_2	90	40	90	60

Show that $P_{X_1} = P_{X_2}$, $P_{Y_1} = P_{Y_2}$, but $P_{X_1,Y_1} \neq P_{X_2,Y_2}$.

Definition 3.14
The **joint distribution function** of X, Y is the function $F_{X,Y} : \mathbb{R}^2 \to [0,1]$ defined by

$$F_{X,Y}(x, y) = P(X \le x, Y \le y).$$

In other words,

$$F_{X,Y}(x, y) = P_{X,Y}((-\infty, x] \times (-\infty, y]).$$

Exercise 3.10   Show that the joint distribution function $(x, y) \mapsto F_{X,Y}(x, y)$ is non-decreasing in each of its arguments and that for any $a, b \in \mathbb{R}$

$$\lim_{y \to \infty} F_{X,Y}(a, y) = F_X(a),$$
$$\lim_{x \to \infty} F_{X,Y}(x, b) = F_Y(b).$$

Exercise 3.11 For $a, b \in \mathbb{R}$ find $P(X > a, Y > b)$ in terms of F_X, F_Y and $F_{X,Y}$.

Definition 3.15
If

$$P_{X,Y}(B) = \int_B f_{X,Y}(x, y) dm_2(x, y)$$

for all $B \in \mathcal{B}(\mathbb{R}^2)$, where $f_{X,Y} : \mathbb{R}^2 \to \mathbb{R}$ is integrable under the Lebesgue measure m_2, then $f_{X,Y}$ is called the **joint density** of X and Y, and the random variables X, Y are said to be **jointly continuous**.

If X, Y are jointly continuous, the joint distribution and joint density are related by

$$F_{X,Y}(a, b) = \int_{(-\infty,a]\times(-\infty,b]} f_{X,Y}(x, y) dm_2(x, y).$$

Example 3.16
The **bivariate normal density** is given by

$$f_{X,Y}(x_1, x_2) = \frac{1}{2\pi \sqrt{1 - \rho^2}} \exp\left(-\frac{x_1^2 - 2\rho x_1 x_2 + x_2^2}{2(1 - \rho^2)}\right), \qquad (3.5)$$

where $\rho \in (-1, 1)$ is a fixed parameter, whose meaning will become clear in due course. To check that it is a density we need to show that

$$\int_{\mathbb{R}^2} f_{X,Y}(x_1, x_2) dm_2(x_1, x_2) = 1.$$

This will be done in Exercise 3.12.

We need techniques for calculating such integrals. We achieve this in the next section by considering product measures.

3.3 Iterated integrals

As in Section 3.1, we consider measure spaces $(\Omega_1, \mathcal{F}_1, \mu_1)$ and $(\Omega_2, \mathcal{F}_2, \mu_2)$. In order to integrate functions defined on $\Omega_1 \times \Omega_2$ with respect to the product measure we seek to exploit integration with respect to the measures μ_1 and μ_2 individually.

For a function $f : \Omega_1 \times \Omega_2 \to [-\infty, \infty]$ the **sections** of f are defined by $\omega_1 \mapsto f(\omega_1, \omega_2)$ for any $\omega_2 \in \Omega_2$ and $\omega_2 \mapsto f(\omega_1, \omega_2)$ for any $\omega_1 \in \Omega_1$. They are functions from Ω_1 and, respectively, from Ω_2 to $[-\infty, \infty]$.

Iterated integrals with respect to finite measures

We first consider the issue of measurability of the sections and their integrals.

Proposition 3.17

Suppose that μ_1 and μ_2 are finite measures. If a non-negative function $f : \Omega_1 \times \Omega_2 \to [0, \infty]$ is measurable with respect to $\mathcal{F}_1 \otimes \mathcal{F}_2$, then:

  (i) *the section $\omega_1 \mapsto f(\omega_1, \omega_2)$ is $\mathcal{F}_1$-measurable for each $\omega_2 \in \Omega_2$, and*
     $\omega_2 \mapsto f(\omega_1, \omega_2)$ *is $\mathcal{F}_2$-measurable for each $\omega_1 \in \Omega_1$;*

  (ii) *the functions*

$$\omega_1 \mapsto \int_{\Omega_2} f(\omega_1, \omega_2) d\mu_2(\omega_2), \qquad \omega_2 \mapsto \int_{\Omega_1} f(\omega_1, \omega_2) d\mu_1(\omega_1)$$

are, respectively, $\mathcal{F}_1$- measurable and $\mathcal{F}_2$-measurable.

Proof   First we approximate f by simple functions

$$f_n(\omega_1, \omega_2) = \begin{cases} \frac{k}{2^n} & \text{if } f(\omega_1, \omega_2) \in [\frac{k}{2^n}, \frac{k+1}{2^n}), k = 0, 1, \ldots, n2^n - 1, \\ 0 & \text{if } f(\omega_1, \omega_2) \geq n, \end{cases}$$

which form a non-decreasing sequence such that $\lim_{n \to \infty} f_n = f$.

(i) The sections of simple functions are also simple functions. It is clear that the sections of f_n converge to those of f, and since measurability is preserved in the limit (Exercise 1.19), the first claim of the theorem is proved.

(ii) If $A \in \mathcal{F}_1 \times \mathcal{F}_2$, we know from Theorem 3.5 (i) that

$$\omega_1 \mapsto \int_{\Omega_2} \mathbf{1}_A(\omega_1, \omega_2) d\mu_2(\omega_2) = \int_{\Omega_2} \mathbf{1}_{A_{\omega_1}}(\omega_2) d\mu_2(\omega_2) = \mu_2(A_{\omega_1}),$$

$$\omega_2 \mapsto \int_{\Omega_1} \mathbf{1}_A(\omega_1, \omega_2) d\mu_1(\omega_1) = \int_{\Omega_1} \mathbf{1}_{A_{\omega_2}}(\omega_1) d\mu_1(\omega_1) = \mu_1(A_{\omega_2})$$

are measurable functions. It follows by linearity (Exercise 1.21) that the integrals of the sections of f_n are measurable functions. By monotone convergence, see Theorem 1.31, the integrals of the sections of f are limits of the integrals of the sections of f_n, and are therefore also measurable. This completes the proof.   □

We are ready to show that the integral over the product space can be computed as an iterated integral.

Theorem 3.18 (Fubini)

Suppose that μ_1 and μ_2 are finite measures. If $f : \Omega_1 \times \Omega_2 \to [-\infty, \infty]$ is integrable under the product measure $\mu_1 \otimes \mu_2$, then the sections

$$\omega_2 \mapsto f(\omega_1, \omega_2), \qquad \omega_1 \mapsto f(\omega_1, \omega_2)$$

are μ_1-a.e. integrable under μ_2 and, respectively, μ_2-a.e. integrable under μ_1, and the functions

$$\omega_1 \mapsto \int_{\Omega_2} f(\omega_1, \omega_2) d\mu_2(\omega_2), \qquad \omega_2 \mapsto \int_{\Omega_1} f(\omega_1, \omega_2) d\mu_1(\omega_1)$$

are integrable under μ_1 and, respectively, under μ_2. Moreover,

$$\int_{\Omega_1 \times \Omega_2} f(\omega_1, \omega_2) d(\mu_1 \otimes \mu_2)(\omega_1, \omega_2)$$

$$= \int_{\Omega_1} \left(\int_{\Omega_2} f(\omega_1, \omega_2) d\mu_2(\omega_2) \right) d\mu_1(\omega_1)$$

$$= \int_{\Omega_2} \left(\int_{\Omega_1} f(\omega_1, \omega_2) d\mu_1(\omega_1) \right) d\mu_2(\omega_2).$$

Proof We prove the first equality. This will be done in a number steps.

- If $f = \mathbf{1}_A$ is the indicator function for some $A \in \mathcal{F}_1 \otimes \mathcal{F}_2$, then the desired equality becomes

$$(\mu_1 \otimes \mu_2)(A) = \int_{\Omega_1} \mu_2(A_{\omega_1}) d\mu_1(\omega_1),$$

  and this is satisfied by the definition of the product measure (Definition 3.6).

- If f is a non-negative simple function, then it is a linear combination of indicator functions, and linearity of the integral for simple functions (Exercise 1.11) verifies the equality in this case.

- Next, if f is a non-negative measurable function, then it can be expressed as the limit of a non-decreasing sequence non-negative simple functions; see Proposition 1.28. Applying the monotone convergence theorem (Theorem 1.31), first to the inner integral over Ω_2 and then to each side of the target equality, verifies the equality.

- If f is a non-negative integrable function, then, in addition, the integral $\int_{\Omega_1 \times \Omega_2} f(\omega_1, \omega_2) d(\mu_1 \otimes \mu_2)(\omega_1, \omega_2)$ on the left-hand side of the equality is finite, and therefore so is the integral $\int_{\Omega_1} \left(\int_{\Omega_2} f(\omega_1, \omega_2) d\mu_2(\omega_2) \right) d\mu_1(\omega_1)$

on the right-hand side. This means that $\omega_1 \mapsto \int_{\Omega_2} f(\omega_1, \omega_2) d\mu_2(\omega_2)$ is integrable under μ_1. This in turn means that the section $\omega_2 \mapsto f(\omega_1, \omega_2)$ is μ_1-a.e. integrable under μ_2.

• Finally, for any function f integrable under $\mu_1 \otimes \mu_2$, we take the decomposition $f = f^+ - f^-$ into the positive and negative parts; see (1.9). Since f^+ and f^- are non-negative integrable functions, they satisfy the equality in question, with the integrals on both sides of the equality being finite. This, in turn, gives the identity for f, along with the conclusion that $\omega_1 \mapsto \int_{\Omega_2} f(\omega_1, \omega_2) d\mu_2(\omega_2)$ is integrable under μ_1 and $\omega_2 \mapsto f(\omega_1, \omega_2)$ is μ_1-a.e. integrable under μ_2.

The proof of the second identity and the integrability of the functions $\omega_2 \mapsto \int_{\Omega_1} f(\omega_1, \omega_2) d\mu_1(\omega_1)$ and $\omega_1 \mapsto f(\omega_1, \omega_2)$ is similar.   □

Iterated integrals with respect to σ-finite measures

Before we can handle iterated integrals with respect to Lebesgue measure, we need to extend Fubini's theorem to σ-finite measures.

Suppose that μ_1, μ_2 are σ-finite measures, and let $f : \Omega_1 \times \Omega_2 \to [-\infty, \infty]$ be an integrable function under the product measure $\mu_1 \otimes \mu_2$. We proceed as follows.

• Take sequences of events A_n and B_n as in part (i) and $\mu_1^{(n)}, \mu_2^{(n)}$ to be the finite measures from part (ii) of Definition 3.9. Then

$$\int_{A_n \times B_n} f(\omega_1, \omega_2) \, d(\mu_1^{(n)} \otimes \mu_2^{(n)})(\omega_1, \omega_2)$$
$$= \int_{B_n} \left(\int_{A_n} f(\omega_1, \omega_2) \, d\mu_1^{(n)}(\omega_1) \right) d\mu_2^{(n)}(\omega_2)$$
$$= \int_{A_n} \left(\int_{B_n} f(\omega_1, \omega_2) \, d\mu_2^{(n)}(\omega_2) \right) d\mu_1^{(n)}(\omega_1).$$

The integrals in these identities can be written as

$$\int_{\Omega_1 \times \Omega_2} \mathbf{1}_{A_n \times B_n}(\omega_1, \omega_2) f(\omega_1, \omega_2) \, d(\mu_1 \otimes \mu_2)(\omega_1, \omega_2)$$
$$= \int_{\Omega_2} \mathbf{1}_{B_n}(\omega_2) \left(\int_{\Omega_1} \mathbf{1}_{A_n}(\omega_1) f(\omega_1, \omega_2) \, d\mu_1(\omega_1) \right) d\mu_2(\omega_2)$$
$$= \int_{\Omega_1} \mathbf{1}_{A_n}(\omega_1) \left(\int_{\Omega_2} \mathbf{1}_{B_n}(\omega_2) f(\omega_1, \omega_2) \, d\mu_2(\omega_2) \right) d\mu_1(\omega_1).$$

• Next, if f is non-negative, we can use monotone convergence, that is,

Theorem 1.31, to obtain

$$\int_{\Omega_1 \times \Omega_2} f(\omega_1, \omega_2) \, d(\mu_1 \otimes \mu_2)(\omega_1, \omega_2)$$

$$= \int_{\Omega_2} \left(\int_{\Omega_1} f(\omega_1, \omega_2) \, d\mu_1(\omega_1) \right) d\mu_2(\omega_2)$$

$$= \int_{\Omega_1} \left(\int_{\Omega_2} f(\omega_1, \omega_2) \, d\mu_2(\omega_2) \right) d\mu_1(\omega_1)$$

in the limit as $n \to \infty$ because A_n, B_n and $A_n \times B_n$ for $n = 1, 2, \dots$ are non-decreasing sequences of sets such that $\bigcup_{n=1}^{\infty} A_n = \Omega_1$, $\bigcup_{n=1}^{\infty} B_n = \Omega_2$ and $\bigcup_{n=1}^{\infty} (A_n \times B_n) = \Omega_1 \times \Omega_2$.

- Finally, for any function $f : \mathbb{R}^2 \to \mathbb{R}$ integrable under $\mu_1 \otimes \mu_2$, we know that the latter identities hold for the positive and negative parts f^+, f^-. Since $f = f^+ - f^-$, we obtain the same identities for f by the linearity of integrals. Moreover, since $\int_{\Omega_1 \times \Omega_2} f(\omega_1, \omega_2) \, d(\mu_1 \otimes \mu_2)(\omega_1, \omega_2) < \infty$, we can conclude that the integrals on the right-hand side are finite, and so the functions

$$\omega_2 \mapsto \int_{\Omega_1} f(\omega_1, \omega_2) \, d\mu_1(\omega_1) \quad \text{and} \quad \omega_1 \mapsto \left(\int_{\Omega_2} f(\omega_1, \omega_2) \, d\mu_2(\omega_2) \right)$$

are integrable.

This extends Fubini's theorem to σ-finite measures and, in particular, to iterated integrals with respect to Lebesgue measure.

Example 3.19
We now apply these results to the joint probability $P_{X,Y}$ of two random variables X, Y. If X, Y are jointly continuous with density $f_{X,Y}$, then

$$P_{X,Y}(B_1 \times B_2) = \int_{B_1 \times B_2} f_{X,Y}(x, y) \, dm_2(x, y)$$

$$= \int_{B_1} \left(\int_{B_2} f_{X,Y}(x, y) \, dm(y) \right) dm(x)$$

for any $B_1, B_2 \in \mathcal{B}(\mathbb{R})$. In particular, when $B_1 = \{X \le a\}$ and $B_2 = \{Y \le b\}$ for some $a, b \in \mathbb{R}$ and the joint density is a continuous function, this becomes

$$F_{X,Y}(a, b) = \int_{-\infty}^{a} \left(\int_{-\infty}^{b} f_{X,Y}(x, y) \, dy \right) dx,$$

with Riemann integrals on the right-hand side, so we obtain

$$f_{X,Y}(a,b) = \frac{\partial^2}{\partial b \partial a} F_{X,Y}(a,b).$$

Proposition 3.20
If X, Y are jointly continuous random variables with density $f_{X,Y}$, then X and Y are (individually) continuous with densities

$$f_X(x) = \int_{\mathbb{R}} f_{X,Y}(x,y)dm(y), \quad f_Y(y) = \int_{\mathbb{R}} f_{X,Y}(x,y)dm(x). \qquad (3.6)$$

Proof By Fubini's theorem,

$$P_X(B) = P_{X,Y}(B \times \mathbb{R})$$
$$= \int_{B \times \mathbb{R}} f_{X,Y}(x,y)dm_2(x,y) = \int_B \left(\int_{\mathbb{R}} f_{X,Y}(x,y)dm(y) \right) dm(x)$$

for any $B \in \mathcal{B}(\mathbb{R})$, where $x \mapsto \int_{\mathbb{R}} f_{X,Y}(x,y)dm(y)$ is a non-negative integrable function. This means that

$$f_X(x) = \int_{\mathbb{R}} f_{X,Y}(x,y)dm(y).$$

The proof of the second identity is similar. $\qquad\qquad\qquad\qquad\square$

We call f_X and f_Y given by (3.6) the **marginal densities** of the joint distribution of X, Y.

Exercise 3.12
Confirm that $f_{X,Y}$ given by (3.5) is a density, that is,

$$\int_{\mathbb{R}^2} f_{X,Y}(x_1, x_2)dm_2(x_1, x_2) = 1$$

and that f_X, f_Y given by (3.6) are standard normal densities.

Exercise 3.13   Suppose X, Y have joint density $f_{X,Y}$. Show that $X + Y$ is a continuous random variable with density

$$f_{X+Y}(z) = \int_{\mathbb{R}} f_{X,Y}(x, z - x)dm(x).$$

> **Exercise 3.14**   Suppose that random variables X, Y have joint density $f_{X,Y}(x,y) = e^{-(x+y)}$ when $x > 0$ and $y > 0$, and $f_{X,Y}(x,y) = 0$ otherwise. Find the density of X/Y.

3.4   Random vectors in $\mathbb{R}^n$

When defining the joint distribution of two random variables, we found it helpful to consider random vectors (Definition 3.12) as functions from Ω to $\mathbb{R}^2$. We can extend this to n random variables. As for $\mathbb{R}^2$, we can define the Borel sets in $\mathbb{R}^n$ by means of products of Borel sets in $\mathbb{R}$, generalising the notation introduced in (3.3).

Definition 3.21
Given $n = 2, 3, \ldots$, define the σ-field of **Borel sets** on $\mathbb{R}^n$ as

$$\mathcal{B}(\mathbb{R}^n) = \underbrace{\mathcal{B}(\mathbb{R}) \otimes \mathcal{B}(\mathbb{R}) \otimes \cdots \otimes \mathcal{B}(\mathbb{R})}_{n},$$

as in Example 3.11. In other words, $\mathcal{B}(\mathbb{R}^n) = \sigma(\mathcal{R}_n)$, the σ-field on $\mathbb{R}^n$ generated by the collection

$$\mathcal{R}_n = \{B_1 \times \cdots \times B_n : B_1, \ldots, B_n \in \mathcal{B}(\mathbb{R})\}.$$

> **Exercise 3.15**   Show that $\mathcal{B}(\mathbb{R}^n) = \sigma(\mathcal{I}_n)$, where
>
> $$\mathcal{I}_n = \{I_1 \times \cdots \times I_n : I_1, \ldots, I_n \text{ are intervals in } \mathbb{R}\}.$$

Definition 3.22
A map $X = (X_1, X_2, \ldots, X_n)$ from $(\Omega, \mathcal{F}, P)$ to $\mathbb{R}^n$ is called a **random vector** if $\{X \in B\} \in \mathcal{F}$ for every $B \in \mathcal{B}(\mathbb{R}^n)$.

> **Exercise 3.16**   Show that $X = (X_1, X_2, \ldots, X_n)$ is a random vector if and only if $X_1, X_2, \ldots, X_n$ are random variables.

Definition 3.23
Let $X = (X_1, X_2, \ldots, X_n)$ be a random vector from Ω to $\mathbb{R}^n$. The **joint**

distribution of X (equivalently, of $X_1, \ldots, X_n$) is the probability P_X on $(\mathbb{R}^n, \mathcal{B}(\mathbb{R}^n))$ defined by

$$P_X(B) = P(X \in B) \quad \text{for each } B \in \mathcal{B}(\mathbb{R}^n).$$

The **joint distribution function** of $X = (X_1, X_2, \ldots, X_n)$ is the function $F_X : \mathbb{R}^n \to [0, 1]$ given by

$$F_X(x_1, \ldots, x_n) = P(X_1 \leq x_1, X_2 \leq x_2, \ldots, X_n \leq x_n)$$

for any $x_1, \ldots, x_n \in \mathbb{R}$.

Having made sense of Lebesgue measure m_n on $\mathbb{R}^n$, we can use it, just as we did for m_2, to define the joint density of n random variables.

Definition 3.24
We say that a random vector $X = (X_1, X_2, \ldots, X_n)$ has **joint density** if the joint distribution P_X can be written as

$$P_X(B) = \int_B f_X(x) \, dm_n(x) \quad \text{for each } B \in \mathcal{B}(\mathbb{R}^n)$$

for some integrable function $f_X : \mathbb{R}^n \to [0, \infty]$, where m_n denotes Lebesgue measure on $\mathbb{R}^n$. In this case the random variables $X_1, X_2, \ldots, X_n$ are said to be **jointly continuous**. The P_{X_i} are called the **marginal distributions** of P_X.

If P_X has a density f_X on $\mathbb{R}^n$, then the marginal distribution P_{X_i} has density on $\mathbb{R}$ given by an integral relative to Lebesgue measure m_{n-1} on $\mathbb{R}^{n-1}$. Indeed, using Fubini's theorem for σ-finite measures repeatedly, we have

$$
\begin{aligned}
P_{X_i}(B) = P(X \in \mathbb{R}^{i-1} \times B \times \mathbb{R}^{n-i}) &= \int_{\mathbb{R}^{i-1} \times B \times \mathbb{R}^{n-i}} f_X(y) \, dm_n(y) \\
&= \int_{\mathbb{R}^{i-1} \times B} \left(\int_{\mathbb{R}^{n-i}} f_X(x', x, x'') \, dm_{n-i}(x'') \right) dm_i(x', x) \\
&= \int_B \left(\int_{\mathbb{R}^{n-i}} \left(\int_{\mathbb{R}^{i-1}} f_X(x', x, x'') \, dm_{i-1}(x') \right) dm_{n-i}(x'') \right) dm(x) \\
&= \int_B \left(\int_{\mathbb{R}^{n-1}} f_X(x', x, x'') \, dm_{n-1}(x', x'') \right) dm(x)
\end{aligned}
$$

for any $B \in \mathcal{B}(\mathbb{R})$, where for any $x' \in \mathbb{R}^{i-1}$, $x \in \mathbb{R}$ and $x'' \in \mathbb{R}^{n-i}$ we identify (x', x, x'') with a point in $\mathbb{R}^n$, (x', x) with a point in $\mathbb{R}^i$, and (x', x'') with a point in $\mathbb{R}^{n-1}$. It follows that

$$f_{X_i}(x) = \int_{\mathbb{R}^{n-1}} f_X(x', x, x'') \, dm_{n-1}(x', x'').$$

This extends the result in Proposition 3.20.

Example 3.25

We call $X = (X_1, X_2, \ldots, X_n)$ a **Gaussian random vector** if it has joint density given for all $x \in \mathbb{R}^n$ by

$$f_X(x) = \frac{1}{\sqrt{(2\pi)^n \det \Sigma}} \exp\left(-\frac{1}{2}(x - \mu)^T \Sigma^{-1}(x - \mu)\right), \qquad (3.7)$$

where $\mu \in \mathbb{R}^n$, Σ is a non-singular positive definite (that is, $x^T \Sigma x > 0$ when $x \in \mathbb{R}^n$ is any non-zero vector) symmetric $n \times n$ matrix, Σ^{-1} is the inverse matrix of Σ, $\det \Sigma$ denotes the determinant of Σ, and $(x - \mu)^T$ is the transpose of the vector $x - \mu$ in $\mathbb{R}^n$. We say that (3.7) is a **multivariate normal density**.

In particular, the bivariate normal density (3.5) from Example 3.16 fits into this pattern since it can be written as

$$\frac{1}{2\pi\sqrt{1-\rho^2}} \exp\left(-\frac{x_1^2 - 2\rho x_1 x_2 + x_2^2}{2(1-\rho^2)}\right) = \frac{1}{\sqrt{(2\pi)^2 \det \Sigma}} \exp\left(-\frac{1}{2} x^T \Sigma^{-1} x\right),$$

where $x = \begin{bmatrix} x_1 \\ x_2 \end{bmatrix}$ and where $\Sigma = \begin{bmatrix} 1 & \rho \\ \rho & 1 \end{bmatrix}$ is a positive definite symmetric matrix with determinant $\det \Sigma = 1 - \rho^2 > 0$ and inverse $\Sigma^{-1} = \frac{1}{1-\rho^2}\begin{bmatrix} 1 & -\rho \\ -\rho & 1 \end{bmatrix}$.

Exercise 3.17 Show that (3.7) is indeed a density, that is,

$$\int_{\mathbb{R}^n} \frac{1}{\sqrt{(2\pi)^n \det \Sigma}} \exp\left(-\frac{1}{2}(x - \mu)^T \Sigma^{-1}(x - \mu)\right) dm_n(x) = 1.$$

3.5 Independence

One of the key concepts in probability theory is that of independence. We consider it in various forms: for random variables, events and σ-fields. Each time we start with just two such objects before moving to the general case.

Two independent random variables

We begin by examining two random variables whose joint distribution is the product of their individual distributions.

Definition 3.26
If random variables X, Y satisfy

$$P_{X,Y}(B_1 \times B_2) = P_X(B_1)P_Y(B_2) \tag{3.8}$$

for all choices of $B_1, B_2 \in \mathcal{B}(\mathbb{R})$, we say that X and Y are **independent**.

In other words, the joint distribution of two independent variables X, Y is the product measure $P_{X,Y} = P_X \otimes P_Y$. We can conveniently express this in terms of distribution functions.

Theorem 3.27
Random variables X, Y are independent if and only if their joint distribution function $F_{X,Y}$ is the product of their individual distribution functions, that is,

$$F_{X,Y}(x, y) = F_X(x)F_Y(y) \quad \text{for any } x, y \in \mathbb{R}.$$

The necessity of this condition is immediate, but the proof of its sufficiency is somewhat technical and is given in Section 3.7.

When X and Y are jointly continuous, their independence can be expressed in terms of densities.

Proposition 3.28
If X, Y are jointly continuous with density $f_{X,Y}$, then they are independent if and only if

$$f_{X,Y}(x, y) = f_X(x)f_Y(y), \quad m_2\text{-a.e.,} \tag{3.9}$$

that is, if and only if

$$m_2\left(\left\{(x, y) \in \mathbb{R}^2 : f_{X,Y}(x, y) \neq f_X(x)f_Y(y)\right\}\right) = 0.$$

Proof   Proposition 3.20 confirms that X and Y have densities f_X, f_Y. For any $B_1, B_2 \in \mathcal{B}(\mathbb{R})$ we have

$$P_{X,Y}(B_1 \times B_2) = \int_{B_1 \times B_2} f_{X,Y}(x, y)dm_2(x, y),$$

while

$$P_X(X \in B_1)P_Y(Y \in B_2) = \left(\int_{B_1} f_X(x)dm(x)\right)\left(\int_{B_2} f_Y(y)dm(y)\right)$$

$$= \int_{B_1}\left(\int_{B_2} f_X(x)f_Y(y)dm(y)\right)dm(x)$$

$$= \int_{B_1 \times B_2} f_X(x)f_Y(y)dm_2(x,y)$$

by Fubini's theorem. Now if (3.9) holds, it follows immediately that (3.8) does too. Conversely, if (3.8) holds, then we see that

$$\int_{B_1 \times B_2} f_{X,Y}(x,y)dm_2(x,y) = \int_{B_1 \times B_2} f_X(x)f_Y(y)dm_2(x,y)$$

for any Borel sets $B_1, B_2 \in \mathcal{B}(\mathbb{R})$. It follows from Lemma 3.58 in Section 3.7 that

$$\int_B f_{X,Y}(x,y)dm_2(x,y) = \int_B f_X(x)f_Y(y)dm_2(x,y)$$

for any Borel set $B \in \mathcal{B}(\mathbb{R}^2)$ because, by Theorem 1.35, the integrals on both sides of the last equality are measures when regarded as functions of $B \in \mathcal{B}(\mathbb{R}^2)$. This implies (3.9) by virtue of Exercise 1.30. □

As a by-product we obtain the following result.

Corollary 3.29
If X and Y are (individually) continuous and independent, then they are also jointly continuous, with joint density given by the product of their individual densities.

This result fails when the random variables are not independent, as the next exercise shows.

Exercise 3.18 Give an example of continuous random variables X, Y defined on the same probability space that are not jointly continuous.

Exercise 3.19 Suppose the joint density $f_{X,Y}$ of random variables X, Y is the bivariate normal density (3.5) with $\rho = 0$. (We call $f_{X,Y}$ the **standard** bivariate normal density when $\rho = 0$.) Show that X and Y are independent.

Exercise 3.20   Show that if X and Y are jointly continuous and independent, then their sum $X + Y$ has density

$$f_{X+Y}(z) = \int_{-\infty}^{\infty} f_X(x) f_Y(z - x) dm(x).$$

This density is called the **convolution** of f_X and f_Y.

Families of independent random variables

The following definition is a natural extension of the concept of independence from 2 to n random variables.

Definition 3.30

Let P_X be the joint distribution of a random vector $X = (X_1, X_2, \ldots, X_n)$. The random variables $X_1, X_2, \ldots, X_n$ are said to be **independent** if for every choice of Borel sets $B_1, B_2, \ldots, B_n \in \mathcal{B}(\mathbb{R})$

$$P_X(B_1 \times B_2 \times \cdots \times B_n) = \prod_{i=1}^{n} P_{X_i}(B_i),$$

or in other words if

$$P_X = P_{X_1} \otimes P_{X_2} \otimes \cdots \otimes P_{X_n}.$$

An arbitrary family $\mathcal{X}$ of random variables are called **independent** if for every finite subset $\{X_1, X_2, \ldots, X_n\} \subset \mathcal{X}$ the random variables $X_1, X_2, \ldots, X_n$ are independent.

For n random variables their independence can again be expressed in terms of the distribution function. The proof follows just like in the previous section, which dealt with the case $n = 2$.

Theorem 3.31

$X_1, X_2, \ldots, X_n$ *are independent if and only if the joint distribution function for the random vector $X = (X_1, X_2, \ldots, X_n)$ satisfies*

$$F_X(x_1, x_2, \ldots, x_n) = \prod_{i=1}^{n} F_{X_i}(x_i) \quad \text{for any } x_1, x_2, \ldots, x_n \in \mathbb{R}.$$

The description in terms of densities follows just as for the case $n = 2$.

Theorem 3.32

If a random vector $X = (X_1, \ldots, X_n)$ has joint density f_X, then $X_1, \ldots, X_n$ are independent if and only if

$$f_X(x_1, x_2, \ldots, x_n) = \prod_{i=1}^{n} f_{X_i}(x_i) \quad m_n\text{-}a.e. \tag{3.10}$$

Exercise 3.21 Prove Theorems 3.31 and 3.32.

Exercise 3.22 Suppose that the random vector $X = (X_1, X_2, \ldots, X_n)$ has joint density (3.7). Show that $E(X_i) = \mu_i$ for each $i = 1, \ldots, n$. Also prove that if Σ is a diagonal matrix, then $X_1, X_2, \ldots, X_n$ are independent.

Two independent events

Our principal interest is in random variables, but the concept of independence can be defined more widely: for $A_1 = \{X \in B_1\}$ and $A_2 = \{Y \in B_2\}$ we see that (3.8) becomes

$$P(A_1 \cap A_2) = P(A_1)P(A_2).$$

We turn this into a general definition for arbitrary events $A_1, A_2 \in \mathcal{F}$.

Definition 3.33

Let $(\Omega, \mathcal{F}, P)$ be a probability space. Events $A_1, A_2 \in \mathcal{F}$ are said to be **independent** if

$$P(A_1 \cap A_2) = P(A_1)P(A_2).$$

Example 3.34

A fair die is thrown twice. Thus $\Omega = \{(i, j) : i, j = 1, 2, 3, 4, 5, 6\}$ and each pair occurs with probability $\frac{1}{36}$. Let A be the event that the first throw is odd, and B the event that the second throw is odd. Then $P(A) = \frac{1}{2} = P(B)$, while $P(A \cap B) = \frac{1}{4}$. Thus A, B are independent events. However, for $D = \{(i, j) \in \Omega : i + j > 6\}$ the events A, D are not independent since $P(D) = \frac{7}{12}$ and $P(A \cap D) = \frac{1}{4} \neq \frac{1}{2} \times \frac{7}{12}$.

Exercise 3.23 Show that A_1, A_2 are independent events if and only if $A_1, \Omega \setminus A_2$ are independent events.

Exercise 3.24 Show that A_1, A_2 are independent events if and only if the indicator functions $\mathbf{1}_{A_1}, \mathbf{1}_{A_2}$ are independent random variables.

Now suppose we know that an event A has occurred. This means that A can take the place of Ω. For any event B only the part of B lying within A matters now, so we replace B by $A \cap B$ in order to compute the probability of B given that A has occurred. We normalise by dividing by $P(A)$ to define the **conditional probability** of B given A as

$$P(B|A) = \frac{P(A \cap B)}{P(A)}. \tag{3.11}$$

This makes sense whenever $P(A) \neq 0$. It is then natural to consider the events A, B as independent if the prior occurrence of A does not influence the probability of B, that is, if

$$P(B|A) = P(B).$$

(It is equivalent to $P(A|B) = P(A)$ when $P(B) \neq 0$ in addition to $P(A) \neq 0$.) In Example 3.34 this is simply the statement that the outcomes of the first throw of the die do not affect the outcome of the second. It is consistent with Definition 3.33 of independent events,

$$P(A \cap B) = P(A)P(B),$$

with the apparent advantage that the latter also applies when $P(B) = 0$ or $P(A) = 0$.

Families of independent events

Extending the definition of independence to more than two events requires some care. It is tempting to propose that A, B, C be called independent if

$$P(A \cap B \cap C) = P(A)P(B)P(C), \tag{3.12}$$

but the following exercises show that this would not be satisfactory.

Exercise 3.25 Find subsets A, B, C of $[0, 1]$ with uniform probability such that (3.12) holds, but A, B are not independent. Can you find three subsets such that each pair is independent, but (3.12) fails?

Exercise 3.26 Find another example by considering the events A, B in Example 3.34 together with a third event C chosen so that each pair of these events is independent, but (3.12) fails.

This leads us to make the following general definition.

Definition 3.35
A finite family of events $A_1, \ldots, A_n \in \mathcal{F}$ are said to be **independent** if

$$P(A_{i_1} \cap A_{i_2} \cap \cdots \cap A_{i_k}) = \prod_{j=1}^{k} P(A_{i_j})$$

for any $k = 2, \ldots, n$ and for any $1 \le i_1 < \cdots < i_k \le n$.

An arbitrary family of events is defined to be **independent** if each of its finite subfamilies is independent.

It is immediate from this definition that a subcollection of a family of independent events is also independent.

Exercise 3.27 Suppose A, B, C are independent events. Show that $A \cup B$ and C are independent.

Exercise 3.28 Show that $A_1, A_2, \ldots, A_n$ are independent events if and only if the indicator functions $\mathbf{1}_{A_1}, \mathbf{1}_{A_2}, \ldots, \mathbf{1}_{A_n}$ are independent random variables.

Example 3.36
Let $(\Omega_i, \mathcal{F}_i, P_i)$ be a probability space for each $i = 1, 2, \ldots, n$, and suppose that $\Omega = \Omega_1 \times \Omega_2 \times \cdots \times \Omega_n$ is equipped with the product σ-field $\mathcal{F} = \mathcal{F}_1 \otimes$

$\cdots \otimes \mathcal{F}_n$ and the product probability $P = P_1 \otimes \cdots \otimes P_n$. **Cylinder sets** are defined in Ω as Cartesian products of the form

$$C_i = \Omega_1 \times \cdots \times \Omega_{i-1} \times A_i \times \Omega_{i+1} \times \cdots \times \Omega_n$$

for some $i = 1, 2, \ldots, n$ and $A_i \in \mathcal{F}_i$. By the definition the product measure, $P(C_i) = P_i(A_i)$. Moreover, for any $i \neq j$

$$
\begin{aligned}
P(C_i \cap C_j) \\
&= P(\Omega_1 \times \cdots \times \Omega_{i-1} \times A_i \times \Omega_{i+1} \times \cdots \times \Omega_{j-1} \times A_j \times \Omega_{j+1} \times \cdots \times \Omega_n) \\
&= P_i(A_i) P_j(A_j) \\
&= P(C_i) P(C_j),
\end{aligned}
$$

so the cylinder sets C_i, C_j are independent. By extending this argument, we can show that $C_1, C_2, \ldots, C_n$ are independent.

Two independent σ-fields

The defining identity (3.8) for independent random variables X, Y can be written as

$$P(A_1 \cap A_2) = P(A_1) P(A_2)$$

for any events of the form $A_1 = \{X \in B_1\}$ and $A_2 = \{Y \in B_2\}$ with $B_1, B_2 \in \mathcal{B}(\mathbb{R})$. In other words, X, Y are independent if and only if for any $A_1 \in \sigma(X)$ and $A_2 \in \sigma(Y)$ the events A_1, A_2 are independent.

As we can see, independence of random variables X, Y can be expressed in terms of the generated σ-fields $\sigma(X), \sigma(Y)$. This suggests that the notion of independence can be extended to arbitrary σ-fields $\mathcal{G}_1, \mathcal{G}_2 \subset \mathcal{F}$.

Definition 3.37
We say that σ-fields $\mathcal{G}_1, \mathcal{G}_2 \subset \mathcal{F}$ are **independent** if for any $A_1 \in \mathcal{G}_1$ and $A_2 \in \mathcal{G}_2$ the events A_1, A_2 are independent.

We can now say that random variables X, Y are independent if and only if the σ-fields $\sigma(X), \sigma(Y)$ are independent. As a simple application, we show the following proposition.

Proposition 3.38
Suppose that X, Y are independent random variables and U, W are random variables measurable with respect to $\sigma(X)$ and, respectively, $\sigma(Y)$. Then U, W are independent.

Proof Since U is measurable with respect to $\sigma(X)$ and W is measurable with respect to $\sigma(Y)$, we have $\sigma(U) \subset \sigma(X)$ and $\sigma(W) \subset \sigma(Y)$. Independence of X, Y means that the σ-fields $\sigma(X), \sigma(Y)$ are independent, which implies immediately that the sub-σ-fields $\sigma(U), \sigma(W)$ are independent, and so the random variables U, W themselves are independent.   □

Corollary 3.39
If X, Y are independent random variables and $g, h : \mathbb{R} \to \mathbb{R}$ are Borel-measurable functions, then $g(X), h(Y)$ are also independent random variables.

Exercise 3.29   Show that A, B are independent events if and only if the σ-fields $\{\varnothing, A, \Omega \setminus A, \Omega\}$ and $\{\varnothing, B, \Omega \setminus B, \Omega\}$ are independent.

Exercise 3.30   What can you say about a σ-field that is independent of itself?

Remark 3.40
Extending Definition 3.26, we can say that two random vectors

$$X = (X_1, \ldots, X_m), \quad Y = (Y_1, \ldots, Y_n)$$

with values, respectively, in $\mathbb{R}^m$ and $\mathbb{R}^n$ are **independent** whenever

$$P_{X,Y}(B_1 \times B_2) = P_X(B_1)P_Y(B_1)$$

for all Borel sets $B_1 \in \mathcal{B}(\mathbb{R}^m)$ and $B_2 \in \mathcal{B}(\mathbb{R}^n)$, where by $P_{X,Y}$ we denote the joint distribution of the random vector $(X_1, \ldots, X_m, Y_1, \ldots, Y_n)$.

Equivalently, we can say that the random vectors X, Y are independent whenever the σ-fields $\sigma(X), \sigma(Y)$ generated by them are independent, where by definition $\sigma(X)$ consists of all events of the form $\{X \in B\}$ with $B \in \mathcal{B}(\mathbb{R}^m)$ and, similarly, $\sigma(X)$ consists of all events of the form $\{Y \in B\}$ with $B \in \mathcal{B}(\mathbb{R}^n)$.

Families of independent σ-fields

The notion of independence is readily extended to any finite number of σ-fields.

Definition 3.41
We say that σ-fields $\mathcal{G}_1, \mathcal{G}_2, \ldots, \mathcal{G}_n \subset \mathcal{F}$ are **independent** if for any $A_1 \in \mathcal{G}_1, A_2 \in \mathcal{G}_2, \ldots, A_n \in \mathcal{G}_n$ the events $A_1, A_2, \ldots, A_n$ are independent.

Exercise 3.31 Show that random variables $X_1, X_2, \ldots, X_n$ are independent if and only if their generated σ-fields $\sigma(X_1), \sigma(X_2), \ldots, \sigma(X_n)$ are independent.

Excrcise 3.32 Show that events $A_1, A_2, \ldots, A_n \in \mathcal{F}$ are independent if and only if the σ-fields $\mathcal{G}_1, \mathcal{G}_2, \ldots, \mathcal{G}_n$ are independent, where $\mathcal{G}_k = \{\varnothing, A_k, \Omega \setminus A_k, \Omega\}$ for $k = 1, 2, \ldots, n$.

Given a random variable Y on a probability space $(\Omega, \mathcal{F}, P)$ and a σ-field $\mathcal{G} \subset \mathcal{F}$ it is now natural to say that Y is independent of $\mathcal{G}$ if $\sigma(Y)$ and $\mathcal{G}$ are independent σ-fields.

Exercise 3.33 Suppose that $X_1, X_2, \ldots, X_n, Y$ are independent random variables. Show that Y is independent of the σ-field $\sigma(X)$ generated by the random vector $X = (X_1, X_2, \ldots, X_n)$. By definition, the σ-field $\sigma(X)$ consists of all sets of the form $\{X \in B\}$ such that $B \in \mathcal{B}((R))$.

Independence: expectation and variance

Theorem 3.42
If X, Y are independent integrable random variables, then the product XY is also integrable and

$$\mathbb{E}(XY) = \mathbb{E}(X)\mathbb{E}(Y).$$

Proof First suppose that $X = \sum_{i=1}^{m} a_i \mathbf{1}_{A_i}$ and $Y = \sum_{j=1}^{n} b_j \mathbf{1}_{B_j}$ are simple functions. Then $XY = \sum_{i=1}^{m} \sum_{j=1}^{n} a_i b_j \mathbf{1}_{A_i \cap B_j}$. We may assume without loss of generality that the a_i are distinct, so $A_i = \{X = a_i\}$ for each $i = 1, \ldots, m$, and that the b_j are also distinct, so $B_j = \{Y = b_j\}$ for each $j = 1, \ldots, n$. If

X, Y are independent, then so are A_i, B_j for each i, j, and

$$\mathbb{E}(XY) = \sum_{i=1}^{m} \sum_{j=1}^{n} a_i b_j P(A_i \cap B_j) = \sum_{i=1}^{m} \sum_{j=1}^{n} a_i b_j P(A_i) P(B_j)$$

$$= \left(\sum_{i=1}^{m} a_i P(A_i) \right) \left(\sum_{j=1}^{n} b_j P(B_j) \right) = \mathbb{E}(X)\mathbb{E}(Y).$$

Now define

$$f_n(x) = \begin{cases} \frac{k-1}{2^n} & \text{for} \quad \frac{k-1}{2^n} \le x < \frac{k}{2^n}, \ k = 1, 2, \ldots, n2^n \\ n & \text{for} \quad x \ge n \end{cases}$$

for each $n = 1, 2, \ldots$. If X is a non-negative random variable, then $X_n = f_n(X)$ is a non-decreasing sequence and $\lim_{n \to \infty} X_n = X$. If X is not necessarily non-negative, we put

$$X_n = f_n(X^+) - f_n(X^-).$$

Then X_n is a sequence of simple functions such that $\lim_{n \to \infty} X_n = X$, and $|X_n|$ is a non-decreasing sequence of simple functions such that $\lim_{n \to \infty} |X_n| = |X|$, so $\lim_{n \to \infty} \mathbb{E}(|X_n|) = \mathbb{E}(|X|)$ by monotone convergence, see Theorem 1.31. Similarly, we put

$$Y_n = f_n(Y^+) - f_n(Y^-),$$

which have similar properties as the X_n. It follows that $|X_n Y_n| = |X_n| |Y_n|$ is a non-decreasing sequence of simple functions such that $\lim_{n \to \infty} |X_n Y_n| = |XY|$. Using monotone convergence once again, we have $\lim_{n \to \infty} \mathbb{E}(|X_n Y_n|) = \mathbb{E}(|XY|)$. If X, Y are independent, then by Corollary 3.39, so are X_n, Y_n and also $|X_n|, |Y_n|$, so the result already established for independent simple random variables yields

$$\mathbb{E}(X_n Y_n) = \mathbb{E}(X_n)\mathbb{E}(Y_n) \quad \text{and} \quad \mathbb{E}(|X_n Y_n|) = \mathbb{E}(|X_n|)\mathbb{E}(|Y_n|),$$

for any n. If, in addition, X and Y are both integrable, then

$$\mathbb{E}(|XY|) = \lim_{n \to \infty} \mathbb{E}(|X_n Y_n|) = \lim_{n \to \infty} \mathbb{E}(|X_n|)\mathbb{E}(|Y_n|) = \mathbb{E}(|X|)\mathbb{E}(|Y|) < \infty,$$

which means that $|XY|$ is integrable. Finally, because $|X_n Y_n| \le |XY|$ and $\lim_{n \to \infty} X_n Y_n = XY$, by dominated convergence, see Theorem 1.43, we can conclude that XY is integrable and

$$\mathbb{E}(XY) = \lim_{n \to \infty} \mathbb{E}(X_n Y_n) = \lim_{n \to \infty} \mathbb{E}(X_n)\mathbb{E}(Y_n) = \mathbb{E}(X)\mathbb{E}(Y),$$

completing the proof. $\qquad\square$

Exercise 3.34   Prove the following version of Theorem 3.42 extended to the case of n random variables.
If $X_1, X_2, \ldots, X_n$ are independent integrable random variables, then the product $\prod_{i=1}^{n} X_i$ is also integrable and

$$\mathbb{E}\left(\prod_{i=1}^{n} X_i\right) = \prod_{i=1}^{n} \mathbb{E}(X_i).$$

Example 3.43
The converse of Theorem 3.42 is false. For a simple counterexample take $X(x) = x$ and $Y(x) = x^2$ on $[-\frac{1}{2}, \frac{1}{2}]$ with Lebesgue measure. Since X and XY are both odd functions, their integrals over $[-\frac{1}{2}, \frac{1}{2}]$ are 0, so that $\mathbb{E}[XY] = \mathbb{E}[X]\mathbb{E}[Y]$. However, X, Y are not independent, as we can verify by taking the inverse images of $B = [-\frac{1}{9}, \frac{1}{9}]$ under X and Y. We see that $\{X \in B\} = [-\frac{1}{9}, \frac{1}{9}]$ and $\{Y \in B\} = [-\frac{1}{3}, \frac{1}{3}]$, and these are not independent events: their intersection has measure $\frac{2}{9}$, whereas the product of their measures is $\frac{2}{9} \times \frac{2}{3} = \frac{4}{27}$.

The following important result illustrates the extent to which knowledge of expectations provides a sufficient condition for independence.

Theorem 3.44
Random variables X, Y are independent if and only if

$$\mathbb{E}[f(X)g(Y)] = \mathbb{E}[f(X)]\mathbb{E}[g(Y)] \tag{3.13}$$

for all choices of bounded Borel measurable functions $f, g : \mathbb{R} \to \mathbb{R}$.

Proof   Suppose (3.13) holds, and apply it with the indicators $\mathbf{1}_B, \mathbf{1}_C$ for Borel sets $B, C \in \mathcal{B}(\mathbb{R})$. Then (3.13) becomes simply

$$P(X \in B, Y \in C) = P(X \in B)P(Y \in C).$$

This holds for arbitrary sets $B, C \in \mathcal{B}(\mathbb{R})$, so X, Y are independent.

Conversely, if X and Y are independent and f, g are real Borel functions, then Corollary 3.39 tells us that $f(X)$ and $g(Y)$ are independent. If f, g are bounded, then $f(X)$ and $g(Y)$ are integrable, so by Theorem 3.42 we have (3.13).   □

Recalling that for a complex-valued $f = \mathrm{Re}f + i\mathrm{Im}f$ we define $\mathbb{E}(f) = \mathbb{E}(\mathrm{Re}f) + i\mathbb{E}(\mathrm{Im}f)$, we can see that (3.13) extends to bounded complex-valued Borel measurable functions. We therefore immediately have the following way of finding the characteristic function of the sum of independent random variables.

Corollary 3.45
If X, Y are independent random variables, then

$$\phi_{X+Y}(t) = \phi_X(t)\phi_Y(t).$$

Exercise 3.35 Recall from Exercise 2.25 the characteristic function of a standard normal random variable. Use this to find the characteristic function of the linear combination $aX + bY$ of independent standard normal random variables X, Y.

Proposition 3.46
If X, Y are independent integrable random variables, then

$$\mathrm{Var}(X + Y) = \mathrm{Var}(X) + \mathrm{Var}(Y).$$

Proof The random variables $V = X - \mathbb{E}(X)$ and $W = Y - \mathbb{E}(Y)$ are integrable because X and Y are. Moreover, since X, Y are independent, so are V, W by Corollary 3.39. It follows that VW is integrable and $\mathbb{E}(VW) = \mathbb{E}(V)\mathbb{E}(W) = 0$. Applying expectation to both sides of the equality

$$(V + W)^2 = V^2 + 2VW + W^2,$$

we get

$$\mathrm{Var}(X + Y) = \mathbb{E}((V + W)^2) = \mathbb{E}(V^2) + 2\mathbb{E}(VW) + \mathbb{E}(W^2)$$
$$= \mathbb{E}(V^2) + \mathbb{E}(W^2) = \mathrm{Var}(X) + \mathrm{Var}(Y).$$

$\square$

Exercise 3.36 Prove the following version of Proposition 3.46 extended to the case of n random variables.
If $X_1, \ldots, X_n$ are independent integrable random variables, then

$$\mathrm{Var}(X_1 + X_2 + \cdots + X_n) = \mathrm{Var}(X_1) + \mathrm{Var}(X_2) + \cdots + \mathrm{Var}(X_n).$$

3.6 Covariance

Covariance and correlation can serve as tools to quantify the dependence between random variables, which in general may or may not be independent.

Definition 3.47
For integrable random variables X, Y whose product XY is also integrable we define the **covariance** as

$$\text{Cov}(X, Y) = \mathbb{E}\left((X - \mathbb{E}(X))(Y - \mathbb{E}(Y))\right) = \mathbb{E}(XY) - \mathbb{E}(X)\mathbb{E}(Y).$$

If, in addition, $\text{Var}(X) \neq 0$ and $\text{Var}(Y) \neq 0$, we can define the **correlation coefficient** of X, Y as

$$\rho_{X,Y} = \frac{\text{Cov}(X, Y)}{\sigma_X \sigma_Y}.$$

It is not hard to verify the following properties of covariance, which are due to the linearity of expectation:

$$\text{Cov}(aX, Y) = a\text{Cov}(X, Y),$$
$$\text{Cov}(W + X, Y) = \text{Cov}(W, Y) + \text{Cov}(X, Y).$$

It is also worth noting that, in general,

$$\text{Var}(X + Y) = \text{Var}(X) + \text{Var}(Y) + 2\text{Cov}(X, Y).$$

Observe further that

$$\text{Cov}(X, Y) = \text{Cov}(Y, X)$$

and

$$\text{Cov}(X, X) = \text{Var}(X).$$

Exercise 3.37   Suppose X, Y have bivariate normal distribution with density (3.5). Compute $\text{Cov}(X, Y)$.

It follows from Definition 3.47 that independent random variables X, Y have zero covariance and zero correlation (when it exists). More generally, we say that X and Y are **uncorrelated** if $\rho_{X,Y} = 0$. Example 3.43 shows that uncorrelated random variables need not be independent. However, for normally distributed random variables the two concepts coincide.

Exercise 3.38 Show that if X, Y have joint distribution with density (3.5) for some constant $\rho \in (-1, 1)$, then their correlation is given by $\rho_{XY} = \rho$. Hence show that if such X, Y are uncorrelated, then they are independent.

Next, we prove an important general inequality which gives a bound for $\text{Cov}(X, Y)$ in terms of $\text{Var}(X)$ and $\text{Var}(Y)$ or, equivalently, a bound for $\rho_{X,Y}$. Anticipating the terminology to be used extensively later, we make the following definition.

Definition 3.48
A random variable X is said to be **square-integrable** if X^2 is integrable.

Lemma 3.49 (Schwarz inequality)
If X and Y are square-integrable random variables, then XY is integrable, and

$$[\mathbb{E}(XY)]^2 \le \mathbb{E}(X^2)\mathbb{E}(Y^2).$$

Proof Observe that for any $t \in \mathbb{R}$ we have obtain $0 \le (X + tY)^2 = X^2 + 2tXY + t^2Y^2$, and these random variables are integrable since X and Y are square-integrable. As a result,

$$0 \le \mathbb{E}((X + tY)^2) = \mathbb{E}(X^2) + 2t\mathbb{E}(XY) + t^2\mathbb{E}(Y^2)$$

for any $t \in \mathbb{R}$. For this quadratic expression in t to be non-negative for all $t \in \mathbb{R}$, its discriminant must be non-positive, that is,

$$[2\mathbb{E}(XY)]^2 - 4\mathbb{E}(X^2)\mathbb{E}(Y^2) \le 0,$$

which proves the Schwarz inequality. □

Applying Lemma 3.49 to the **centred** random variables $X - \mathbb{E}(X)$ and $Y - \mathbb{E}(Y)$ it is now easy to verify the following bounds for $\text{Cov}(X, Y)$ and $\rho_{X,Y}$.

Corollary 3.50
The following inequalities hold:

$$[\text{Cov}(X, Y)]^2 \le \text{Var}(X)\text{Var}(Y),$$
$$-1 \le \rho_{X,Y} \le 1.$$

Exercise 3.39 Suppose that $|\rho_{X,Y}| = 1$. What is the relationship between X and Y?

Finally, we can quantify the dependencies between n random variables by means of the covariance matrix defined as follows.

Definition 3.51

For a random vector $X = (X_1, X_2, \ldots, X_n)$ consisting of integrable random variables such that the product $X_i X_j$ is integrable for each $i, j = 1, 2, \ldots, n$ we define the **covariance matrix** to be the $n \times n$ square matrix with entries $\mathrm{Cov}(X_i, X_j)$ for $i, j = 1, 2, \ldots, n$, that is, the matrix

$$
\mathbf{C} = \begin{pmatrix}
\mathrm{Cov}(X_1, X_1) & \mathrm{Cov}(X_1, X_2) & \cdots & \mathrm{Cov}(X_1, X_n) \\
\mathrm{Cov}(X_2, X_1) & \mathrm{Cov}(X_2, X_2) & \cdots & \mathrm{Cov}(X_2, X_n) \\
\vdots & \vdots & \ddots & \vdots \\
\mathrm{Cov}(X_n, X_1) & \mathrm{Cov}(X_n, X_2) & \cdots & \mathrm{Cov}(X_n, X_n)
\end{pmatrix}.
$$

Since $\mathrm{Cov}(X_i, X_j) = \mathrm{Cov}(X_j, X_i)$, the covariance matrix is symmetric. The diagonal elements are $\mathrm{Cov}(X_i, X_i) = \mathrm{Var}(X_i)$. Also note that for any vector $a = (a_1, a_2, \ldots, a_n) \in \mathbb{R}^n$ we have

$$
\begin{aligned}
0 &\leq \mathrm{Var}(a_1 X_1 + \cdots + a_n X_n) \\
&= \mathrm{Cov}(a_1 X_1 + \cdots + a_n X_n, a_1 X_1 + \cdots + a_n X_n) \\
&= a^T \mathbf{C} a,
\end{aligned}
$$

which means that the covariance matrix is non-negative definite.

3.7   Proofs by means of d-systems

The idea behind the proof of Theorem 3.5 is to observe that the desired properties hold for all sets in the σ-field generated by $\mathcal{R}$, the class of measurable rectangles. For example, setting

$$
\mathcal{D} = \{A \in \sigma(\mathcal{R}) : \omega_1 \mapsto \mu_2(A_{\omega_1}) \text{ is } \mathcal{F}_1\text{-measurable}\},
$$

we wish to show that $\mathcal{D} = \sigma(\mathcal{R})$ in order to prove that $\omega_1 \mapsto \mu_2(A_{\omega_1})$ is $\mathcal{F}_1$-measurable for every $A \in \sigma(\mathcal{R})$ (and similarly for the function $\omega_2 \mapsto \mu_1(A_{\omega_2})$). It is clear that $\mathcal{R} \subset \mathcal{D}$ since for $A_1 \times A_2 \in \mathcal{R}$ we have $\mu_2(A_{\omega_1}) = \mathbf{1}_{A_1}(\omega_1)\mu_2(A_2)$. It would therefore suffice to prove that $\mathcal{D}$ is a σ-field in order to verify part (i) of the theorem

Similarly, to ensure that μ is uniquely determined on $\mathcal{F}_1 \otimes \mathcal{F}_2$ by its defining property (3.2) on $\mathcal{R}$, it would suffice to prove that, given two finite measures ν_1, ν_2 that agree on $\mathcal{R}$, the collection of all sets on which they agree is a σ-field.

Here we have two examples of a general proof technique which finds frequent use in measure theory. First we observe that a certain property holds on a given collection C of subsets, and show that the collection $\mathcal{D}$ of all sets that satisfy this property is a σ-field. Since the σ-field $\mathcal{D}$ contains C, it must contain $\sigma(C)$, so the property holds on $\sigma(C)$. Rather than verifying directly that $\mathcal{D}$ satisfies the definition of a σ-field, it is often easier to check that $\mathcal{D}$ meets the following requirements.

Definition 3.52
A system $\mathcal{D}$ of subsets of Ω is called a d-**system** on Ω when the following conditions are satisfied:
  (i) $\Omega \in \mathcal{D}$;
  (ii) if $A, B \in \mathcal{D}$ with $A \subset B$, then $B \setminus A \in \mathcal{D}$;
  (iii) if $A_i \subset A_{i+1}$ and $A_i \in \mathcal{D}$ for $i = 1, 2, \ldots$, then $\bigcup_{i=1}^{\infty} A_i \in \mathcal{D}$.

Similarly as for σ-fields, the smallest d-system on Ω that contains a family C of subsets of Ω is given by

$$d(C) = \bigcap \{\mathcal{D} : \mathcal{D} \text{ is a } d\text{-system on } \Omega, C \subset \mathcal{D}\}$$

and called the d-**system generated by** C.

It is clear that the conditions defining a d-system are weaker than those for a σ-field; compare Definitions 1.10 (ii) and 3.52.

Since every σ-field is a d-system, for any collection C we have $d(C) \subset \sigma(C)$. If, for a particular collection C, we can prove the opposite inclusion, our task of checking that the desired property holds on $\sigma(C)$ will be accomplished by checking the conditions defining a d-system.

Of course, we cannot expect this to be true for an arbitrary collection C. However, the following simple property of C is sufficient.

Definition 3.53
A family C is **closed under intersection** if $A, B \in C$ implies $A \cap B \in C$.

An immediate example of such a collection is given by the measurable rectangles.

Exercise 3.40 Show that the family $\mathcal{R}$ of measurable rectangles is closed under intersection.

When a family C of subsets of a given set Ω is closed under intersection, the d-system and the σ-field generated by C turn out to be the same. We prove this below.

Lemma 3.54

Suppose a family C of subsets of Ω is closed under intersection. Then $d(C)$ is closed under intersection.

Proof Consider the family of sets

$$\mathcal{G} = \{A \in d(C) : A \cap C \in d(C) \text{ for all } C \in C\}.$$

Since C is closed under intersection and $C \subset d(C)$, we have $C \subset \mathcal{G}$. We claim that $\mathcal{G}$ is a d-system. Obviously, $\Omega \cap C = C \in C$ for each $C \in C$, so $\Omega \in \mathcal{G}$. If $A, B \in \mathcal{G}$ and $A \subset B$, then for any $C \in C$

$$(B \setminus A) \cap C = (B \cap C) \setminus (A \cap C) \in d(C)$$

since $A \cap C, B \cap C \in d(C)$ and $A \cap C \subset B \cap C$. Thus $B \setminus A \in \mathcal{G}$.

   Finally, suppose that $A_i \subset A_{i+1}$ and $A_i \in d(C)$ for $i = 1, 2, \dots$. Then for any $C \in C$ we have $A_i \cap C \subset A_{i+1} \cap C$ and $A_i \cap C \in d(C)$, so

$$\left(\bigcup_{i=1}^{\infty} A_i \right) \cap C = \bigcup_{i=1}^{\infty} (A_i \cap C) \in d(C),$$

implying that $\bigcup_{i=1}^{\infty} A_i \in \mathcal{G}$. We have shown that $\mathcal{G}$ is a d-system such that $C \subset \mathcal{G} \subset d(C)$, hence $\mathcal{G} = d(C)$.

   Now consider the family of sets

$$\mathcal{H} = \{A \in d(C) : A \cap B \in d(C) \text{ for all } B \in d(C)\}.$$

Because $\mathcal{G} = d(C)$, we know that $C \subset \mathcal{H}$. Moreover, $\mathcal{H}$ is a d-system, which can be verified in a very similar way as for $\mathcal{G}$. Since $\mathcal{H} \subset d(C)$, we conclude that $\mathcal{H} = d(C)$, and this proves the lemma.   □

Lemma 3.55

A family $\mathcal{D}$ of subsets of Ω is a σ-field if and only if it is a d-system closed under intersection.

Proof If $\mathcal{D}$ is a σ-field, it obviously is a d-system closed under intersection. Conversely, if $\mathcal{D}$ is a d-system closed under intersection and $A, B \in \mathcal{D}$, then $\Omega, \Omega \setminus A, \Omega \setminus B \in \mathcal{D}$. Hence $\Omega \setminus (A \cup B) = (\Omega \setminus A) \cap (\Omega \setminus B)$ is in $\mathcal{D}$. But then so is its complement $A \cup B$ since $\Omega \in \mathcal{D}$. Finally, if $A_i \in \mathcal{D}$ for all $i = 1, 2, \dots$, then the sets $B_k = \bigcup_{i=1}^{k} A_i$ belong to $\mathcal{D}$ by induction on what has just been proved for $k = 2$. The B_k increase to $\bigcup_{i=1}^{\infty} A_i$, so this union also belongs to the d-system $\mathcal{D}$. We have verified that $\mathcal{D}$ is a σ-field.   □

   Together, these two lemmas imply the result we seek.

Proposition 3.56

If a family C of subsets of Ω is closed under intersection, then $d(C) = \sigma(C)$.

Proof Since C is closed under intersection, it follows by Lemma 3.54 that $d(C)$ is also closed under intersection. According to Lemma 3.55, $d(C)$ is therefore a σ-field. Because $C \subset d(C) \subset \sigma(C)$ and $\sigma(C)$ is the smallest σ-field containing C we can therefore conclude that $d(C) = \sigma(C)$. □

By Exercise 3.40 we have an immediate consequence for measurable rectangles.

Corollary 3.57

The family of measurable rectangles on $\Omega_1 \times \Omega_2$ satisfies

$$d(\mathcal{R}) = \sigma(\mathcal{R}).$$

Exercise 3.41 Show that

$$d(\mathcal{I}) = \sigma(\mathcal{I}),$$

where $\mathcal{I}$ is the family of open intervals in $\mathbb{R}$.

The final step in our preparation for the proof Theorem 3.5 will ensure that the measure μ is uniquely defined on $\mathcal{F}_1 \otimes \mathcal{F}_2$ by the requirement that for all measurable rectangles $A_1 \times A_2$,

$$\mu(A_1 \times A_2) = \mu_1(A_1)\mu_2(A_2).$$

Again, we shall phrase the result in terms of general families of sets to enable us to use it in a variety of settings. Assume that C is a family of subsets of a non-empty set Ω.

Lemma 3.58

Suppose that C is closed under intersection. If μ and ν are measures defined on the σ-field $\sigma(C)$ such that $\mu(A) = \nu(A)$ for every $A \in C$ and $\mu(\Omega) = \nu(\Omega) < \infty$, then $\mu(A) = \nu(A)$ for every $A \in \sigma(C)$.

Proof Consider the family of sets

$$\mathcal{D} = \{A \in \sigma(C) : \mu(A) = \nu(A)\}.$$

Since the measures agree on C we know that $C \subset \mathcal{D}$. Let us verify that $\mathcal{D}$ is a d-system. Since $\mu(\Omega) = \nu(\Omega)$, it follows that $\Omega \in \mathcal{D}$. For any $A, B \in \mathcal{D}$ such that $B \subset A$ we have

$$\mu(A \setminus B) = \mu(A) - \mu(B) = \nu(A) - \nu(B) = \nu(A \setminus B).$$

(Here it is important that μ and ν are finite measures.) Hence $A \setminus B \in \mathcal{D}$. Moreover, for any non-decreasing sequence $A_i \subset A_{i+1}$ with $A_i \in \mathcal{D}$ for $i = 1, 2, \ldots$ we have

$$\mu\left(\bigcup_{i=1}^{\infty} A_i\right) = \lim_{i \to \infty} \mu(A_i) = \lim_{i \to \infty} \nu(A_i) = \nu\left(\bigcup_{i=1}^{\infty} A_i\right),$$

which shows that $\bigcup_{i=1}^{\infty} A_i \in \mathcal{D}$. We have shown that $\mathcal{D}$ is a d-system such that $C \subset \mathcal{D} \subset \sigma(C)$. Hence $d(C) \subset \mathcal{D} \subset \sigma(C)$. Because C is closed under intersection, it follows by Lemma 3.56 that $\mathcal{D} = \sigma(C)$, that is, the measures μ and ν coincide on $\sigma(C)$. $\qquad \square$

To prove Theorem 3.5 we now need to apply these general results to the family $\mathcal{R}$ of measurable rectangles on $\Omega_1 \times \Omega_2$.

Theorem 3.5
Suppose that μ_1 and μ_2 are finite measures defined on the σ-fields $\mathcal{F}_1$ and $\mathcal{F}_2$, respectively. Then:
  (i) *for any $A \in \mathcal{F}_1 \otimes \mathcal{F}_2$ the functions*

$$\omega_1 \mapsto \mu_2(A_{\omega_1}), \qquad \omega_2 \mapsto \mu_1(A_{\omega_2})$$

  are measurable, respectively, with respect to $\mathcal{F}_1$ and $\mathcal{F}_2$;
  (ii) *for any $A \in \mathcal{F}_1 \otimes \mathcal{F}_2$ the following integrals are well defined and equal to one another:*

$$\int_{\Omega_1} \mu_2(A_{\omega_1}) d\mu_1(\omega_1) = \int_{\Omega_2} \mu_1(A_{\omega_2}) d\mu_2(\omega_2);$$

  (iii) *the function $\mu : \mathcal{F}_1 \otimes \mathcal{F}_2 \to [0, \infty)$ defined by*

$$\mu(A) = \int_{\Omega_1} \mu_2(A_{\omega_1}) d\mu_1(\omega_1) = \int_{\Omega_2} \mu_1(A_{\omega_2}) d\mu_2(\omega_2) \qquad (3.4)$$

  for each $A \in \mathcal{F}_1 \otimes \mathcal{F}_2$ is a measure on the σ-field $\mathcal{F}_1 \otimes \mathcal{F}_2$;
  (iv) *μ is the only measure on $\mathcal{F}_1 \otimes \mathcal{F}_2$ such that*

$$\mu(A_1 \times A_2) = \mu_1(A_1)\mu_2(A_2)$$

  for each $A_1 \in \mathcal{F}_1$ and $A_2 \in \mathcal{F}_2$.

Proof (i) Define the family of sets

$$\mathcal{D} = \{A \in \sigma(\mathcal{R}) : \omega_1 \mapsto \mu_2(A_{\omega_1}) \text{ is } \mathcal{F}_1\text{-measurable}\}.$$

In order to prove that $\omega_1 \mapsto \mu_2(A_{\omega_1})$ is $\mathcal{F}_1$-measurable for any $A \in \mathcal{F}_1 \otimes \mathcal{F}_2 = \sigma(\mathcal{R})$ it is enough to show that $\mathcal{D} = \sigma(\mathcal{R})$. Since $\mu_2(A_{\omega_1}) = \mathbf{1}_{A_1}(\omega_1)\mu_2(A_2)$ for $A = A_1 \times A_2$, it follows that $\mathcal{R} \subset \mathcal{D}$. To show that $\mathcal{D}$ is a d-system note first that $\Omega_1 \times \Omega_2$ belongs to $\mathcal{R}$, hence it belongs to $\mathcal{D}$. If $A \subset B$ and $A, B \in \mathcal{D}$, then for any $\omega_1 \in \Omega_1$

$$(B \setminus A)_{\omega_1} = B_{\omega_1} \setminus A_{\omega_1} \quad \text{and} \quad A_{\omega_1} \subset B_{\omega_1},$$

so

$$\mu_2((B \setminus A)_{\omega_1}) = \mu_2(B_{\omega_1}) - \mu_2(A_{\omega_1}),$$

where $\omega_1 \mapsto \mu_2(A_{\omega_1})$ and $\omega_1 \mapsto \mu_2(B_{\omega_1})$ are measurable functions. Hence $\omega_1 \mapsto \mu_2((B \setminus A)_{\omega_1})$ is a measurable function, so $B \setminus A \in \mathcal{D}$. Finally, given an non-decreasing sequence $A_i \subset A_{i+1}$ with $A_i \in \mathcal{D}$ for $i = 1, 2, \ldots$, we see that $(A_i)_{\omega_1} \subset (A_{i+1})_{\omega_1}$ for any $\omega_1 \in \Omega_1$, so

$$\mu_2 \left(\left(\bigcup_{i=1}^{\infty} A_i \right)_{\omega_1} \right) = \mu_2 \left(\bigcup_{i=1}^{\infty} (A_i)_{\omega_1} \right) = \lim_{i \to \infty} \mu_2((A_i)_{\omega_1}).$$

By Exercise 1.19, this means that $\bigcup_{i=1}^{\infty} A_n \in \mathcal{D}$. We have shown that $\mathcal{D}$ is a d-system containing $\mathcal{R}$. Hence $d(\mathcal{R}) \subset \mathcal{D}$. By Corollary 3.57 it follows that $\mathcal{D} = \sigma(\mathcal{R})$, completing the proof. The same argument works for the function $\omega_2 \mapsto \mu_1(A_{\omega_2})$.

(ii) For any $A \in \mathcal{F}_1 \otimes \mathcal{F}_2$ put

$$\nu_1(A) = \int_{\Omega_1} \mu_2(A_{\omega_1}) d\mu_1(\omega_1), \quad \nu_2(A) = \int_{\Omega_2} \mu_1(A_{\omega_2}) d\mu_2(\omega_2).$$

The integrals are well defined by part (i) of the theorem. We show that ν_1 and ν_2 are finite measures on $\mathcal{F}_1 \otimes \mathcal{F}_2$. Let $A_i \in \mathcal{F}_1 \otimes \mathcal{F}_2$ for $i = 1, 2, \ldots$ be a sequence of pairwise disjoint sets. Then the sections $(A_i)_{\omega_2}$ are also pairwise disjoint for any $\omega_2 \in \Omega_2$, and

$$\nu_1 \left(\bigcup_{i=1}^{\infty} A_i \right) = \int_{\Omega_1} \mu_2 \left(\left(\bigcup_{i=1}^{\infty} A_i \right)_{\omega_1} \right) d\mu_1(\omega_1) = \int_{\Omega_1} \mu_2 \left(\bigcup_{i=1}^{\infty} (A_i)_{\omega_1} \right) d\mu_1(\omega_1)$$

$$= \int_{\Omega_1} \sum_{i=1}^{\infty} \mu_2((A_i)_{\omega_1}) d\mu_1(\omega_1) = \sum_{i=1}^{\infty} \int_{\Omega_1} \mu_2((A_i)_{\omega_1}) d\mu_1(\omega_1)$$

$$= \sum_{i=1}^{\infty} \nu_1(A_i)$$

by the monotone convergence theorem for a series (Exercise 1.24). Moreover, ν_1 is a finite measure since

$$\nu_1(\Omega_1 \times \Omega_2) = \mu_1(\Omega_1)\mu_2(\Omega_2) < \infty.$$

A similar argument applies to v_2. For measurable rectangles $A_1 \times A_2 \in \mathcal{R}$, where $A_1 \in \mathcal{F}_1$ and $A_2 \in \mathcal{F}_2$, we have

$$v_1(A_1 \times A_2) = \mu_1(A_1)\mu_2(A_2) = v_2(A_1 \times A_2).$$

By Lemma 3.58, the measures v_1 and v_2 therefore coincide on $\mathcal{F}_1 \otimes \mathcal{F}_2 = \sigma(\mathcal{R})$.

(iii) Since $\mu = v_1 = v_2$, we have already proved in part (ii) that μ is a measure on $\mathcal{F}_1 \otimes \mathcal{F}_2$.

(iv) Uniqueness of μ follows directly from Lemma 3.58.   □

Exercise 3.42   Let X be an integrable random variable on the probability space $\Omega = [0, 1]$ with Borel sets and Lebesgue measure. Show that if

$$\int_{(i2^{-n}, j2^{-n}]} X \, dm = 0$$

for any $n = 0, 1, \ldots$ and for any $i, j = 0, 1, \ldots, 2^n$ with $i \leq j$, then

$$\int_A X \, dm = 0$$

for every Borel set $A \subset [0, 1]$, and deduce that $X = 0$, m-a.s.

The proof of Theorem 3.27 is based on a similar technique, making use of d-systems.

Theorem 3.27
Random variables X, Y are independent if and only if their joint distribution function $F_{X,Y}$ is the product of their individual distribution functions, that is,

$$F_{X,Y}(x, y) = F_X(x)F_Y(y) \quad \text{for any } x, y \in \mathbb{R}.$$

Proof   Since intervals are Borel sets, the necessity is obvious. For sufficiency, the claim is that we need only check (3.8) for intervals of the form $B_1 = (-\infty, x)$, $B_2 = (-\infty, y)$. We are then given that for all $x, y \in \mathbb{R}$

$$P(X \leq x, Y \leq y) = P(X \leq x)P(Y \leq y). \tag{3.14}$$

Now consider the class C of all Borel sets $A \in \mathcal{B}(\mathbb{R})$ such that for all $y \in \mathbb{R}$

$$P(X \in A, Y \leq y) = P(X \in A)P(Y \leq y), \tag{3.15}$$

and the class $\mathcal{D}$ of Borel sets $B \in \mathcal{B}(\mathbb{R})$ such that for all $A \in C$

$$P(X \in A, Y \in B) = P(X \in A)P(Y \in B). \tag{3.16}$$

Our aim is to show that C and $\mathcal{D}$ are both equal to the Borel σ-field $\mathcal{B}(\mathbb{R})$. By our assumption (3.14), C contains the collection of all intervals $(-\infty, x)$, and this collection is closed under intersection, we only need to check that C is a d-system. This will mean that it contains all Borel sets, and so (3.15) holds for all Borel sets. This in turn will mean that $\mathcal{D}$ contains all intervals $(-\infty, x)$, hence to show that it contains $\mathcal{B}(\mathbb{R})$ we again only need to make sure that $\mathcal{D}$ is a d-system.

We now check that $\mathcal{D}$ satisfies the conditions for a d-system; the proof for C is almost identical. We have $\Omega \in \mathcal{D}$ since for all $A \in C$

$$P(X \in A, Y \in \Omega) = P(X \in A) = P(X \in A)P(Y \in \Omega).$$

If $B \in \mathcal{D}$, then

$$\begin{aligned} P(X \in A, Y \in \Omega \setminus B) &= P(X \in A, Y \in \Omega) - P(X \in A, Y \in B) \\ &= P(X \in A)P(Y \in \Omega) - P(X \in A)P(Y \in B) \\ &= P(X \in A)P(Y \in \Omega \setminus B). \end{aligned}$$

Finally, if $B_n \subset B_{n+1}$ with $B_n \in \mathcal{D}$ for all $n = 1, 2, \ldots$ and $\bigcup_{n=1}^{\infty} B_n = B$, then

$$\begin{aligned} P(X \in A, Y \in B) &= P\left(\bigcup_{n=1}^{\infty} \{X \in A, Y \in B_n\}\right) \\ &= \lim_{n \to \infty} P(X \in A, Y \in B_n) \\ &= P(X \in A) \lim_{n \to \infty} P(Y \in B_n) \\ &= P(X \in A)P(Y \in B). \end{aligned}$$

Thus $\mathcal{D}$ is a d-system. By Proposition 3.56, $\mathcal{D}$ is a σ-field containing all intervals $(-\infty, y)$, and so contains all Borel sets, which proves that (3.16) holds for all pairs of Borel sets, that is, X and Y are independent. □

4

Conditional expectation

We turn our attention to the concept of **conditioning,** which involves adjusting our expectations in the light of the knowledge we have gained of certain events or random variables. Building on the notion of the conditional probability defined in (3.11), we describe how knowledge of one random variable Y may cause us to review how likely the various outcomes of another random variable X are going to be. We adjust the probabilities for the values of X in the light of the information provided by the values of Y, by focusing on those scenarios for which these values of Y have occurred. This becomes especially important when we have a sequence, or even a continuous-parameter family, of random variables, and we consider how knowledge of the earlier terms will affect the later ones. We first illustrate these ideas in the simplest multi-step financial market model, since our main applications come from finance.

4.1   Binomial stock prices

Consider the binomial model of stock prices in order to illustrate the probabilistic ideas we will develop. This model, studied in detail in [DMFM], combines simplicity with flexibility. The general multi-step binomial model consists of repetitions of the single-step model.

Single-step model Suppose that the current price $S(0)$ of some risky asset (stock) is known, and its future price $S(T)$ at some fixed $T > 0$ is a random variable $S(T) : \Omega \to [0, +\infty)$, taking just two values:

$$S(T) = \begin{cases} S(0)(1 + U) & \text{with probability } p, \\ S(0)(1 + D) & \text{with probability } 1 - p, \end{cases}$$

where $-1 < D < U$. The return

$$K = \frac{S(T) - S(0)}{S(0)}$$

is a random variable such that

$$K = \begin{cases} U & \text{with probability } p, \\ D & \text{with probability } 1 - p. \end{cases}$$

As the sample space we take a two-element set $\Omega = \{U, D\}$ equipped with a probability P determined by a single number $p \in (0, 1)$ such that $P(U) = p$ and $P(D) = 1 - p$.

Multi-step model All the essential features of a general multi-step model are contained in a model with three time steps, where we take time to be $0, h, 2h, 3h = T$. We simplify the notation by just specifying the number of a step, ignoring its length h. The model involves stock prices $S(0), S(1), S(2), S(3)$ at these four time instants, where $S(0)$ is a constant, and $S(1), S(2), S(3)$ are random variables. The returns

$$K_n = \frac{S(n) - S(n - 1)}{S(n - 1)}$$

at each step $n = 1, 2, 3$ are independent random variables, and each has the same distribution as the return K in the single-step model. For the probability space we take $\Omega = \{U, D\}^3$, which consists of eight triples, called scenarios (or paths):

$$\Omega = \{UUU, UUD, UDU, UDD, DUU, DUD, DDU, DDD\}.$$

As K_1, K_2, K_3 are independent random variables, the probability of each path is the product of the probabilities of the up/down price movements along that path, namely

$$P(UUU) = p^3,$$
$$P(DUU) = P(UDU) = P(UUD) = p^2(1 - p),$$
$$P(UDD) = P(DUD) = P(DDU) = p(1 - p)^2,$$
$$P(DDD) = (1 - p)^3.$$

The emerging binomial tree is recombining, as can be seen in the next example.

Example 4.1

Let $S(0) = 100$, $U = 0.1$, $D = -0.1$ and $p = 0.6$. The corresponding binomial tree is

$$S(0) \qquad S(1) \qquad S(2) \qquad S(3)$$

The number X of upward movements in this binomial tree is a random variable with distribution

$$P(X = 3) = P(\{UUU\}) = p^3,$$
$$P(X = 2) = P(\{DUU, UDU, UUD\}) = 3p^2(1 - p),$$
$$P(X = 1) = P(\{UDD, DUD, DDU\}) = 3p(1 - p)^2,$$
$$P(X = 0) = P(\{DDD\}) = (1 - p)^3,$$

that is, X has binomial distribution (see Example 2.2). The expected price after three steps is $\mathbb{E}(S(3)) \simeq 106.12$.

We use this example to analyse the changes of this expectation corresponding to the flow of information over time.

Partitions and expectation

Conditioning on the first step Suppose we know that the stock has gone up in the first step. This means that the collection of available scenarios is reduced to those beginning with U, which we denote by

$$\Omega_U = \{UUU, UUD, UDU, UDD\}.$$

This set now plays the role of the probability space, which we need to equip with a probability measure (the events will be all the subsets of Ω_U). This is done by adjusting the original probabilities so that the new probability of Ω_U is 1. For $A \subset \Omega_U$ we put

$$P_U(A) = \frac{P(A)}{P(\Omega_U)}.$$

Of course $P_U(\Omega_U) = 1$. Since $A \subset \Omega_U$, it follows that

$$P_U(A) = \frac{P(A \cap \Omega_U)}{P(\Omega_U)} = P(A \,|\, \Omega_U),$$

so the measure P_U is the conditional probability $A \mapsto P(A \,|\, \Omega_U)$ considered for subsets $A \subset \Omega_U$.

If we know that the stock went down in the first step, we replace Ω_U by the set Ω_D of all paths beginning with D, and for $A \subset \Omega_D$ we put

$$P_D(A) = P(A \,|\, \Omega_D).$$

We have decomposed the set $\Omega = \Omega_U \cup \Omega_D$ of all scenarios into two disjoint subsets Ω_U, Ω_D, which motivates the following general definition.

Definition 4.2
Let Ω be a non-empty set. A family $\mathcal{P} = \{B_1, B_2, \ldots\}$ such that $B_i \subset \Omega$ for $i = 1, 2, \ldots$ is called a **partition** of Ω if $B_i \cap B_j = \varnothing$ whenever $i \neq j$ and $\Omega = \bigcup_{i=1}^{\infty} B_i$.

Note that we allow for the possibility that $B_i = \varnothing$ when $i > n$ for some n, so the partition may be finite or countably infinite.

Example 4.3
$\mathcal{P} = \{\Omega_U, \Omega_D\}$ is a partition of $\Omega = \{U, D\}^3$.

For any discrete random variable X with values $x_1, x_2, \ldots \in \mathbb{R}$ the family of all sets of the form $\{X = x_i\}$ for $i = 1, 2, \ldots$ is a partition of Ω. We call it the partition **generated** by X.

Example 4.4

In $\Omega = \{U, D\}^3$ the partition generated by $S(1)$ from Example 4.1 is $\{\Omega_U, \Omega_D\}$.

Recall from Definition 3.2 that for any collection C of subsets of Ω, the σ-field generated by C is the smallest σ-field containing C.

Exercise 4.1   Show that the σ-field $\sigma(\mathcal{P})$ generated by a partition $\mathcal{P}$ consists of all possible countable unions of the sets belonging to $\mathcal{P}$.

Not all σ-fields are generated by partitions. For example, the σ-field of Borel sets $\mathcal{B}(\mathbb{R})$ is not generated by a partition.

Although σ-fields are more general, we will work with partitions for the present to develop better intuition in a relatively simple case.

Exercise 4.2   We call A an **atom** in a σ-field $\mathcal{F}$ if $A \in \mathcal{F}$ is non-empty and there are no non-empty sets $B, C \in \mathcal{F}$ such that $A = B \cup C$. Show that if the family $\mathcal{A}$ of all atoms in $\mathcal{F}$ is a partition, then $\mathcal{F} = \sigma(\mathcal{A})$.

Example 4.5

Continuing Example 4.1, we compute the expectation of $S(3)$ in the new probability space $\Omega_U = \{S(1) = 110\}$ with probability P_U. Since the paths beginning with D are excluded, $S(3)$ takes three values on Ω_U, and this expectation, which we denote by $\mathbb{E}(S(3)|\Omega_U)$ and call the conditional expectation of $S(3)$ given Ω_U, is equal to

$$\mathbb{E}(S(3)|\Omega_U) = 131.1 \times 0.6^2 + 108.9 \times 2 \times 0.6 \times 0.4 + 89.1 \times 0.4^2 \simeq 114.44.$$

In a similar manner we can compute the expectation of $S(3)$ on $\Omega_D = \{S(1) = 90\}$ with probability P_D, denote it by $\mathbb{E}(S(3)|\Omega_D)$ and call it the conditional expectation of $S(3)$ given Ω_D. We obtain

$$\mathbb{E}(S(3)|\Omega_D) = 108.9 \times 0.6^2 + 89.1 \times 2 \times 0.6 \times 0.4 + 72.9 \times 0.4^2 \simeq 93.64.$$

These two cases can be combined by setting up a new random variable, denoted by $\mathbb{E}(S(3)|S(1))$ and called the conditional expectation of $S(3)$ given $S(1)$:

$$\mathbb{E}(S(3)|S(1)) = \begin{cases} \mathbb{E}(S(3)|\Omega_U) & \text{on } \Omega_U, \\ \mathbb{E}(S(3)|\Omega_D) & \text{on } \Omega_D, \end{cases}$$

$$\simeq \begin{cases} 114.44 & \text{on } \{S(1) = 110\}, \\ 93.64 & \text{on } \{S(1) = 90\}. \end{cases}$$

Conditioning on the first two steps Suppose now that we know the price moves for the first two steps. There are four possibilities, which can be described by specifying a partition of Ω into four disjoint sets:

$$\Omega_{UU} = \{UUU, UUD\},$$
$$\Omega_{UD} = \{UDU, UDD\},$$
$$\Omega_{DU} = \{DUU, DUD\},$$
$$\Omega_{DD} = \{DDU, DDD\}.$$

Each of these sets can be viewed as a probability space equipped with a measure adjusted in a similar manner as before, for instance in Ω_{UU} we have $P_{UU}(A) = P(A|\Omega_{UU})$ for any $A \subset \Omega_{UU}$, and similarly for P_{UD}, P_{DU} and P_{DD}. We follow the setup in Example 4.1 to illustrate how this leads to the conditional expectation of $S(3)$ given $S(2)$.

Example 4.6
We compute the expected value of $S(3)$ on each of the sets $\Omega_{UU}, \Omega_{UD}, \Omega_{DU}, \Omega_{DD}$ under the respective probability:

$$\mathbb{E}(S(3)|\Omega_{UU}) = 131.1 \times 0.6 + 108.9 \times 0.4 \simeq 123.42,$$
$$\mathbb{E}(S(3)|\Omega_{UD}) = 108.9 \times 0.6 + 89.1 \times 0.4 \simeq 100.98,$$
$$\mathbb{E}(S(3)|\Omega_{DU}) = 108.9 \times 0.6 + 89.1 \times 0.4 \simeq 100.98,$$
$$\mathbb{E}(S(3)|\Omega_{DD}) = 89.1 \times 0.6 + 72.9 \times 0.4 \simeq 82.62,$$

introducing similar notation for these expectations as in Example 4.5. We can see, in particular, that $\mathbb{E}(S(3)|\Omega_{UD}) = \mathbb{E}(S(3)|\Omega_{DU})$. Since $S(2)$ has the same value on Ω_{UD} and Ω_{DU}, this allows us to employ a random variable denoted by $\mathbb{E}(S(3)|S(2))$. To this end, note that the partition generated by $S(2)$ consists of three sets

$$\Omega_{UU} = \{S(2) = 121\}, \quad \Omega_{UD} \cup \Omega_{DU} = \{S(2) = 99\}, \quad \Omega_{DD} = \{S(2) = 81\},$$

and the random variable $\mathbb{E}(S(3)\,|\,S(2))$ takes three different values

$$\mathbb{E}(S(3)\,|\,S(2)) = \begin{cases} \mathbb{E}(S(3)\,|\,\Omega_{UU}) & \text{on } \Omega_{UU}, \\ \mathbb{E}(S(3)\,|\,\Omega_{UD}) = \mathbb{E}(S(3)\,|\,\Omega_{DU}) & \text{on } \Omega_{UD} \cup \Omega_{DU}, \\ \mathbb{E}(S(3)\,|\,\Omega_{DD}) & \text{on } \Omega_{DD}, \end{cases}$$

$$\simeq \begin{cases} 123.42 & \text{on } \{S(2) = 121\}, \\ 100.98 & \text{on } \{S(2) = 99\}, \\ 82.62 & \text{on } \{S(2) = 81\}. \end{cases}$$

The actual values of $S(2)$ are irrelevant here since they do not appear in the computations. What matters is the partition related to these values.

4.2 Conditional expectation: discrete case

The binomial example motivates a more general definition. Recall that for any event $B \in \mathcal{F}$ such that $P(B) > 0$ and for any $A \in \mathcal{F}$ we know from (3.11) that the conditional probability of A given B is

$$P(A\,|\,B) = \frac{P(A \cap B)}{P(B)}.$$

Exercise 4.3 Show that

$$P_B(A) = P(A\,|\,B)$$

is a probability measure on B defined on the σ-field $\mathcal{F}_B$ consisting of all events $A \in \mathcal{F}$ such that $A \subset B$.

Definition 4.7
If X is a discrete random variable on Ω with finitely many distinct values $x_1, x_2, \ldots, x_n$ and $B \in \mathcal{F}$ is an event such that $P(B) > 0$, the **conditional expectation** of X given B, denoted by $\mathbb{E}(X\,|\,B)$, can be defined as the expectation of X restricted to B under the probability P_B.

This follows the same pattern as in Examples 4.5 and 4.6, and gives

$$\mathbb{E}(X \mid B) = \frac{1}{P(B)} \sum_{i=1}^{n} x_i P(\{X = x_i\} \cap B)$$

$$= \frac{1}{P(B)} \sum_{i=1}^{n} x_i P(\mathbf{1}_B X = x_i) = \frac{1}{P(B)} \mathbb{E}(\mathbf{1}_B X).$$

We use this to extend the definition to any integrable random variable X.

Definition 4.8
Given an integrable random variable X on Ω and an event $B \in \mathcal{F}$ with $P(B) > 0$, the **conditional expectation** of X given B is defined as

$$\mathbb{E}(X \mid B) = \frac{1}{P(B)} \mathbb{E}(\mathbf{1}_B X). \tag{4.1}$$

Exercise 4.4 For a random variable X with Poisson distribution find the conditional expectation of X given that the value of X is an odd number.

As noted in the binomial example, given a partition of Ω we can piece together the conditional expectations of X relative to the members of the partition to obtain a random variable.

Definition 4.9
Given a partition $\mathcal{P} = \{B_1, B_2, \ldots\}$ of Ω, the random variable $\mathbb{E}(X \mid \mathcal{P})$: $\Omega \to \mathbb{R}$ such that for each $i = 1, 2, \ldots$

$$\mathbb{E}(X \mid \mathcal{P})(\omega) = \mathbb{E}(X \mid B_i) \quad \text{if } \omega \in B_i \text{ and } P(B_i) > 0$$

is called the **conditional expectation** of X with respect to the partition $\mathcal{P}$.

Note that in this definition the random variable $\mathbb{E}(X \mid \mathcal{P})$ remains undefined when $P(B_i) = 0$. Since $\mathcal{P}$ is a partition, this means that the function $\mathbb{E}(X \mid \mathcal{P})$ is well defined P-a.s.

Applying (4.1), we can write

$$\mathbb{E}(X \mid \mathcal{P}) = \sum_{\substack{i=1,2,\ldots \\ P(B_i)>0}} \frac{1}{P(B_i)} \mathbb{E}(\mathbf{1}_{B_i} X) \mathbf{1}_{B_i}. \tag{4.2}$$

The above definition, applied to the partition of Ω generated by a discrete random variable Y, leads to the following one.

Definition 4.10

If X is an integrable random variable and Y is a discrete random variable with values $y_1, y_2, \ldots$, then the **conditional expectation** $\mathbb{E}(X\,|\,Y)$ of X given Y is the conditional expectation of X with respect to the partition $\mathcal{P}$ generated by Y, that is, for each $i = 1, 2, \ldots$

$$\mathbb{E}(X\,|\,Y)(\omega) = \mathbb{E}(X\,|\,\{Y = y_i\}) \quad \text{if } Y(\omega) = y_i \text{ and } P(Y = y_i) > 0.$$

Exercise 4.5 On $[0, 1]$ equipped with its Borel subsets and Lebesgue measure, let Z be the random variable taking just two values, -1 on $[0, \frac{1}{2})$ and 1 on $[\frac{1}{2}, 1]$, and let X be the random variable defined as $X(\omega) = \omega$ for each $\omega \in [0, 1]$. Compute $\mathbb{E}(X\,|\,Z)$.

Exercise 4.6 Suppose that Z is the same random variable on $[0, 1]$ as in Exercise 4.5, and Y is the random variable defined as $Y(\omega) = 1 - \omega$ for each $\omega \in [0, 1]$. Compute $\mathbb{E}(Y\,|\,Z)$.

Observe that if Y is constant on a subset of Ω, then $\mathbb{E}(X\,|\,Y)$ is also constant on that subset. The values of $\mathbb{E}(X\,|\,Y)$ depend only on the subsets on which Y is constant, not on the actual values of Y. For discrete random variables Y and Z generating the same partition we always have the same conditional expectations,

$$\mathbb{E}(X\,|\,Y) = \mathbb{E}(X\,|\,Z).$$

Exercise 4.7 Construct an example to show that, for random variables V and W defining different partitions, in general we have

$$\mathbb{E}(X\,|\,V) \neq \mathbb{E}(X\,|\,W).$$

Exercise 4.8 Let X, Y be random variables on $\Omega = \{1, 2, \ldots\}$ equipped with the σ-field of all subsets of Ω and a probability measure P such that $P(\{n\}) = 2 \times 3^{-n}$, $X(n) = 2^n$ and $Y(n) = (-1)^n$ for each $n = 1, 2, \ldots$. Compute $\mathbb{E}(X\,|\,Y)$.

Properties of conditional expectation: discrete case

We establish some of the basic properties of the random variable $\mathbb{E}(X\,|\,Y)$, where X is an arbitrary integrable random variable (so that $\mathbb{E}(X)$ is well-defined) and Y is any discrete random variable.

First, note that conditional expectation preserves linear combinations: for any integrable random variables X_1, X_2 and a discrete random variable Y, and for any numbers $a, b \in \mathbb{R}$

$$\mathbb{E}(aX_1 + bX_2\,|\,Y) = a\mathbb{E}(X_1\,|\,Y) + b\mathbb{E}(X_2\,|\,Y).$$

This is an easy consequence of the definition of conditional expectation and the linearity of expectation. If $y_1, y_2, \ldots$ are the values of Y, then on each set $B_n = \{Y = y_n\}$ such that $P(B_n) > 0$ we have

$$\mathbb{E}(aX_1 + bX_2\,|\,Y) = \mathbb{E}(aX_1 + bX_2\,|\,B_n) = \frac{1}{P(B_n)}\mathbb{E}(\mathbf{1}_{B_n}(aX_1 + bX_2))$$

$$= \frac{1}{P(B_n)}(a\mathbb{E}(\mathbf{1}_{B_n}X_1) + b\mathbb{E}(\mathbf{1}_{B_n}X_2))$$

$$= a\mathbb{E}(X_1\,|\,B_n) + b\mathbb{E}(X_2\,|\,B_n) = a\mathbb{E}(X_1\,|\,Y) + b\mathbb{E}(X_2\,|\,Y).$$

Example 4.11
To illustrate some further properties of $\mathbb{E}(X\,|\,Y)$, again consider stock price evolution through a binomial tree. Starting with $S(0) = 100$, with returns $\pm 20\%$ in the first step and $\pm 10\%$ in the second, we obtain four values $S(2) = 132, 108, 88, 72$. (You may find it helpful to draw the tree.) Suppose that $p = \frac{3}{4}$ at each step. Conditioning $S(2)$ on $S(1)$, we observe that $\mathbb{E}(S(2)|S(1))$ is constant on each of the sets $\Omega_U = \{UU, UD\}$ and $\Omega_D = \{DU, DD\}$ in this two-step model, with values

$$\mathbb{E}(S(2)|\Omega_U) = 132p + 108(1-p) = 126,$$
$$\mathbb{E}(S(2)|\Omega_D) = 88p + 72(1-p) = 84.$$

Hence $\mathbb{E}(S(2)|S(1))$ equals 126 on Ω_U and 84 on Ω_D. The expectation of this random variable is $\mathbb{E}(\mathbb{E}(S(2)|S(1))) = 115.5$. This equals $\mathbb{E}(S(2))$, as you may check.

In this example, therefore, the 'average of the averages' of $S(2)$ over the sets in the partition generated by $S(1)$ coincides with its overall average. This is true in general.

Proposition 4.12
When X is an integrable and Y a discrete random variable, the expectation of $\mathbb{E}(X \mid Y)$ *is equal to the expectation of X:*

$$\mathbb{E}(\mathbb{E}(X \mid Y)) = \mathbb{E}(X). \tag{4.3}$$

Proof Let $y_1, y_2 \ldots$ be the values of Y. Writing $B_n = \{Y = y_n\}$, we can assume without loss of generality that $P(B_n) > 0$ for all $n = 1, 2, \ldots$. Then $\sum_{n=1}^{\infty} \mathbf{1}_{B_n} = 1$, and we obtain

$$\mathbb{E}(\mathbb{E}(X \mid Y)) = \sum_{n=1}^{\infty} \mathbb{E}(X \mid B_n) P(B_n) = \sum_{n=1}^{\infty} \frac{1}{P(B_n)} \mathbb{E}(\mathbf{1}_{B_n} X) P(B_n)$$

$$= \sum_{n=1}^{\infty} \mathbb{E}(\mathbf{1}_{B_n} X) = \mathbb{E}(X).$$

Note that dominated convergence in the form stated in Exercise 1.34 is used in the last equality.   □

Exercise 4.9   Let X be an integrable random variable and Y a discrete random variable. Verify that for any $B \in \sigma(Y)$

$$\mathbb{E}(\mathbf{1}_B \mathbb{E}(X \mid Y)) = \mathbb{E}(\mathbf{1}_B X).$$

Example 4.13
The two-step stock-price model in Example 4.11 provides two partitions of $\Omega = \{U, D\}^2$, partition $\mathcal{P}_1$ defined by $S(1)$ consisting of two sets Ω_U, Ω_D, and $\mathcal{P}_2$ determined by $S(2)$ consisting of four sets $\Omega_{UU}, \Omega_{UD}, \Omega_{DU}, \Omega_{DD}$ (as defined earlier). Notice that $\Omega_U = \Omega_{UU} \cup \Omega_{UD}$ and $\Omega_D = \Omega_{DU} \cup \Omega_{DD}$. It reflects the fact that $S(2)$ carries more information than $S(1)$, that is, if the value of $S(2)$ becomes known, then we will also know the value of $S(1)$.

This gives rise to the following definition.

Definition 4.14
Given two partitions $\mathcal{P}_1, \mathcal{P}_2$, we say $\mathcal{P}_2$ is **finer** than (or **refines**) $\mathcal{P}_1$ (equivalently, that $\mathcal{P}_1$ is **coarser** than $\mathcal{P}_2$) whenever each element of $\mathcal{P}_1$ can be represented as a union of sets from $\mathcal{P}_2$.

Remark 4.15

The tree constructed in Example 4.11 is not recombining, which results in partition $\mathcal{P}_2$ being finer than $\mathcal{P}_1$. In a recombining binomial tree, as in Example 4.1, the partition defined by $S(2)$, which consists of the sets $\Omega_{UU}, \Omega_{UD} \cup \Omega_{DU}, \Omega_{DD}$, is *not* finer than that generated by $S(1)$, which consists of the sets $\Omega_U = \Omega_{UU} \cup \Omega_{UD}, \Omega_D = \Omega_{DU} \cup \Omega_{DD}$. In a recombining tree $S(2)$ has only three values, and its middle value gives us no information about the value of $S(1)$.

Exercise 4.10 Suppose $\mathcal{P}_1$ and $\mathcal{P}_2$ are partitions of some set Ω. Show that the coarsest partition which refines them both is that consisting of all intersections $A \cap B$, where $A \in \mathcal{P}_1$ and $B \in \mathcal{P}_2$.

Example 4.16

We extend Example 4.11 by adding a third step with returns $\pm 10\%$. The stock price $S(3)$ then takes the values $145.2, 118.8, 97.2, 96.8, 79.2, 64.8$, as you may confirm. (Note that there are only six values as the tree recombines in two of its nodes.) The conditional expectation $\mathbb{E}(S(3)\,|\,S(2))$ is calculated in a similar manner as for $\mathbb{E}(S(2)\,|\,S(1))$. Its sets of constancy are those of the partition $\mathcal{P}_2$ generated by $S(2)$, that is, $\Omega_{UU}, \Omega_{UD}, \Omega_{DU}, \Omega_{DD}$. The corresponding values of $\mathbb{E}(S(3)\,|\,S(2))$ are $138.6, 113.4, 92.4, 75.6$. We now condition the random variable $\mathbb{E}(S(3)\,|\,S(2))$ on the values of $S(1)$:

$$\mathbb{E}(\mathbb{E}(S(3)\,|\,S(2))\,|\,\Omega_U) = 138.60 \times p + 113.40 \times (1-p) = 132.3,$$
$$\mathbb{E}(\mathbb{E}(S(3)\,|\,S(2))\,|\,\Omega_D) = 92.40 \times p + 75.60 \times (1-p) = 88.2,$$

given that $p = \frac{3}{4}$. We compare this with the constant values taken by $\mathbb{E}(S(3)\,|\,S(1))$ on these two sets:

$$\mathbb{E}(S(3)\,|\,\Omega_U) = 145.20 \times p^2 + 118.80 \times 2p(1-p) + 97.20 \times (1-p)^2$$
$$= 138.60 \times p + 113.40 \times (1-p) = 132.3,$$
$$\mathbb{E}(S(3)\,|\,\Omega_D) = 96.80 \times p^2 + 79.20 \times 2p(1-p) + 64.80 \times (1-p)^2$$
$$= 92.40 \times p + 75.60 \times (1-p) = 88.2.$$

Hence $\mathbb{E}(\mathbb{E}(S(3)\,|\,S(2))\,|\,S(1)) = \mathbb{E}(S(3)\,|\,S(1))$, which is again a particular case of an important general result.

Proposition 4.17 (tower property)

Let X be an integrable random variable and let Y, Z be discrete random variables such that Y generates a finer partition than Z. Then

$$\mathbb{E}(\mathbb{E}(X \,|\, Y) \,|\, Z) = \mathbb{E}(X \,|\, Z). \tag{4.4}$$

Proof Let $y_1, y_2, \ldots$ be the values of Y and $z_1, z_2, \ldots$ the values of Z. We can assume without loss of generality that the sets $B_i = \{Y = y_i\}$ and $C_j = \{Z = z_j\}$ in the partitions generated, respectively, by Y and Z are such that $P(B_i), P(C_j) > 0$ for each $i, j = 1, 2, \ldots$. Because Y generates a finer partition than Z, for any $j = 1, 2, \ldots$ we can write $C_j = \bigcup_{i \in I_j} B_i$ for some set of indices $I_j \subset \{1, 2, \ldots\}$. For any $\omega \in C_j$, by (4.1) and (4.2),

$$
\mathbb{E}(\mathbb{E}(X \,|\, Y) \,|\, Z)(\omega) = \frac{1}{P(C_j)} \mathbb{E}(\mathbb{E}(X \,|\, Y)\mathbf{1}_{C_j})
$$

$$
= \frac{1}{P(C_j)} \mathbb{E}\left(\sum_{i \in I_j} \frac{1}{P(B_i)} \mathbb{E}(\mathbf{1}_{B_i} X) \mathbf{1}_{B_i} \mathbf{1}_{C_j} \right).
$$

But $B_i \subset C_j$ for $i \in I_j$, so $\mathbf{1}_{B_i} \mathbf{1}_{C_j} = \mathbf{1}_{B_i}$. Moreover, $\sum_{i \in I_j} \mathbf{1}_{B_i} = \mathbf{1}_{C_j}$. It follows that

$$
\frac{1}{P(C_j)} \mathbb{E}\left(\sum_{i \in I_j} \frac{1}{P(B_i)} \mathbb{E}(\mathbf{1}_{B_i} X) \mathbf{1}_{B_i} \right) = \frac{1}{P(C_j)} \sum_{i \in I_j} \frac{1}{P(B_i)} \mathbb{E}(\mathbf{1}_{B_i} X) \mathbb{E}(\mathbf{1}_{B_i})
$$

$$
= \frac{1}{P(C_j)} \sum_{i \in I_j} \mathbb{E}(\mathbf{1}_{B_i} X) = \frac{1}{P(C_j)} \mathbb{E}\left(\sum_{i \in I_j} \mathbf{1}_{B_i} X \right)
$$

$$
= \frac{1}{P(C_j)} \mathbb{E}(\mathbf{1}_{C_j} X) = \mathbb{E}(X \,|\, Z)(\omega).
$$

Once again, dominated convergence in the form stated in Exercise 1.34 is used here. $\square$

Example 4.18

To motivate the next property, we return to Example 4.16 and consider $\mathbb{E}(S(1)S(3) \,|\, \Omega_{UU})$. This conditional expectation boils down to summation over $\omega \in \Omega_{UU}$, but for such scenarios $S(1)$ is constant (and equal to 120), so it can be taken outside the sum, which gives $\mathbb{E}(S(1)S(3) \,|\, \Omega_{UU}) = S(1)\mathbb{E}(S(3) \,|\, \Omega_{UU})$. If we repeat the same argument for Ω_{UD}, Ω_{DU} and Ω_{DD}, we discover that $\mathbb{E}(S(1)S(3) \,|\, S(2)) = S(1)\mathbb{E}(S(3) \,|\, S(2))$. In other words, when conditioning on the second step, we can take out the 'known' value $S(1)$. This is again a general feature of conditioning.

Proposition 4.19 (taking out what is known)
Assume that X is integrable and Y, Z are discrete random variables such that Y generates a finer partition than Z. In this case

$$\mathbb{E}(ZX \mid Y) = Z\mathbb{E}(X \mid Y). \tag{4.5}$$

Proof Fix a set B belonging to the partition generated by Y such that $P(B) > 0$, and notice that Z is constant on B, taking value z, say. Then

$$\mathbb{E}(ZX \mid B) = \frac{1}{P(B)}\mathbb{E}(\mathbf{1}_B ZX) = \frac{1}{P(B)}\mathbb{E}(z\mathbf{1}_B X) = \frac{1}{P(B)}z\mathbb{E}(\mathbf{1}_B X) = z\mathbb{E}(X \mid B)$$

so the result holds on B. By gluing together the formulae obtained for each such B we complete the argument. □

The intuition behind this result is that once the value of Y becomes known, we will also know that of Z, and therefore can treat it as if it were a constant rather than a random variable, moving it out in front of the conditional expectation. In particular, for $X \equiv 1$, we have $\mathbb{E}(Z \mid Y) = Z$.

The final property we consider here extends a familiar feature of independent events, namely the fact that the conditional probability of an event A is not sensitive to conditioning on an event B that is independent of A, that is, $P(A \mid B) = P(A)$.

Exercise 4.11 Prove that $\mathbb{E}(X \mid Y) = \mathbb{E}(X)$ if X and Y are independent random variables and Y is discrete.

4.3 Conditional expectation: general case

Let Y be a uniformly distributed random variable on $[0, 1]$. Then the event $B_y = \{Y = y\}$ has probability $P(B_y) = 0$ for every $y \in [0, 1]$. In such situations the definition of conditional probability $P(A \mid B_y)$ as $\frac{P(A \cap B_y)}{P(B_y)}$ no longer makes sense, nor is there a partition generated by Y, and we need a different approach. This can be achieved by turning matters on their head, defining conditional expectation in the general case by means of certain properties which follow from the special case of conditioning with respect to a discrete random variable or a partition.

Suppose Y is a discrete random variable and B is a set from the partition generated by Y. From Proposition 4.19 we know that

$$\mathbf{1}_B \mathbb{E}(X \mid Y) = \mathbb{E}(\mathbf{1}_B X \mid Y).$$

Applying expectation to both sides and using Proposition 4.12, we get

$$\mathbb{E}(\mathbf{1}_B \mathbb{E}(X \mid Y)) = \mathbb{E}(\mathbf{1}_B X). \qquad (4.6)$$

These equalities are also valid for each $B \in \sigma(Y)$, since each such B can be expressed as a countable union of disjoint sets from the partition generated by Y. We also note that the conditional expectation $\mathbb{E}(X \mid Y)$ is $\sigma(Y)$-measurable and does not depend on the actual values of Y but just on the partition generated by Y, or equivalently on the σ-field $\sigma(Y)$. We could, therefore denote $\mathbb{E}(X \mid Y)$ by $\mathbb{E}(X \mid \sigma(Y))$.

These observations are very useful in the general case of an arbitrary random variable Y, when there may be no partition generated by Y, but we do have the σ-field $\sigma(Y)$ generated by Y. This gives rise to the following definition of conditional expectation with respect to a σ-field.

Definition 4.20
Let X be an integrable random variable on a probability space $(\Omega, \mathcal{F}, P)$. The **conditional expectation** of X with respect to a σ-field $\mathcal{G} \subset \mathcal{F}$ is defined as a random variable, denoted by $\mathbb{E}(X \mid \mathcal{G})$, that satisfies the following two conditions:
  (i) $\mathbb{E}(X \mid \mathcal{G})$ is $\mathcal{G}$-measurable;
  (ii) for each $B \in \mathcal{G}$

$$\mathbb{E}(\mathbf{1}_B \mathbb{E}(X \mid \mathcal{G})) = \mathbb{E}(\mathbf{1}_B X).$$

When $\mathcal{G} = \sigma(Y)$ for some random variable Y on the same probability space, then we shall write $\mathbb{E}(X \mid Y)$ in place of $\mathbb{E}(X \mid \mathcal{G})$ and call it the **conditional expectation** of X given Y. In other words,

$$\mathbb{E}(X \mid Y) = \mathbb{E}(X \mid \sigma(Y)).$$

The first condition is a general counterpart of the condition that the conditional expectation should be constant on the atoms of $\mathcal{G}$ in the discrete case, the second extends (4.6).

At this point we have no guarantee that a random variable with the properties (i), (ii) exists, nor that it is uniquely defined if it does exist. We defer this question for the moment, and will return to it after discussing the properties implied by Definition 4.20.

> **Exercise 4.12** On the probability space $[0, 1]$ with Borel sets and Lebesgue measure compute $\mathbb{E}(X \mid Y)$ when $X(\omega) = \left|\omega - \frac{1}{3}\right|$ and $Y(\omega) = \left|\omega - \frac{1}{2}\right|$ for $\omega \in [0, 1]$.

Properties of conditional expectation: general case

All the properties we proved for the discrete case can also be proved with Definition 4.20. We summarise them in the following exercises and propositions.

> **Exercise 4.13** Let X, Y be integrable random variables on $(\Omega, \mathcal{F}, P)$ and let $\mathcal{G}$ be a sub-σ-field of $\mathcal{F}$. Show that, P-a.s.,
> (1) $\mathbb{E}((aX + bY) \mid \mathcal{G}) = a\mathbb{E}(X \mid \mathcal{G}) + b\mathbb{E}(Y \mid \mathcal{G})$ for any $a, b \in \mathbb{R}$ (**linearity**);
> (2) $\mathbb{E}(X \mid \mathcal{G}) \geq 0$ if $X \geq 0$ (**positivity**).

Remark 4.21

As in Exercise 4.13, identities and inequalities involving conditional expectation (as a random variable) should be read as holding up to P-a.s in what follows.

Proposition 4.22 (tower property)

If X is integrable and $\mathcal{H} \subset \mathcal{G}$, then

$$\mathbb{E}(\mathbb{E}(X \mid \mathcal{G}) \mid \mathcal{H}) = \mathbb{E}(X \mid \mathcal{H}).$$

Proof Write $Y = \mathbb{E}(X \mid \mathcal{G})$ and take any $A \in \mathcal{H}$. We need to show that $\mathbb{E}(\mathbf{1}_A Y) = \mathbb{E}(\mathbf{1}_A \mathbb{E}(X \mid \mathcal{H}))$. By the definition of conditional expectation with respect to $\mathcal{G}$ ($A \in \mathcal{G}$ since $\mathcal{H} \subset \mathcal{G}$), we have

$$\mathbb{E}(\mathbf{1}_A Y) = \mathbb{E}(\mathbf{1}_A \mathbb{E}(X \mid \mathcal{G})) = \mathbb{E}(\mathbf{1}_A X).$$

By the definition of conditional expectation with respect to $\mathcal{H}$,

$$\mathbb{E}(\mathbf{1}_A \mathbb{E}(X \mid \mathcal{H})) = \mathbb{E}(\mathbf{1}_A X),$$

which concludes the proof. □

Corollary 4.23

For any integrable random variable X

$$\mathbb{E}(\mathbb{E}(X \mid \mathcal{G})) = \mathbb{E}(X).$$

Proof Since $\mathbf{1}_\Omega = 1$ and $\Omega \in \mathcal{G}$, the definition of conditional expectation with respect to $\mathcal{G}$ applies:

$$\mathbb{E}(\mathbb{E}(X \mid \mathcal{G})) = \mathbb{E}(\mathbf{1}_\Omega \mathbb{E}(X \mid \mathcal{G})) = \mathbb{E}(\mathbf{1}_\Omega X) = \mathbb{E}(X).$$

$\square$

Exercise 4.14   Prove the following **monotone convergence** theorem for conditional expectations.

If X_n for $n = 1, 2, \ldots$ is a non-decreasing sequence of integrable random variables such that $\lim_{n \to \infty} X_n = X$, P-a.s., then their conditional expectations $\mathbb{E}(X_n \mid \mathcal{G})$ form a non-decreasing sequence of non-negative integrable random variables such that $\lim_{n \to \infty} \mathbb{E}(X_n \mid \mathcal{G}) = \mathbb{E}(X \mid \mathcal{G})$, P-a.s.

If Z is a $\mathcal{G}$-measurable random variable, we can 'take it outside' the conditional expectation of the product XZ; this accords with the intuition that Z is 'known' once we know $\mathcal{G}$ and can therefore be treated like a constant when conditioning on $\mathcal{G}$, exactly as in the discrete case.

Proposition 4.24 (taking out what is known)
If both X and XZ are integrable and Z is $\mathcal{G}$-measurable, then

$$\mathbb{E}(ZX \mid \mathcal{G}) = Z\mathbb{E}(X \mid \mathcal{G}).$$

Proof We may assume $X \geq 0$ by linearity. Take any $B \in \mathcal{G}$. We have to show that

$$\mathbb{E}(\mathbf{1}_B ZX) = \mathbb{E}(\mathbf{1}_B Z\mathbb{E}(X \mid \mathcal{G})).$$

Let $Z = \mathbf{1}_A$ for some $A \in \mathcal{G}$. Then, since $A \cap B \in \mathcal{G}$,

$$\mathbb{E}(\mathbf{1}_B ZX) = \mathbb{E}(\mathbf{1}_B \mathbf{1}_A X) = \mathbb{E}(\mathbf{1}_{A \cap B} X) = \mathbb{E}(\mathbf{1}_{A \cap B}\mathbb{E}(X \mid \mathcal{G}))$$
$$= \mathbb{E}(\mathbf{1}_B \mathbf{1}_A \mathbb{E}(X \mid \mathcal{G})) = \mathbb{E}(\mathbf{1}_B Z\mathbb{E}(X \mid \mathcal{G})).$$

By linearity, we have $\mathbb{E}(ZX \mid \mathcal{G}) = Z\mathbb{E}(X \mid \mathcal{G})$ for any simple $\mathcal{G}$-measurable random variable Z. For any $\mathcal{G}$-measurable $Z \geq 0$ we use Exercise 4.14 and a sequence $Z_1, Z_2, \ldots$ of non-negative simple $\mathcal{G}$-measurable functions increasing to Z to conclude that $\mathbb{E}(Z_n X \mid \mathcal{G})$ increases to $\mathbb{E}(ZX \mid \mathcal{G})$, while $Z_n \mathbb{E}(X \mid \mathcal{G})$ increases to $Z\mathbb{E}(X \mid \mathcal{G})$. Since $\mathbb{E}(Z_n X \mid \mathcal{G}) = Z_n \mathbb{E}(X \mid \mathcal{G})$ for each n, and the limit on the left as $n \to \infty$ is P-a.s. finite by our integrability assumption, we have $\mathbb{E}(ZX \mid \mathcal{G}) = Z\mathbb{E}(X \mid \mathcal{G})$ as required. For general Z we can take positive and negative parts of Z and apply linearity of the conditional expectation. $\square$

Corollary 4.25
$\mathbb{E}(Z \mid \mathcal{G}) = Z$ *if Z is integrable and $\mathcal{G}$-measurable.*

Proof   Take $X = 1$ in Proposition 4.24.   □

At the other extreme, independence of random variables X, Y means that knowing one 'tells us nothing' about the other. Recall that random variables X, Y are independent if and only if their generated σ-fields $\sigma(X), \sigma(Y)$ are independent, see Exercise 3.31. Moreover, recall that X is independent of a σ-field $\mathcal{G} \subset \mathcal{F}$ precisely when the σ-fields $\sigma(X)$ and $\mathcal{G}$ are independent. In that case $\mathbb{E}(X \mid \mathcal{G})$ is constant, as the next result shows.

Proposition 4.26 (independence)
If X is integrable and independent of $\mathcal{G}$, then

$$\mathbb{E}(X \mid \mathcal{G}) = \mathbb{E}(X).$$

Proof   For any $B \in \mathcal{G}$ the random variables $\mathbf{1}_B, X$ are independent, so

$$\mathbb{E}(\mathbf{1}_B X) = \mathbb{E}(\mathbf{1}_B)\mathbb{E}(X) = \mathbb{E}(\mathbf{1}_B \mathbb{E}(X)),$$

which shows that the constant random variable $\mathbb{E}(X)$ satisfies (4.6). Since $\mathbb{E}(X)$ is also $\mathcal{G}$-measurable, it satisfies the definition of $\mathbb{E}(X \mid \mathcal{G})$.   □

In the next two results we use the fact that for independent random variables or random vectors their joint distribution is simply the product of the individual distributions. The first result will be used in the analysis of the Black–Scholes model in [BSM]; the second is a special case which becomes crucial for the development of Markov processes in [SCF]. Both follow easily from the Fubini theorem.

Theorem 4.27
Let $(\Omega, \mathcal{F}, P)$ be a probability space, and let $\mathcal{G} \subset \mathcal{F}$ be a σ-field. Suppose that $X : \Omega \to \mathbb{R}$ is a $\mathcal{G}$-measurable random variable and $Y : \Omega \to \mathbb{R}$ is a random variable independent of $\mathcal{G}$. If $f : \mathbb{R}^2 \to \mathbb{R}$ is a bounded Borel measurable function, then $g_f : \mathbb{R} \to \mathbb{R}$ defined for any $x \in \mathbb{R}$ by

$$g_f(x) = \mathbb{E}(f(x, Y)) = \int_{\mathbb{R}} f(x, y) \, dP_Y(y)$$

is a bounded Borel measurable function, and we have

$$\mathbb{E}(f(X, Y) \mid \mathcal{G})) = g_f(X), \quad P\text{-a.s.} \tag{4.7}$$

Proof   We know from Proposition 3.17 that g_f is a Borel measurable function. If follows that $g_f(X)$ is $\sigma(X)$-measurable. By the definition of conditional expectation it suffices to show that

$$\mathbb{E}[\mathbf{1}_G f(X, Y)] = \mathbb{E}[g_f(X)\mathbf{1}_G]$$

for each $G \in \mathcal{G}$.

By hypothesis, $\sigma(Y)$ and $\mathcal{G}$ are independent σ-fields. For any bounded $\mathcal{G}$-measurable random variable Z the σ-field $\sigma(X, Z)$ generated by the random vector (X, Z) is contained in $\mathcal{G}$, hence Y and (X, Z) are independent. This means that their joint distribution is the product measure $P_{X,Z} \otimes P_Y$ (see Remark 3.40). Applying Fubini's theorem, we obtain

$$
\begin{aligned}
\mathbb{E}(f(X, Y)Z) &= \int_{\mathbb{R}^3} f(x, y)z \, d(P_{X,Z} \otimes P_Y)(x, z, y) \\
&= \int_{\mathbb{R}^2} \left(\int_{\mathbb{R}} f(x, y)z \, dP_Y(y) \right) dP_{X,Z}(x, z) \\
&= \int_{\mathbb{R}} g_f(x)z \, dP_{X,Z}(x, z) \\
&= \mathbb{E}(g_f(X)Z).
\end{aligned}
$$

Applying this with $Z = \mathbf{1}_G$ proves (4.7).   □

In the special case where $\mathcal{G} = \sigma(X)$ for some random variable $X : \Omega \to \mathbb{R}$, the theorem reduces to the following

Corollary 4.28
Let $(\Omega, \mathcal{F}, P)$ be a probability space, and suppose that $X : \Omega \to \mathbb{R}$ and $Y : \Omega \to \mathbb{R}$ are independent random variables. If $f : \mathbb{R}^2 \to \mathbb{R}$ is a bounded Borel measurable function, then $g_f : \mathbb{R} \to \mathbb{R}$ defined for any $x \in \mathbb{R}$ by

$$g_f(x) = \mathbb{E}(f(x, Y)) = \int_{\mathbb{R}} f(x, y) \, dP_Y(y)$$

is a bounded Borel measurable function, and we have

$$\mathbb{E}(f(X, Y) \mid \sigma(X)) = g_f(X).$$

Exercise 4.15   Extend Theorem 4.27 to the case of random vectors X, Y with values in $\mathbb{R}^m$ and $\mathbb{R}^n$, respectively, and a function $f : \mathbb{R}^m \times \mathbb{R}^n \to \mathbb{R}$.

Now suppose that $Z \geq 0$ is a non-negative random variable on a probability space $(\Omega, \mathcal{F}, P)$ such that $\mathbb{E}(Z) = 1$. It can be used to define a new probability measure Q such that for each $A \in \mathcal{F}$

$$Q(A) = \mathbb{E}(\mathbf{1}_A Z).$$

We know from Theorem 1.35 that Q is indeed a measure. It is a probability measure because $Q(\Omega) = \mathbb{E}(Z) = 1$.

Since we now have two probability measures P and Q, we need to distinguish between the corresponding expectations by writing $\mathbb{E}_P$ and $\mathbb{E}_Q$, respectively. For any $B \in \mathcal{F}$ we have

$$\mathbb{E}_Q(\mathbf{1}_B) = Q(B) = \mathbb{E}_P(\mathbf{1}_B Z).$$

By linearity this extends to

$$\mathbb{E}_Q(s) = \mathbb{E}_P(sZ)$$

for any simple function s. Approximating any non-negative random variable X by a non-decreasing sequence of simple functions, we obtain by monotone convergence that

$$\mathbb{E}_Q(X) = \mathbb{E}_P(XZ). \tag{4.8}$$

Finally, we can extend the last identity to any random variable X integrable under Q by considering X^+ and X^- and using linearity once again. This gives a relationship between the expectation under Q and that under P. The next result, which will be needed in [BSM], extends this to conditional expectation.

Lemma 4.29 (Bayes formula)
Let $Z \geq 0$ be a random variable such that $\mathbb{E}_P(Z) = 1$ and let $Q(A) = \mathbb{E}_P(\mathbf{1}_A Z)$ for each $A \in \mathcal{F}$. For any integrable random variable X under Q and for any σ-field $\mathcal{G} \subset \mathcal{F}$

$$\mathbb{E}_Q(X \mid \mathcal{G}) \mathbb{E}_P(Z \mid \mathcal{G}) = \mathbb{E}_P(XZ \mid \mathcal{G}).$$

Proof For any $B \in \mathcal{G}$ we apply (4.8) and the definition of conditional expectation to get

$$\mathbb{E}_P(\mathbf{1}_B \mathbb{E}_P(XZ \mid \mathcal{G})) = \mathbb{E}_P(\mathbf{1}_B XZ) = \mathbb{E}_Q(\mathbf{1}_B X) = \mathbb{E}_Q(\mathbf{1}_B \mathbb{E}_Q(X \mid \mathcal{G})).$$

Now we use (4.8) again and then the tower property and the fact that $\mathbf{1}_B$

and $\mathbb{E}_Q(X \mid \mathcal{G})$ are $\mathcal{G}$-measurable to write the last expression as

$$
\begin{aligned}
\mathbb{E}_Q(\mathbf{1}_B \mathbb{E}_Q(X \mid \mathcal{G})) &= \mathbb{E}_P(\mathbf{1}_B \mathbb{E}_Q(X \mid \mathcal{G}) Z) \\
&= \mathbb{E}_P(\mathbb{E}_P(\mathbf{1}_B \mathbb{E}_Q(X \mid \mathcal{G}) Z \mid \mathcal{G})) \\
&= \mathbb{E}_P(\mathbf{1}_B \mathbb{E}_Q(X \mid \mathcal{G}) \mathbb{E}_P(Z \mid \mathcal{G})).
\end{aligned}
$$

Since $\mathbb{E}_Q(X \mid \mathcal{G}) \mathbb{E}_P(Z \mid \mathcal{G})$ is $\mathcal{G}$-measurable, this proves the Bayes formula.

$\square$

Conditional density

When X is a continuous random variable with density f_X and $g : \mathbb{R} \to \mathbb{R}$ is a Borel measurable function such that $g(X)$ is integrable, the expectation of $g(X)$ can be written as

$$
\mathbb{E}(g(X)) = \int_{\mathbb{R}} g(x) f_X(x) \, dm(x). \tag{4.9}
$$

For two jointly continuous random variables X, Y we would like to write the conditional expectation $\mathbb{E}(g(X) \mid Y)$ in a similar manner. Since the conditional expectation is a $\sigma(Y)$-measurable random variable, we need to express it as a Borel measurable function of Y. We know that for any Borel set $B \in \mathcal{B}(\mathbb{R})$

$$
\mathbb{E}(\mathbf{1}_B(Y) g(X)) = \mathbb{E}(\mathbf{1}_B(Y) \mathbb{E}(g(X) \mid Y)).
$$

We can write the left-hand side in terms of the joint density $f_{X,Y}$ and use Fubini's theorem to transform it as follows:

$$
\begin{aligned}
\mathbb{E}(\mathbf{1}_B(Y) g(X)) &= \int_{\mathbb{R} \times B} g(x) f_{X,Y}(x, y) \, dm_2(x, y) \\
&= \int_B \left(\int_{\mathbb{R}} g(x) f_{X,Y}(x, y) \, dm(x) \right) dm(y) \\
&= \int_B \left(\int_{\mathbb{R}} g(x) \frac{f_{X,Y}(x, y)}{f_Y(y)} \, dm(x) \right) dP_Y(y). \tag{4.10}
\end{aligned}
$$

Dividing by the marginal density f_Y is all right because $f_Y \neq 0$, P_Y-a.s., that is, for $C = \{y \in \mathbb{R} : f_Y(y) = 0\}$ we have

$$
P_Y(C) = \int_C f_Y(y) \, dm(y) = 0.
$$

The fraction appearing in (4.10) is what we are looking for to play a role similar to the density $f_Y(y)$ in (4.9).

Definition 4.30

We define the **conditional density** of X given Y as

$$h(x, y) = \frac{f_{X,Y}(x, y)}{f_Y(y)}$$

for any $x, y \in \mathbb{R}$ such that $f_Y(y) \neq 0$, and put $h(x, y) = 0$ otherwise.

This allows us write

$$\mathbb{E}(\mathbf{1}_B(Y)g(X)) = \mathbb{E}\left(\mathbf{1}_B(Y) \int_{\mathbb{R}} g(x)h(x, Y) \, dm(x)\right).$$

Since $h(x, Y)$ is a $\sigma(Y)$-measurable random variable for each $x \in \mathbb{R}$, it follows that $\int_{\mathbb{R}} g(x)h(x, Y) \, dm(x)$ is $\sigma(Y)$-measurable. We have just proved the following result.

Proposition 4.31

If X, Y are jointly continuous random variables and $g : \mathbb{R} \to \mathbb{R}$ is a Borel measurable function such that $g(X)$ is integrable, then

$$\mathbb{E}(g(X) \mid Y) = \int_{\mathbb{R}} g(x)h(x, Y) \, dm(x),$$

where $h(x, y)$ for $x, y \in \mathbb{R}$ is the conditional density of X given Y.

Note that this result provides an immediate alternative proof (valid only for jointly continuous random variables, of course) of Proposition 4.26: if X, Y are jointly continuous and independent, and X is integrable, then $f_{X,Y}(x, y) = f_X(x)f_Y(y)$, so $h(x, y) = \frac{f_{X,Y}(x,y)}{f_Y(y)} = f_X(x)$, hence

$$\mathbb{E}(X \mid Y) = \int_{\mathbb{R}} xh(x, Y)dx = \int_{\mathbb{R}} xf_X(x) \, dm(x) = \mathbb{E}(X).$$

Exercise 4.16   Let $f_{X,Y}(x, y)$ be the bivariate normal density given in Example 3.16. Find a formula for the corresponding conditional density $h(x, y)$ and use it to compute $\mathbb{E}(X \mid Y)$.

Jensen's inequality

The next property of expectation requires some facts concerning convex functions. Many common inequalities have their origin in the notion of convexity. First we recall the definition of a convex function.

Definition 4.32

A function $\phi : (a, b) \to \mathbb{R}$, where $-\infty \le a < b \le \infty$, is called **convex** if the inequality

$$\phi(\lambda x + (1 - \lambda)y) \le \phi(x) + (1 - \lambda)\phi(y)$$

holds whenever $x, y \in (a, b)$ and $0 \le \lambda \le 1$.

Such functions have right- and left-hand derivatives at each point in the open interval (a, b). We recall some of their properties, including a proof of this well-known fact.

Suppose that $x, y, z \in (a, b)$ and $x < y < z$. Taking $\lambda = \frac{z-y}{z-x}$, we have $y = \lambda x + (1 - \lambda)z$, so the convexity of ϕ gives

$$\phi(y) \le \frac{z - y}{z - x}\phi(x) + \frac{y - x}{z - x}\phi(z).$$

Rearranging, we get

$$\frac{\phi(y) - \phi(x)}{y - x} \le \frac{\phi(z) - \phi(y)}{z - y}.$$

The next exercise shows that the one-sided derivatives of ϕ exist and are finite.

Exercise 4.17   Show that if $\phi : (a, b) \to \mathbb{R}$ is convex and $h > 0$ with $x - h, x + h \in (a, b)$, then

$$\frac{\phi(x) - \phi(x - h)}{h} \le \frac{\phi(x + h) - \phi(x)}{h}.$$

Explain why the ratio $\frac{1}{h}[\phi(x + h) - \phi(x)]$ decreases as $h \searrow 0$, and is bounded below by a constant. Similarly, explain why $\frac{1}{h}[\phi(x) - \phi(x - h)]$ increases as $h \searrow 0$, and is bounded above by a constant.

This exercise shows that the right- and left-derivatives

$$\phi'_+(x) = \lim_{h \searrow 0} \frac{\phi(x + h) - \phi(x)}{h}, \quad \phi'_-(x) = \lim_{h \searrow 0} \frac{\phi(x) - \phi(x - h)}{h} \qquad (4.11)$$

are well defined for each $x \in (a, b)$. We also obtain

$$\phi'_-(x) \le \phi'_+(x).$$

Moreover, for any $x < y$ in (a, b)

$$\phi'_+(x) \le \frac{\phi(y) - \phi(x)}{y - x} \le \phi'_-(y),$$

which ensures that both one-sided derivatives are non-decreasing on (a, b). Since ϕ has finite one-sided derivatives at each point, it is a continuous function on (a, b).

Lemma 4.33

Any convex function $\phi : (a, b) \to \mathbb{R}$ is the supremum of some sequence of affine functions $L_n : \mathbb{R} \to \mathbb{R}$ of the form $L_n(x) = a_n x + b_n$ for $x \in \mathbb{R}$, where $a_n, b_n \in \mathbb{R}$ and $n = 1, 2, \ldots$.

Proof Consider the set of rational numbers in (a, b). It is a countable set, which we can therefore write as a sequence $q_1, q_2, \ldots$. For each $n = 1, 2, \ldots$ we take any $a_n \in [\phi'_-(q_n), \phi'_+(q_n)]$, put $b_n = \phi(q_n) - a_n q_n$ and consider the straight line $a_n x + b_n$ for $x \in \mathbb{R}$. Clearly, $a_n q_n + b_n = \phi(q_n)$ for each $n = 1, 2, \ldots$, and it follows from the above inequalities that $a_n x + b_n \le \phi(x)$ for each $x \in (a, b)$ and for each $n = 1, 2, \ldots$. As a result, for each $x \in (a, b)$

$$\sup_{n=1,2,\ldots} (a_n x + b_n) \le \phi(x).$$

Now, for any $x \in (a, b)$ we can take a subsequence $q_{i_1}, q_{i_2}, \ldots$ of the rationals in (a, b) such that $\lim_{n \to \infty} q_{i_n} = x$. Then, since ϕ is continuous,

$$\lim_{n \to \infty} (a_{i_n} q_{i_n} + b_{i_n}) = \lim_{n \to \infty} \phi(q_{i_n}) = \phi(x).$$

It follows that for each $x \in (a, b)$

$$\sup_{n=1,2,\ldots} (a_n x + b_n) = \phi(x).$$

This completes the proof. □

Proposition 4.34 (Jensen's inequality)

Let $-\infty \le a < b \le \infty$. Suppose that $X : \Omega \to (a, b)$ is an integrable random variable on $(\Omega, \mathcal{F}, P)$ and take a σ-field $\mathcal{G} \subset \mathcal{F}$. If $\phi : (a, b) \to \mathbb{R}$ is a convex function such the random variable $\phi(X)$ is also integrable, then

$$\phi(\mathbb{E}(X \mid \mathcal{G})) \le \mathbb{E}(\phi(X) \mid \mathcal{G}).$$

Proof We must show that $\mathbb{E}(X \mid \mathcal{G}) \in (a, b)$, P-a.s. before we can even write $\phi(\mathbb{E}(X \mid \mathcal{G}))$ on the left-hand side of the inequality. By assumption, $X > a$. The set $B = \{\mathbb{E}(X \mid \mathcal{G}) \le a\}$ is $\mathcal{G}$-measurable, so by the definition of conditional expectation,

$$0 \le \mathbb{E}(\mathbf{1}_B(X - a)) = \mathbb{E}(\mathbf{1}_B(\mathbb{E}(X - a \mid \mathcal{G}))) = \mathbb{E}(\mathbf{1}_B(\mathbb{E}(X \mid \mathcal{G}) - a)) \le 0,$$

implying that $\mathbb{E}(\mathbf{1}_B(X - a)) = 0$. Because, $X > a$, it means that $P(B) = 0$, or in other words, $\mathbb{E}(X|\mathcal{G}) > a$, P-a.s. We can show similarly that $\mathbb{E}(X|\mathcal{G}) < b$, P-a.s.

By Lemma 4.33, since ϕ is the supremum of a sequence of affine functions $L_n(x) = a_n x + b_n$, we have $a_n X + b_n \leq \phi(X)$ for each $n = 1, 2, \ldots$, hence by the linearity and positivity of conditional expectation (Exercise 4.13) we obtain

$$a_n \mathbb{E}(X|\mathcal{G}) + b_n \leq \mathbb{E}(\phi(X)|\mathcal{G})$$

for each $n = 1, 2, \ldots$, and taking the supremum over n completes the proof.

□

Applying this to the trivial σ-field $\mathcal{G} = \{\Omega, \varnothing\}$, we have the following corollary.

Corollary 4.35
Suppose the random variable X is integrable, ϕ is convex on an open interval containing the range of X and $\phi(X)$ is also integrable. Then

$$\phi(\mathbb{E}(X)) \leq \mathbb{E}(\phi(X)).$$

The next special case is equally important for the applications we have in mind. It follows from Jensen's inequality by taking $\phi(x) = x^2$.

Corollary 4.36
If X^2 is integrable, then $(\mathbb{E}(X|\mathcal{G}))^2 \leq \mathbb{E}(X^2|\mathcal{G})$.

4.4 The inner product space $L^2(P)$

We turn to some unfinished business: establishing the existence of conditional expectation in the general setting of Definition 4.20. We do this first for square-integrable random variables, that is, random variables X such that $\mathbb{E}(X^2)$ is finite.

We shall identify random variables which are equal to one another P-a.s. Given two random variables X, Y, observe that if $a \in \mathbb{R}$ and both $\mathbb{E}(X^2)$ and $\mathbb{E}(Y^2)$ are finite, then $\mathbb{E}((aX)^2) = a^2 \mathbb{E}(X^2)$ and $\mathbb{E}((X + Y)^2) \leq 2(\mathbb{E}(X^2) + \mathbb{E}(Y^2))$ are also finite. This shows that the collection of such random variables is a vector space. Moreover, by the Schwarz inequality, see Lemma 3.49, $|\mathbb{E}(XY)| \leq \sqrt{\mathbb{E}(X^2)\mathbb{E}(Y^2)}$ is finite too. We introduce some notation to reflect this.

Definition 4.37

We denote by

$$L^2(P) = L^2(\Omega, \mathcal{F}, P)$$

the vector space of all square-integrable random variables on a probability space $(\Omega, \mathcal{F}, P)$. For any $X, Y \in L^2(P)$ we define their **inner product** by

$$\langle X, Y \rangle = \mathbb{E}(XY).$$

Remark 4.38

In abstract texts on functional analysis it is customary to eliminate the non-uniqueness due to identifying random variables equal to one another P-a.s., by considering the vector space of equivalence classes of elements of $L^2(P)$ under the equivalence relation

$$X \sim Y \quad \text{if and only if} \quad X = Y, P\text{-a.s.}$$

We prefer to work directly with functions rather than equivalence classes for the results we require.

We note some immediate properties of the inner product.

(i) The inner product is **linear** in its first argument: given $a, b \in \mathbb{R}$ and $X_1, X_2, Y \in L^2(P)$, we have (by the linearity of expectation)

$$\langle aX_1 + bX_2, Y \rangle = a\langle X_1, Y \rangle + b\langle X_2, Y \rangle.$$

(ii) The inner product is **symmetric**:

$$\langle Y, X \rangle = \mathbb{E}(YX) = \mathbb{E}(XY) = \langle X, Y \rangle.$$

Hence it is also linear in its second argument.

(iii) The inner product is **non-negative**:

$$\langle X, X \rangle = \mathbb{E}(X^2) \geq 0.$$

(iv) $\langle X, X \rangle = 0$ if and only if $X = 0$, P-a.s.; this is so because $\langle X, X \rangle = \mathbb{E}(X^2)$, and $\mathbb{E}(X^2) = 0$ if and only if $X = 0$, P-a.s., see Proposition 1.36.

Since we do not distinguish between random variables equal to one another P-a.s., we interpret this as saying that $\langle X, X \rangle = 0$ means $X = 0$, and with this proviso the last two properties together say that the inner product is **positive definite**.

The inner product induces a notion of 'length', or **norm**, on vectors in $L^2(P)$.

Definition 4.39

For any $X \in L^2(P)$ define the L^2-norm as

$$\|X\|_2 = \sqrt{\langle X, X \rangle} = \sqrt{\mathbb{E}(X^2)}.$$

This should look familiar. For $x = (x_1, \ldots, x_n) \in \mathbb{R}^n$ the Euclidean norm

$$\|x\|_2 = \sqrt{\sum_{i=1}^{n} x_i^2}$$

is related in the same manner to the scalar product

$$\langle x, y \rangle = \sum_{i=1}^{n} x_i y_i.$$

The sum is now replaced by an integral.

The L^2-norm shares the following properties of the Euclidean norm.

(i) For any $X \in L^2(P)$

$$\|X\|_2 \geq 0,$$

with $\|X\|_2 = 0$ if and only $X = 0$, P-a.s.

(ii) For any $a \in \mathbb{R}$ and $X \in L^2(P)$

$$\|aX\|_2 = |a| \, \|X\|_2.$$

(iii) For any $X, Y \in L^2(P)$

$$\|X + Y\|_2 \leq \|X\|_2 + \|Y\|_2.$$

The first two claims are obvious, while the third follows from the Schwarz inequality, using the definition of the norm:

$$\|X + Y\|_2^2 = \mathbb{E}((X + Y)^2) = \mathbb{E}(X^2) + 2\mathbb{E}(XY) + \mathbb{E}(Y^2)$$
$$\leq \|X\|_2^2 + 2\,\|X\|_2\,\|Y\|_2 + \|Y\|_2^2 = (\|X\|_2 + \|Y\|_2)^2.$$

The Schwarz inequality is key to many properties of the inner product space $L^2(P)$. First, since a constant random variable is square-integrable, the Schwarz inequality implies that

$$(\mathbb{E}(|X|))^2 = (\mathbb{E}(1|X|))^2 \leq \|1\|_2^2 \|X\|_2^2 = \mathbb{E}(X^2),$$

so $\mathbb{E}(|X|)$ must be finite if $\mathbb{E}(X^2)$ is. In other words, any square-integrable X is also an integrable random variable, hence $\mathbb{E}(X)$ is well-defined for each $X \in L^2(P)$.

Second, the Schwarz inequality implies continuity of the inner product and L^2-norm.

Definition 4.40
We say that $f : L^2(P) \to \mathbb{R}$ is **norm continuous** if for any $X \in L^2(P)$ and any sequence $X_1, X_2, \ldots \in L^2(P)$

$$\lim_{n\to\infty} \|X_n - X\|_2 = 0 \quad \text{implies} \quad \lim_{n\to\infty} |f(X_n) - f(X)| \to 0.$$

Exercise 4.18 Show that the maps $X \mapsto \langle X, Y \rangle$ and $X \mapsto \|X\|_2$ are norm continuous functions.

For our purposes, the most important property of $L^2(P)$ is its **completeness**. The terminology is borrowed from the real line: recall that $x_1, x_2, \ldots \in \mathbb{R}$ is called a **Cauchy sequence** if $\sup_{m,n\geq k} |x_n - x_m| \to 0$ as $k \to \infty$. The key property that distinguishes $\mathbb{R}$ from $\mathbb{Q}$ is that $\mathbb{R}$ is complete while $\mathbb{Q}$ is not: every Cauchy sequence $x_1, x_2, \ldots \in \mathbb{R}$ has a limit $\lim_{n\to\infty} x_n \in \mathbb{R}$, but this is not the case in $\mathbb{Q}$. For example, take any Cauchy sequence $r_1, r_2, \ldots \in \mathbb{Q}$ of rationals with $\lim_{n\to\infty} r_n = \sqrt{2}$, which is not in $\mathbb{Q}$.

The definition of a Cauchy sequence and the notion of completeness also make sense in $L^2(P)$.

Definition 4.41
We say that $X_1, X_2, \ldots \in L^2(P)$ is a **Cauchy sequence** whenever

$$\sup_{m,n\geq k} \|X_n - X_m\|_2 \to 0 \quad \text{as} \quad k \to \infty.$$

By saying that $L^2(P)$ is **complete** we mean that for every Cauchy sequence $X_1, X_2, \ldots \in L^2(P)$ there is an $X \in L^2(P)$ such that

$$\|X_n - X\|_2 \to 0 \quad \text{as} \quad n \to \infty.$$

Theorem 4.42
$L^2(P)$ *is complete.*

The proof makes essential use of the first Fatou lemma (Lemma 1.41 (i)). We leave the details to the end of the chapter, Section 4.6.

Exercise 4.19 Show that any convergent sequence $X_1, X_2, \ldots \in L^2(P)$ is a Cauchy sequence, that is, show that if $\lim_{n\to\infty} \|X_n - X\|_2 = 0$ for some $X \in L^2(P)$, then $X_1, X_2, \ldots$ is a Cauchy sequence.

Orthogonal projection and conditional expectation in $L^2(P)$

The conditional expectation of $X \in L^2(P)$ with respect to a σ-field $\mathcal{G} \subset \mathcal{F}$ is given in Definition 4.20 as a $\mathcal{G}$-measurable random variable $\mathbb{E}(X \,|\, \mathcal{G})$ such that for all $B \in \mathcal{G}$

$$\mathbb{E}(\mathbf{1}_B \mathbb{E}(X \,|\, \mathcal{G})) = \mathbb{E}(\mathbf{1}_B X).$$

We denote the set of all $\mathcal{G}$-measurable square-integrable random variables by $L^2(\mathcal{G}, P)$, and write $L^2(\mathcal{F}, P)$ instead of $L^2(P)$ when there is some danger of ambiguity. Then $L^2(\mathcal{G}, P)$ is an example of a linear subspace of $L^2(\mathcal{F}, P)$, that is, a subset $L^2(\mathcal{G}, P) \subset L^2(\mathcal{F}, P)$ such that $X, Y \in L^2(\mathcal{G}, P)$ implies $aX + bY \in L^2(\mathcal{G}, P)$ for all $a, b \in \mathbb{R}$. The inner product and norm for any $X, Y \in L^2(\mathcal{G}, P)$ coincide with those in $L^2(\mathcal{F}, P)$ and can be denoted by the same symbols $\langle X, Y \rangle$ and $\|X\|_2$.

Since Theorem 4.42 applies to the family of square-integrable random variables on any probability space, we know that $L^2(\mathcal{G}, P)$ is also complete. It is often useful to state this property slightly differently, using the notion of a closed set.

Definition 4.43
We say that a subset $C \subset L^2(\mathcal{F}, P)$ is **closed** whenever it has the following property: for any sequence $X_1, X_2, \ldots \in C$ and $X \in L^2(\mathcal{F}, P)$

$$\lim_{n \to \infty} \|X_n - X\|_2 = 0 \quad \text{implies} \quad X \in C.$$

Proposition 4.44
For any σ-field $\mathcal{G} \subset \mathcal{F}$, the family $L^2(\mathcal{G}, P)$ of $\mathcal{G}$-measurable square-integrable random variables is a closed subset of $L^2(\mathcal{F}, P)$.

Proof Suppose that $X_1, X_2, \ldots \in L^2(\mathcal{G}, P)$ and $\lim_{n \to \infty} \|X_n - X\|_2 = 0$ for some $X \in L^2(\mathcal{F}, P)$. By Exercise 4.19, it is a Cauchy sequence in $L^2(\mathcal{F}, P)$. Because the norms in $L^2(\mathcal{G}, P)$ and $L^2(\mathcal{F}, P)$ coincide, it follows that $X_1, X_2, \ldots$ is a Cauchy sequence in $L^2(\mathcal{G}, P)$. Because $L^2(\mathcal{G}, P)$ is complete, there is a $Y \in L^2(\mathcal{G}, P)$ such that $\lim_{n \to \infty} \|X_n - Y\|_2 = 0$. To conclude that $X \in L^2(\mathcal{G}, P)$ it remains to show that $X = Y$, P-a.s. This is so because

$$0 \le \|X - Y\|_2 = \|(X - X_n) - (Y - X_n)\|_2 \le \|X - X_n\|_2 + \|Y - X_n\|_2 \to 0$$

as $n \to \infty$, hence $\|X - Y\|_2 = 0$. $\square$

The analogy with the geometric structure of $\mathbb{R}^n$ can be taken further. Using the centered random variables $X_c = X - \mathbb{E}(X)$, $Y_c = Y - \mathbb{E}(Y)$, we can write the variance of X as

$$\mathrm{Var}(X) = \mathbb{E}(X_c^2) = \|X_c\|_2 ,$$

and similarly for Y. Their covariance is given by

$$\text{Cov}(X, Y) = \mathbb{E}(X_c Y_c) = \langle X_c, Y_c \rangle.$$

Thus, if we define the **angle** θ between two random variables X, Y in $L^2(\mathcal{F}, P)$ by setting

$$\cos \theta = \frac{\langle X, Y \rangle}{\|X\|_2 \|Y\|_2}$$

(which makes sense as long as neither X nor Y are 0, P-a.s.), we recover the correlation between non-constant random variables $X, Y \in L^2(\mathcal{F}, P)$ as the angle between the centred random variables X_c, Y_c:

$$\rho_{X,Y} = \frac{\langle X_c, Y_c \rangle}{\|X_c\|_2 \|Y_c\|_2}.$$

In particular, X and Y are uncorrelated if and only if $\langle X_c, Y_c \rangle = 0$.

Clearly, as defined above, in general we have $\cos \theta = 0$ if $\langle X_1, X_2 \rangle = 0$. It seems natural to use this to define orthogonality with respect to the inner product.

Definition 4.45
Whenever random variables $X, Y \in L^2(\mathcal{F}, P)$ satisfy $\langle X, Y \rangle = 0$, we say that they are **orthogonal.**

The next two exercises show how the geometry of the vector space $L^2(\mathcal{F}, P)$ reflects Euclidean geometry, even though $L^2(\mathcal{F}, P)$ is not necessarily finite-dimensional.

Exercise 4.20 Prove the following **Pythagoras theorem** in $L^2(\mathcal{F}, P)$.
If $X, T \in L^2(\mathcal{F}, P)$ *and* $\langle X, Y \rangle = 0$, *then*

$$\|X + Y\|_2^2 = \|X\|_2^2 + \|Y\|_2^2.$$

Exercise 4.21 Prove the following **parallelogram law** in $L^2(\mathcal{F}, P)$.
For any $X, Y \in L^2(\mathcal{F}, P)$

$$\|X + Y\|_2^2 + \|X - Y\|_2^2 = 2\|X\|_2^2 + 2\|Y\|_2^2.$$

Exercise 4.22 Show that $X_n(\omega) = \sin n\omega$ and $Y_m(\omega) = \cos m\omega$ are orthogonal in $L^2[-\pi, \pi]$ for any $m, n = 1, 2, \ldots$.

More generally, if $X_1, X_2, \ldots, X_n \in L^2(\mathcal{F}, P)$ are mutually orthogonal, then the linearity of the inner product yields

$$\left\langle \sum_{i=1}^{n} X_i, \sum_{j=1}^{n} X_j \right\rangle = \sum_{i,j=1}^{n} \langle X_i, X_j \rangle = \sum_{i=1}^{n} \langle X_i, X_i \rangle.$$

so that

$$\left\| \sum_{i=1}^{n} X_i \right\|_2^2 = \sum_{i=1}^{n} \|X_i\|_2^2.$$

(With $n = 2$ we recover the Pythagoras theorem.)

In $\mathbb{R}^3$ the nearest point to (x, y, z) in the (x, y)-plane is its orthogonal projection $(x, y, 0)$. We can write $(x, y, z) = (x, y, 0) + (0, 0, z)$ and note that the vector $(0, 0, z)$ is orthogonal to $(x, y, 0)$, as their scalar product is 0.

We wish to define orthogonal projections in $L^2(\mathcal{F}, P)$ similarly, using the inner product $\langle X, Y \rangle$. Suppose that M is a closed linear subspace in $L^2(\mathcal{F}, P)$; that is, M is a closed subset of $L^2(\mathcal{F}, P)$ such that $aX + bY \in M$ for any $X, Y \in M$ and $a, b \in \mathbb{R}$. First we introduce the **nearest point** in M to an $X \in L^2(\mathcal{F}, P)$. It is by definition the random variable $Y \in M$ whose existence and uniqueness is asserted in the next theorem.

Theorem 4.46 (nearest point)
Let M be a closed linear subspace in $L^2(\mathcal{F}, P)$. For any $X \in L^2(\mathcal{F}, P)$ there is a $Y \in M$ such that

$$\|X - Y\|_2 = \inf \{\|X - Z\|_2 : Z \in M\}.$$

Such a random variable Y is unique to within equality P-a.s.

The proof is again deferred to the end of the chapter, Section 4.6.

Suppose that $X \in L^2(\mathcal{F}, P)$ and let Y be its nearest point in M in the sense of Theorem 4.46. We claim that $X - Y$ is orthogonal to every $Z \in M$. Indeed, for any $c \in \mathbb{R}$ we have $Y + cZ \in M$, hence

$$\|X - Y\|_2 \leq \|X - (Y + cZ)\|_2^2 = \|X - Y\|_2^2 - 2c\langle X - Y, Z \rangle + c^2 \|Z\|_2^2.$$

It follows that $2c\langle X - Y, Z \rangle \leq c^2 \|Z\|_2^2$ for any $c \in \mathbb{R}$. As a result, $-c \|Z\|_2^2 \leq 2\langle X - Y, Z \rangle \leq c \|Z\|_2^2$ for any $c > 0$, which implies that $\langle X - Y, Z \rangle = 0$, proving that $X - Y$ and Z are orthogonal.

The converse is easy to check.

Exercise 4.23 Let M be a closed linear subspace in $L^2(\mathcal{F}, P)$. Show that if $Y \in M$ satisfies $\langle X - Y, Z \rangle = 0$ for all $Z \in M$, then

$$\|X - Y\|_2 = \inf \{ \|X - Z\|_2 : Z \in M \}.$$

Because of these properties, for any $X \in L^2(\mathcal{F}, P)$ its nearest point in M is also called the **orthogonal projection** of X onto M.

We already know that $L^2(\mathcal{G}, P)$ is a closed linear subspace in $L^2(\mathcal{F}, P)$. This makes it possible to relate orthogonal projection onto $L^2(\mathcal{G}, P)$ to conditional expectation.

Proposition 4.47
For any σ-field $\mathcal{G} \subset \mathcal{F}$ and any $X \in L^2(\mathcal{F}, P)$, the orthogonal projection of X onto $L^2(\mathcal{G}, P)$ is P-a.s. equal to the conditional expectation $\mathbb{E}(X \mid \mathcal{G})$.

Proof Let Y be the orthogonal projection of X onto $L^2(\mathcal{G}, P)$. Since $Y \in L^2(\mathcal{G}, P)$, it is $\mathcal{G}$-measurable. Moreover, for any $B \in \mathcal{G}$ we have $\mathbf{1}_B \in L^2(\mathcal{G}, P)$, so $X - Y$ and $\mathbf{1}_B$ are orthogonal,

$$0 = \langle \mathbf{1}_B, X - Y \rangle = \mathbb{E}(\mathbf{1}_B X) - \mathbb{E}(\mathbf{1}_B Y),$$

which means that

$$\mathbb{E}(\mathbf{1}_B Y) = \mathbb{E}(\mathbf{1}_B X) = \mathbb{E}(\mathbf{1}_B \mathbb{E}(X \mid \mathcal{G})).$$

We have shown that $Y = \mathbb{E}(X \mid \mathcal{G})$, P-a.s.   □

Because we have established the existence and uniqueness of the orthogonal projection, this immediately gives the existence and uniqueness (to within equality P-a.s.) of the conditional expectation $\mathbb{E}(X \mid \mathcal{G})$ for any square-integrable random variable X and any σ-field $\mathcal{G} \subset \mathcal{F}$. For many applications in finance this will suffice.

4.5 Existence of $\mathbb{E}(X \mid \mathcal{G})$ for integrable X

In this section we construct $\mathbb{E}(X \mid \mathcal{G})$ for any integrable random variable X and σ-field $\mathcal{G} \subset \mathcal{F}$. The next result is a vital stepping stone in this task.

We observed in Exercise 4.18 that, for a fixed $Y \in L^2(P)$, the linear map on $L^2(P)$ given by $X \mapsto \langle X, Y \rangle$ is norm continuous. Remarkably, all continuous linear maps from $L^2(P)$ to $\mathbb{R}$ have this form.

Theorem 4.48

If $L : L^2(P) \to \mathbb{R}$ is linear and norm continuous, then there exists (uniquely to within equality P-a.s.) a $Y \in L^2(P)$ such that for all $X \in L^2(P)$

$$L(X) = \langle X, Y \rangle = \mathbb{E}(XY).$$

Proof Since L is linear and norm continuous,

$$M = \{X \in L^2(P) : L(X) = 0\}$$

is a closed linear subspace in $L^2(P)$. If $L(X) = 0$ for all $X \in L^2(P)$, then we take $Y = 0$. Otherwise, there is an $X \in L^2(P)$ such that $L(X) \neq 0$. Let Z be the orthogonal projection of X onto M. It follows that $X \neq Z$ and $X - Z$ is orthogonal to every random variable in M. We put

$$E = \frac{X - Z}{\|X - Z\|_2}$$

and

$$U = L(X)E - L(E)X.$$

Then $L(U) = L(X)L(E) - L(E)L(X) = 0$, so $U \in M$. As a result,

$$0 = \langle U, E \rangle = L(X) - \langle X, L(E)E \rangle.$$

Hence $Y = L(E)E$ satisfies $L(X) = \langle X, Y \rangle$ for all $X \in L^2(P)$. This proves the existence part.

To prove uniqueness, suppose that $V \in L^2(P)$ satisfies $\langle X, Y \rangle = \langle X, V \rangle$ for all $X \in L^2(P)$. Then $\langle X, Y - V \rangle = 0$ for all $X \in L^2(P)$. Apply this with $X = Y - V$. Then $\langle Y - V, Y - V \rangle = \mathbb{E}((Y - V)^2) = 0$, hence $Y = V$, P-a.s. by Proposition 1.36. $\qquad\square$

The set of all integrable random variables on a given probability space is a vector space due to the linearity of expectation. We continue to identify X and Y if they are equal to one another P-a.s., and define a natural norm on this vector space.

Definition 4.49

Let $(\Omega, \mathcal{F}, P)$ be a probability space. We denote by $L^1(P) = L^1(\Omega, \mathcal{F}, P)$ the vector space consisting all integrable random variables, and define

$$\|X\|_1 = \mathbb{E}(|X|)$$

for any $X \in L^1(P)$. We say that $\|X\|_1$ is the L^1-**norm** of X.

Like the L^2-norm in the previous section, the L^1-norm satisfies the following conditions.

(i) For any $X \in L^1(P)$

$$\|X\|_1 \geq 0,$$

with $\|X\|_1 = 0$ if and only if $X = 0$, *P*-a.s.

(ii) For any $a \in \mathbb{R}$ and $X \in L^1(P)$

$$\|aX\|_1 = |a|\,\|X\|_1\,.$$

(iii) For any $X, Y \in L^1(P)$

$$\|X + Y\|_1 \leq \|X\|_1 + \|Y\|_1\,.$$

The first two properties are obvious, while the last one follows by applying expectation to both sides of the inequality $|X + Y| \leq |X| + |Y|$.

In the same manner as for the L^2-norm, we can consider Cauchy sequences in the L^1-norm, that is, sequences $X_1, X_2, \ldots \in L^1(P)$ such that

$$\sup_{m,n \geq k} \|X_n - X_m\|_1 \to 0 \quad \text{as} \quad k \to \infty,$$

and define completeness of $L^1(P)$ by the condition that every Cauchy sequence $X_1, X_2, \ldots \in L^1(P)$ should converge to some $X \in L^1(P)$, that is,

$$\|X_n - X\|_1 \to 0 \quad \text{as} \quad n \to \infty.$$

Theorem 4.50

$L^1(P)$ *is complete.*

The proof is very similar to that of Theorem 4.42 and can be found in Section 4.6.

Even though $L^1(P)$ and $L^2(P)$ have some similar features such as completeness, the L^1-norm does not share the geometric properties of the L^2-norm, as the next exercise confirms.

Exercise 4.24 Show that the parallelogram law stated in Exercise 4.21 fails for the L^1-norm, by considering the random variables $X(\omega) = \omega$ and $Y(\omega) = 1 - \omega$ defined on the probability space $[0, 1]$ with Borel sets and Lebesgue measure. Explain why this means that the L^1-norm is not induced by an inner product.

To compensate for the lack of an inner product in $L^1(P)$ we shall use a result that comes close to representing a particular linear map on $L^1(P)$ in a manner resembling the representation in Theorem 4.48 of any norm continuous linear map on $L^2(P)$ by the inner product. To introduce this result, we need the following definition.

Definition 4.51
Given measures μ, ν defined on the same σ-field $\mathcal{F}$ on Ω, we write $\nu \ll \mu$ and say that ν is **absolutely continuous** with respect to μ if for any $A \in \mathcal{F}$

$$\mu(A) = 0 \quad \text{implies} \quad \nu(A) = 0.$$

Example 4.52
Any random variable X with continuous distribution provides an example. In that case, for any Borel set $A \in \mathcal{B}(\mathbb{R})$ we have $P_X(A) = \int_A f_X \, dm$, where f_X is the density of X and m is Lebesgue measure. Then $P_X \ll m$, since $m(A) = 0$ implies $P_X(A) = \int_{\mathbb{R}} 1_A f_X \, dm = 0$, as follows from Exercise 1.30.

Example 4.53
At the other extreme we may consider Lebesgue measure m and the Dirac measure δ_a for any $a \in \mathbb{R}$, defined in Example 1.12 and restricted to the Borel sets. We have $m(\{a\}) = 0$ while $\delta_a(\{a\}) = 1$, so δ_a is not absolutely continuous with respect to m. On the other hand, $m(\mathbb{R} \setminus \{a\}) = \infty$ while $\delta_a(\mathbb{R} \setminus \{a\}) = 0$, so m is not absolutely continuous with respect to δ_a either.

If $Z \in L^1(P)$ is a non-negative random variable such that $\mathbb{E}(Z) = 1$, then $Q(A) = \int_A Z \, dP$ for each $A \in \mathcal{F}$ defines a probability measure Q on the same σ-field $\mathcal{F}$ as P. It follows that $Q \ll P$. The following theorem shows that the converse is also true.

Theorem 4.54 (Radon–Nikodym)
If P, Q are probability measures defined on the same σ-field $\mathcal{F}$ on Ω and such that $Q \ll P$, then there exists a random variable $Z \in L^1(P)$ such that for each $A \in \mathcal{F}$

$$Q(A) = \int_A Z \, dP.$$

The proof of this theorem, based on a brilliant argument due to John von Neumann, is given in Section 4.6.

Exercise 4.25 Under the assumptions of Theorem 4.54, show that the expectation of any random variable $X \in L^1(Q)$ with respect to Q can be written as

$$\mathbb{E}_Q(X) = \mathbb{E}_P(XZ). \qquad (4.12)$$

The right-hand side of (4.12) resembles the inner product of X and Z. (We cannot write it as $\langle X, Z \rangle$ unless we know, in addition, that $X, Z \in L^2(P)$.) This is the result which compensates for the lack of an inner product behind the L^1-norm as alluded above. It enables us to establish the existence of conditional expectation for any random variable in $L^1(P)$.

Proposition 4.55
For any σ-field $\mathcal{G} \subset \mathcal{F}$ and any random variable $X \in L^1(\mathcal{F}, P)$, the conditional expectation $\mathbb{E}(X|\mathcal{G})$ exists and is unique to within equality P-a.s.

Proof First suppose that X is non-negative and $\mathbb{E}(X) = 1$. The probability measure Q defined on the σ-field $\mathcal{G}$ as

$$Q(A) = \mathbb{E}(\mathbf{1}_A X) \quad \text{for each } A \in \mathcal{G}$$

is absolutely continuous with respect to P (to be precise, with respect to the restriction of P to the σ-field $\mathcal{G}$, denoted here by the same symbol P by a slight abuse of notation). By the Radon–Nikodym theorem, we know that there is a random variable $Z \in L^1(\mathcal{G}, P)$ such that

$$Q(A) = \mathbb{E}(\mathbf{1}_A Z) \quad \text{for each } A \in \mathcal{G}.$$

We therefore have

$$\mathbb{E}(\mathbf{1}_A X) = \mathbb{E}(\mathbf{1}_A Z) \quad \text{for each } A \in \mathcal{G}.$$

If $X \in L^1(\mathcal{F}, P)$ is non-negative but $\mathbb{E}(X)$ is not necessarily equal to 1, then we can apply the above to $\bar{X} = \frac{X}{\mathbb{E}(X)}$ so that $\mathbb{E}(\bar{X}) = 1$, obtain $\bar{Z} \in L^1(\mathcal{G}, P)$ for $\bar{X}$ as above, and put $Z = \mathbb{E}(X)\bar{Z}$. This works when $\mathbb{E}(X) > 0$. If $\mathbb{E}(X) = 0$, we simply take $Z = 0$. Finally, for an arbitrary $X \in L^1(\mathcal{F}, P)$ we write $X = X^+ - X^-$, where $X^+, X^- \in L^1(\mathcal{F}, P)$ are non-negative random variables, obtain Z^+ and Z^- for X^+ and, respectively, X^- as above, and take $Z = Z^+ - Z^-$.

This enables us to conclude that for any $X \in L^1(\mathcal{F}, P)$ there is a random variable $Z \in L^1(\mathcal{G}, P)$ such that

$$\mathbb{E}(\mathbf{1}_A X) = \mathbb{E}(\mathbf{1}_A Z) \quad \text{for each } A \in \mathcal{G}.$$

It follows from Definition 4.20 that $Z = \mathbb{E}(X \mid \mathcal{G})$, P-a.s., which proves the existence of conditional expectation as well as its uniqueness to within equality P-a.s. $\qquad\square$

The Radon–Nikodym theorem has much wider application, of course. If $Q \ll P$, we refer to $Z \geq 0$ such that $Q(A) = \int_A Z\,dP$ for each $A \in \mathcal{F}$ as the **Radon–Nikodym derivative** (often also referred to as the density) of Q with respect to P, and write $Z = \frac{dQ}{dP}$. In finance, the principal application occurs when the probabilities P, Q have the same collections of sets of measure 0, so that $Q \ll P$ and $P \ll Q$. We then write $P \sim Q$ and say that P and Q are **equivalent** probabilities. An important application of this can be found, for example, in the fundamental theorem of asset pricing, asserting that the lack of arbitrage is equivalent to the existence of a risk neutral probability, see [DMFM] and [BSM].

Some elementary relationships between Radon–Nikodym derivatives appear in the next exercise.

Exercise 4.26 Suppose that P, Q, R are probabilities defined on the same σ-field $\mathcal{F}$. Verify the following conditions.

(1) If $Q \ll P$, $R \ll P$ and $\lambda \in (0, 1)$, then $\lambda Q + (1 - \lambda)R \ll P$ and

$$\frac{d(\lambda Q + (1 - \lambda)R)}{dP} = \lambda \frac{dQ}{dP} + (1 - \lambda)\frac{dR}{dP}.$$

(2) If $Q \ll P$ and $R \ll Q$, then $R \ll P$ and

$$\frac{dR}{dP} = \frac{dR}{dQ}\frac{dQ}{dP}.$$

(3) If $P \sim Q$, then

$$\frac{dP}{dQ} = \left(\frac{dQ}{dP}\right)^{-1}.$$

4.6 Proofs

Theorem 4.42

$L^2(P)$ *is complete.*

Proof First, note that if $X_1, X_2, \ldots$ is a Cauchy sequence in $L^2(P)$, then we can find n_1 such that

$$\|X_k - X_l\|_2 \leq \frac{1}{2} \quad \text{whenever } k, l \geq n_1.$$

Next, find $n_2 > n_1$ such that

$$\|X_k - X_l\|_2 \leq \frac{1}{2^2} \quad \text{whenever } k, l \geq n_2,$$

and continue in this fashion to find a sequence of natural numbers $n_1 < n_2 < \cdots$ such that for each $i = 1, 2, \ldots$

$$\|X_k - X_l\|_2 \leq \frac{1}{2^i} \quad \text{whenever } k, l \geq n_i.$$

In particular, for every $i = 1, 2, \ldots$

$$\mathbb{E}\left(\left|X_{n_{i+1}} - X_{n_i}\right|\right) \leq \|X_{n_{i+1}} - X_{n_i}\|_2 \leq \frac{1}{2^i}.$$

This means that, starting with a Cauchy sequence in the L^2-norm, we have a subsequence $X_{n_1}, X_{n_2}, \ldots$ for which

$$\mathbb{E}\left(\left|X_{n_{i+1}} - X_{n_i}\right|\right) \leq \frac{1}{2^i} \text{ for each } i = 1, 2, \ldots .$$

Since $Y_i = \left|X_{n_{i+1}} - X_{n_i}\right|$ is a non-negative $\mathcal{F}$-measurable function on Ω, the monotone convergence theorem, applied to the partial sums $\sum_{i=1}^{n} Y_i$, ensures that

$$\mathbb{E}\left(\sum_{i=1}^{\infty} Y_i\right) = \sum_{i=1}^{\infty} \mathbb{E}(Y_i) \leq 1.$$

This means that P-a.s. the series $\sum_{i=1}^{\infty} \left|X_{n_{i+1}} - X_{n_i}\right|$ converges in $\mathbb{R}$, hence P-a.s. the series $\sum_{i=1}^{\infty} (X_{n_{i+1}} - X_{n_i})$ converges absolutely, and so, P-a.s., it converges in $\mathbb{R}$. We put

$$X = X_{n_1} + \sum_{i=1}^{\infty} (X_{n_{i+1}} - X_{n_i}) = \lim_{i \to \infty} X_{n_i}$$

on the subset of Ω on which $\sum_{i=1}^{\infty} (X_{n_{i+1}} - X_{n_i})$ converges, and $X = 0$ on the subset of P-measure 0 on which it possibly does not converge.

Finally, we must show that X_n also converges to X in L^2-norm. First note that

$$|X_k - X|^2 = \lim_{i \to \infty} \left|X_k - X_{n_i}\right|^2 = \liminf_{i \to \infty} \left|X_k - X_{n_i}\right|^2.$$

So we can apply Fatou's lemma to obtain

$$\|X_k - X\|_2^2 = \mathbb{E}\left(\liminf_{i\to\infty}\left|X_k - X_{n_i}\right|^2\right) \leq \liminf_{i\to\infty}\mathbb{E}\left(\left|X_k - X_{n_i}\right|^2\right)$$

$$= \liminf_{i\to\infty}\left\|X_k - X_{n_i}\right\|_2^2 \to 0 \quad \text{as} \quad k \to \infty,$$

where the last step employs the fact that $X_1, X_2, \ldots$ is a Cauchy sequence in the L^2-norm. $\square$

Theorem 4.46 (nearest point)
Let M be a closed linear subspace in $L^2(\mathcal{F}, P)$. For any $X \in L^2(\mathcal{F}, P)$ there is a $Y \in M$ such that

$$\|X - Y\|_2 = \inf\{\|X - Z\|_2 : Z \in M\}.$$

Such a random variable Y is unique to within equality P-a.s.

Proof   Let

$$\delta = \inf\{\|X - Z\|_2 : Z \in M\}.$$

There is a sequence $Y_1, Y_2, \ldots \in M$ such that $\delta \leq \|X - Y_k\|_2 < \delta + \frac{1}{k}$ for each $k = 1, 2, \ldots$. We will show that the Y_k form a Cauchy sequence in the L^2-norm and then use completeness and the fact that M is closed to obtain $Y \in M$ as a limit of the sequence Y_n.

The parallelogram law (Exercise 4.21), applied to $Y_n - X$ and $Y_m - X$ for any $m, n = 1, 2, \ldots$, provides that

$$\|Y_n + Y_m - 2X\|_2^2 + \|Y_n - Y_m\|_2^2 = 2\|Y_n - X\|_2^2 + 2\|Y_m - X\|_2^2.$$

Now, $\|Y_n - X\|_2^2 \to \delta^2$ and $\|Y_m - X\|_2^2 \to \delta^2$ as $m, n \to \infty$. Moreover, $\|Y_n + Y_m - 2X\|_2^2 \to 4\delta^2$ as $m, n \to \infty$ because $\frac{1}{2}(Y_n + Y_m) \in M$ and

$$2\delta \leq \|Y_n + Y_m - 2X\|_2 \leq \|Y_n - X\|_2 + \|Y_n - X\|_2 \leq 2\delta + \frac{1}{n} + \frac{1}{m}.$$

This means that $\|Y_n - Y_m\|_2^2 \to 0$ as $m, n \to \infty$, showing that $Y_1, Y_2, \ldots$ is a Cauchy sequence. By completeness, the sequence converges in the L^2-norm to a random variable $Y \in L^2(\mathcal{F}, P)$ and, since M is closed, $Y \in M$. Finally, the continuity of the L^2-norm shows that $\|X - Y_k\|_2 \to \|X - Y\|_2$ as $k \to \infty$, and this means that $\|X - Y\|_2 = \delta$.

To see that Y is unique, take any $W \in M$ such that $\|X - W\|_2 = \delta$. Using the parallelogram law with $Y - X$ and $W - X$ we then have

$$\|Y + W - 2X\|_2^2 + \|Y - W\|_2^2 = 2\|Y - X\|_2^2 + 2\|W - X\|_2^2 = 4\delta^2,$$

while, since $\frac{1}{2}(Y + W) \in M$, it follows that $\|Y + W - 2X\|_2^2 \geq 4\delta^2$, so $\|Y - W\|_2^2 = 0$ and therefore $Y = W$, P-a.s. $\square$

Theorem 4.50

$L^1(P)$ is complete.

Proof The argument in the proof of Theorem 4.42, which shows that $L^2(P)$ is complete, can be repeated in the case of $L^1(P)$, with the L^1-norm instead of the L^2-norm and with the squares dropped in the final paragraph. $\qquad\square$

Theorem 4.54 (Radon–Nikodym)

If P, Q are probability measures defined on the same σ-field $\mathcal{F}$ on Ω and such that $Q \ll P$, then there exists a random variable $Z \in L^1(P)$ such that for each $A \in \mathcal{F}$

$$Q(A) = \int_A Z\,dP.$$

Proof Consider a third probability measure defined for each $A \in \mathcal{F}$ as

$$R(A) = \frac{1}{2}Q(A) + \frac{1}{2}P(A).$$

By the Schwarz inequality, see Lemma 3.49, for any $X \in L^2(R)$

$$\left|\mathbb{E}_Q(X)\right| \le \mathbb{E}_Q(|X|) \le 2\mathbb{E}_R(|X|) = 2\mathbb{E}_R(1\,|X|)$$

$$\le 2\sqrt{\mathbb{E}_R(1^2)\mathbb{E}_R(|X|^2)} = 2\sqrt{\mathbb{E}_R(|X|^2)} = 2\,\|X\|_{2,R}\,,$$

where $\|X\|_{2,R}$ denotes the norm in $L^2(R)$. This means that $L : L^2(R) \to \mathbb{R}$ defined as $L(X) = \frac{1}{2}\mathbb{E}_Q(X)$ for each $X \in L^2(R)$ is a norm continuous linear map on $L^2(R)$. Therefore, by Theorem 4.48, there is a $U \in L^2(R)$ such that

$$\frac{1}{2}\mathbb{E}_Q(X) = \mathbb{E}_R(XU) \quad \text{for each } X \in L^2(R).$$

Since $R = \frac{1}{2}Q + \frac{1}{2}P$, this can be written as

$$\mathbb{E}_Q(X(1 - U)) = \mathbb{E}_P(XU) \quad \text{for each } X \in L^2(R). \qquad (4.13)$$

Applying this to $X = \mathbf{1}_A$ for any $A \in \mathcal{F}$ gives $\frac{1}{2}Q(A) = \mathbb{E}_R(\mathbf{1}_A U)$, and since $0 \le \frac{1}{2}Q(A) \le R(A)$, we have

$$0 \le \mathbb{E}_R(\mathbf{1}_A U) \le R(A).$$

Because this holds for any $A \in \mathcal{F}$, it follows that $0 \le U \le 1$, R-a.s. This in turn implies that $0 \le U \le 1$, P-a.s. and therefore also Q-a.s. Moreover, taking $X = \mathbf{1}_{\{U=1\}}$ in (4.13), we get

$$0 = \mathbb{E}_Q(\mathbf{1}_{\{U=1\}}(1 - U)) = \mathbb{E}_P(\mathbf{1}_{\{U=1\}}U) = P(U = 1),$$

and since $Q \ll P$, we also have $Q(U = 1) = 0$. This means that $0 \leq U < 1$, P-a.s. and Q-a.s.

We put $Y_n = 1 + U + U^2 + \cdots + U^n$. For any $A \in \mathcal{F}$, taking $X = 1_A Y_n$, which belongs to $L^2(R)$ because U is bounded R-a.s. and therefore Y_n is bounded R-a.s., we get from (4.13) that

$$\mathbb{E}_Q(1_A(1 - U^{n+1})) = \mathbb{E}_Q(1_A Y_n(1 - U)) = \mathbb{E}_P(1_A Y_n U) = \mathbb{E}_P(1_A(Y_{n+1} - 1)).$$

Since $0 \leq U < 1$, Q-a.s., it follows that $1 - U^{n+1}$ is a Q-a.s. non-decreasing sequence with limit 1. Moreover, since $0 \leq U < 1$, P-a.s., it follows that $Y_{n+1} - 1$ is a P-a.s. non-decreasing sequence, whose limit we denote by Z. By monotone convergence, Theorem 1.31, this gives

$$Q(A) = \mathbb{E}_Q(1_A) = \mathbb{E}_P(1_A Z),$$

completing the proof. $\square$

5

Sequences of random variables

Although financial markets can support only finitely many trades, finite sequences of random variables are hardly sufficient for modelling financial reality. For instance, to model frequent trading we might consider the binomial model with a large but finite number of short steps. However, it would be rather restrictive to place an arbitrary lower bound on the step length. We prefer to consider infinite sequences of random variables (and in due course families of random variables indexed by a continuous time parameter, as in [BSM]). In doing so we need to be aware that convergence questions for random variables are more complex than for a sequence of numbers.

5.1 Sequences in $L^2(P)$

Continuing a theme developed in Chapter 4, we study sequences of square-integrable random variables. The properties of the inner product allow us to construct families of mutually orthogonal random variables, which can play a similar role as an orthogonal basis in a finite-dimensional vector space. Then we move our attention to approximating square-integrable ran-

dom variables on [0, 1] by sequences of continuous functions, a useful result because of the familiar properties of continuous functions.

Orthonormal sequences

Recall from Definition 4.45 that $X, Y \in L^2(P)$ are called orthogonal if
$\langle X, Y \rangle = \mathbb{E}(XY) = 0$. This leads naturally to the notion of an **orthonormal set**, that is, a subset of $L^2(P)$ whose members are pairwise orthogonal
and each has L^2-norm 1. A natural question arises how to approximate
an arbitrary element of $L^2(P)$ by linear combinations of the elements of a
given finite orthonormal set.

Proposition 5.1
*Given $Y \in L^2(P)$ and a finite orthonormal set $\{X_1, X_2, \ldots, X_n\}$ in $L^2(P)$, the
norm $\|Y - \sum_{i=1}^{n} a_i X_i\|_2$ attains its minimum when $a_i = \langle Y, X_i \rangle$ for $i = 1, \ldots, n$.*

Proof By definition, linearity and symmetry of the inner product, and
since the X_i are orthonormal,

$$\left\| Y - \sum_{i=1}^{n} a_i X_i \right\|_2^2 = \left\langle Y - \sum_{i=1}^{n} a_i X_i, Y - \sum_{j=1}^{n} a_j X_j \right\rangle$$

$$= \|Y\|_2^2 - 2 \sum_{i=1}^{n} a_i \langle X_i, Y \rangle + \sum_{i=1}^{n} \sum_{j=1}^{n} a_i a_j \langle X_i, X_j \rangle$$

$$= \|Y\|_2^2 - 2 \sum_{i=1}^{n} a_i \langle X_i, Y \rangle + \sum_{i=1}^{n} a_i^2$$

$$= \|Y\|_2^2 + \sum_{i=1}^{n} [a_i^2 - 2a_i \langle X_i, Y \rangle].$$

Note that for each i

$$[a_i - \langle X_i, Y \rangle]^2 = a_i^2 - 2a_i \langle X_i, Y \rangle + \langle X_i, Y \rangle^2$$

so that in each term of the sum on the right we can replace $a_i^2 - 2a_i \langle X_i, Y \rangle$
by $[a_i - \langle X_i, Y \rangle]^2 - \langle X_i, Y \rangle^2$. In other words

$$\left\| Y - \sum_{i=1}^{n} a_i X_i \right\|_2^2 = \|Y\|_2^2 - \sum_{i=1}^{n} \langle X_i, Y \rangle^2 + \sum_{i=1}^{n} [a_i - \langle X_i, Y \rangle]^2, \qquad (5.1)$$

and the right-hand side attains its minimum if and only if $a_i = \langle X_i, Y \rangle$ for
each i.   □

This choice of coefficients leads to a very useful inequality when we let $n \to \infty$ and consider an **orthonormal sequence**, that is, a sequence $X_1, X_2, \ldots \in L^2(P)$ of random variables with $\|X_i\|_2 = 1$ for all $i = 1, 2, \ldots$ and with $\langle X_i, X_j \rangle = 0$ for all $i, j = 1, 2, \ldots$ such that $i \neq j$.

Corollary 5.2 (Bessel inequality)
Given $Y \in L^2(P)$ and an orthonormal sequence $X_1, X_2, \ldots \in L^2(P)$, we have

$$\sum_{i=1}^{\infty} \langle X_i, Y \rangle^2 \leq \|Y\|_2^2. \tag{5.2}$$

Equality holds precisely when $\sum_{i=1}^{n} \langle X_i, Y \rangle X_i$ converges to Y in L^2-norm, i.e. when $\|Y - \sum_{i=1}^{n} \langle X_i, Y \rangle X_i\|_2 \to 0$ as $n \to \infty$.

Proof Take $X_1, \ldots, X_n$ from the given orthonormal sequence. Putting $a_i = \langle X_i, Y \rangle$ in (5.1), we can see that

$$0 \leq \left\| Y - \sum_{i=1}^{n} \langle X_i, Y \rangle X_i \right\|_2^2 = \|Y\|_2^2 - \sum_{i=1}^{n} \langle X_i, Y \rangle^2.$$

Thus $\|Y\|_2^2$ is an upper bound for the increasing sequence of partial sums $\sum_{i=1}^{n} \langle X_i, Y \rangle^2$, hence also for its limit $\sum_{i=1}^{\infty} \langle X_i, Y \rangle^2$.

The identity

$$\left\| Y - \sum_{i=1}^{n} \langle X_i, Y \rangle X_i \right\|_2^2 = \|Y\|_2^2 - \sum_{i=1}^{n} \langle X_i, Y \rangle^2$$

holds for each n, and so, if the partial sums $\sum_{i=1}^{n} \langle X_i, Y \rangle X_i$ converge to Y in L^2-norm, then

$$0 = \lim_{n \to \infty} \left\| Y - \sum_{i=1}^{n} \langle X_i, Y \rangle X_i \right\|_2^2 = \|Y\|_2^2 - \lim_{n \to \infty} \sum_{i=1}^{n} \langle X_i, Y \rangle^2, \tag{5.3}$$

which shows that $\sum_{i=1}^{\infty} \langle X_i, Y \rangle^2 = \|Y\|_2^2$.

Conversely, if we have equality in (5.2), then the right-hand side of (5.3) is 0, and since the left-hand side is also 0, it means that $\sum_{i=1}^{n} \langle X_i, Y \rangle X_i$ converges to Y in the L^2-norm as $n \to \infty$. □

In the Euclidean space $\mathbb{R}^n$, the standard orthonormal basis $e_1, e_2, \ldots e_n$ provides the representation $x = \sum_{i=1}^{n} x_i e_i$ with $\langle x, e_i \rangle = x_i$, for each $x = (x_1, x_2, \ldots, x_n) \in \mathbb{R}^n$. The basis is maximal in the sense that we cannot add further non-zero vectors to it and retain an orthonormal set. This idea can be used to provide an analogue for a basis in $L^2(P)$.

Definition 5.3

We say that $D \subset L^2(P)$ is a **complete orthonormal set** whenever

$$\langle X, Y \rangle = \begin{cases} 1 & \text{if } X = Y, \ P\text{-a.s.} \\ 0 & \text{otherwise} \end{cases}$$

for any $X, Y \in D$, and $\langle X, Z \rangle = 0$ for all $X \in D$ implies that $Z = 0$, P-a.s.

The case when there is a countable complete orthonormal set $\{E_1, E_2, \ldots\}$ is of particular interest. We then say that $E_1, E_2, \ldots$ is a **complete orthonormal sequence** or **orthonormal basis**.

Given a sequence $a_1, a_2, \ldots \in \mathbb{R}$ such that $\sum_{i=1}^{\infty} a_i^2$ converges, the partial sums $Y_n = \sum_{i=1}^{n} a_i E_i$ satisfy $\|Y_n - Y_m\|_2^2 = \sum_{i=m+1}^{n} a_i^2$ (by Pythagoras), and this becomes arbitrarily small as $m, n \to \infty$. So $Y_1, Y_2, \ldots$ is a Cauchy sequence in the L^2-norm, and therefore by Theorem 4.42 there is a $Y \in L^2(P)$ such that

$$\left\| Y - \sum_{i=1}^{n} a_i E_i \right\|_2 \to 0 \quad \text{as } n \to \infty. \tag{5.4}$$

We define the sum of the infinite series $\sum_{i=1}^{\infty} a_i E_i$ in L^2-norm as $\sum_{i=1}^{\infty} a_i E_i = Y$ (to within equality P-a.s.) whenever (5.4) holds (see also Remark 5.10). In particular, when $a_i = \langle Y, E_i \rangle$, the Bessel inequality (5.2) ensures that $\sum_{i=1}^{\infty} a_i^2 \le \|Y\|_2^2 < \infty$. This yields a representation of Y analogous to that for a basis in a finite-dimensional vector space.

Theorem 5.4

Given a complete orthonormal sequence $E_1, E_2, \ldots \in L^2(P)$, every $Y \in L^2(P)$ satisfies

$$Y = \sum_{i=1}^{\infty} \langle Y, E_i \rangle E_i. \tag{5.5}$$

This is known as the **Fourier representation** of Y. The $\langle Y, E_i \rangle$ are called the **Fourier coefficients** of Y relative to the complete orthonormal sequence $E_1, E_2, \ldots$.

Remark 5.5

The classical representation of functions by their Fourier series uses (5.5) in the case of $\Omega = [-\pi.\pi]$ with Borel sets and uniform probability $P = \frac{1}{2\pi} m_{[-\pi,\pi]}$, where $m_{[-\pi,\pi]}$ is the restriction of Lebesgue measure to $[-\pi, \pi]$, and with the sequence of functions

$$E_0(t) = \frac{1}{\sqrt{2\pi}}, \quad E_{2n-1}(t) = \frac{\cos nt}{\sqrt{\pi}}, \quad E_{2n}(t) = \frac{\sin nt}{\sqrt{\pi}}$$

for each $t \in [-\pi, \pi]$ and $n = 1, 2, \ldots$. We are not going to prove the completeness of this well-known sequence, but focus instead on an example which has direct applications in stochastic calculus.

Proposition 5.6 (Parseval identity)
An orthonormal sequence $E_1, E_2, \ldots \in L^2(P)$ *is complete if and only if for each* $Y \in L^2(P)$

$$\|Y\|_2^2 = \sum_{n=1}^{\infty} \langle Y, E_i \rangle^2. \tag{5.6}$$

Proof If $Y \in L^2(P)$ and $E_1, E_2, \ldots \in L^2(P)$ is a complete orthonormal sequence, then (5.5) holds, so

$$\|Y\|_2^2 = \left\langle \sum_{i=1}^{\infty} \langle Y, E_i \rangle E_i, \sum_{i=1}^{\infty} \langle Y, E_i \rangle E_i \right\rangle = \sum_{i=1}^{\infty} \langle Y, E_i \rangle^2 \langle E_i, E_i \rangle = \sum_{i=1}^{\infty} \langle Y, E_i \rangle^2$$

since $\langle E_i, E_j \rangle = 1$ if $i = j$, and 0 otherwise. Conversely, if $\langle Z, E_i \rangle = 0$ for each $i = 1, 2, \ldots$, then (5.6) implies that $\|Z\|_2^2 = 0$, hence $Z = 0$, P-a.s., so $E_1, E_2, \ldots$ is a complete orthonormal sequence. □

Exercise 5.1 Show that if $E_1, E_2, \ldots \in L^2(P)$ is a complete orthonormal sequence, then for any $X, Y \in L^2(P)$

$$\langle X, Y \rangle = \sum_{i=0}^{\infty} \langle X, E_i \rangle \langle Y, E_i \rangle.$$

Example 5.7
Let $\Omega = [0, 1]$ with Borel sets and Lebesgue measure. A complete orthonormal sequence is given by the **Haar functions**:

$$H_0 = 1,$$
$$H_n = 2^{\frac{j}{2}} 1_{\left(\frac{2k}{2^{j+1}}, \frac{2k+1}{2^{j+1}} \right]} - 2^{\frac{j}{2}} 1_{\left(\frac{2k+1}{2^{j+1}}, \frac{2k+2}{2^{j+1}} \right]} \quad \text{for } n = 1, 2, \ldots,$$

where $j = 0, 1, \ldots$ and $k = 0, 1, \ldots, 2^j - 1$ are such that $n = 2^j + k$. The Haar functions are useful, for example in the construction of the Wiener process, see [SCF].

The Haar functions form a complete orthonormal sequence. The calculations showing that these functions are orthogonal to one another and each has L^2-norm 1 are left as Exercise 5.2 below. We show that this sequence is complete. Suppose that a square-integrable random variable X on $[0, 1]$ is orthogonal to every member of the sequence of Haar functions. We need to show that X is zero m-a.s.

To do this, we first show by induction on $j = 0, 1, \ldots$ that

$$I_{2^j+k} = \int_{\left(\frac{k}{2^j}, \frac{k+1}{2^j}\right]} X \, dm = 0 \quad \text{for each } k = 0, 1, \ldots, 2^j - 1. \tag{5.7}$$

Since X is orthogonal to H_0,

$$0 = \langle X, H_0 \rangle = \int_{(0,1]} X \, dm = I_1,$$

so (5.7) is true for $j = 0$. Now suppose that (5.7) holds for some $j = 0, 1, \ldots$. Then for any $k = 0, 1, \ldots, 2^j - 1$

$$0 = I_{2^j+k} = \int_{\left(\frac{k}{2^j}, \frac{k+1}{2^j}\right]} X \, dm$$

$$= \int_{\left(\frac{2k}{2^{j+1}}, \frac{2k+1}{2^{j+1}}\right]} X \, dm + \int_{\left(\frac{2k+1}{2^{j+1}}, \frac{2k+2}{2^{j+1}}\right]} X \, dm = I_{2^{j+1}+2k} + I_{2^{j+1}+2k+1}$$

and

$$0 = \langle X, H_{2^j+k} \rangle = 2^{\frac{j}{2}} \int_{\left(\frac{2k}{2^{j+1}}, \frac{2k+1}{2^{j+1}}\right]} X \, dm - 2^{\frac{j}{2}} \int_{\left(\frac{2k+1}{2^{j+1}}, \frac{2k+2}{2^{j+1}}\right]} X \, dm$$

$$= 2^{\frac{j}{2}} \left(I_{2^{j+1}+2k} - I_{2^{j+1}+2k+1} \right).$$

It follows that

$$I_{2^{j+1}+2k} = I_{2^{j+1}+2k+1} = 0 \quad \text{for each } k = 0, 1, \ldots, 2^j - 1,$$

completing the induction argument. As a result,

$$\int_{\left(\frac{k}{2^j}, \frac{l}{2^j}\right]} X \, dm = 0$$

for each $j = 0, 1, \ldots$ and each $k, l = 0, 1, \ldots, 2^j$ such that $k \leq l$. By Exercise 3.42 we can conclude that $X = 0$, m-a.s. This shows that the Haar functions form a complete orthonormal sequence.

> **Exercise 5.2**   Verify that the Haar functions H_n for $n = 0, 1, \ldots$ form an orthonormal sequence, as claimed in Example 5.7.

Approximation by continuous functions

From the construction of Lebesgue integral we know that functions that are integrable, and therefore also square-integrable, can be approximated by a sequence of simple functions. Here we consider the special case of square-integrable functions on $\Omega = [0, 1]$, equipped with Borel sets and Lebesgue measure, and show that they can be also be approximated by a sequence of continuous functions.

Lemma 5.8
For every square-integrable function f on $\Omega = [0, 1]$ (with Borel sets and Lebesgue measure) there is a sequence of continuous functions f_n on $[0.1]$ approximating f in the L^2-norm, that is,

$$\|f - f_n\|_2 \to 0 \quad as \quad n \to \infty.$$

Proof It suffices to show that for every square-integrable function f on $[0, 1]$ and for every $\varepsilon > 0$ there is a continuous function g defined on $[0, 1]$ such that $\|f - g\|_2 \le \varepsilon$.

First, take $f(x) = \mathbf{1}_{(a,b)}(x)$ for any $x \in \mathbb{R}$, with $a, b \in \mathbb{R}$ such that $a < b$. For any $\varepsilon > 0$ put

$$g(x) = \frac{x - a + \varepsilon}{\varepsilon} \mathbf{1}_{[a-\varepsilon,a]}(x) + \mathbf{1}_{(a,b)}(x) + \frac{b - x + \varepsilon}{\varepsilon} \mathbf{1}_{[b,b+\varepsilon]}(x)$$

for each $x \in \mathbb{R}$, which defines a continuous function. We denote the restrictions of f and g to $[0, 1]$ by the same symbols f, g. Then

$$\|f - g\|_2^2 = \int_{[0,1]} (f - g)^2 \, dm \le \int_{\mathbb{R}} (f - g)^2 \, dm$$

$$= \int_{[a-\varepsilon,a]} g^2 \, dm + \int_{[b,b+\varepsilon]} g^2 \, dm$$

$$= \int_{a-\varepsilon}^{a} \left(\frac{x - a + \varepsilon}{\varepsilon}\right)^2 dx + \int_{b}^{b+\varepsilon} \left(\frac{b - x + \varepsilon}{\varepsilon}\right)^2 dx = \frac{2}{3}\varepsilon < \varepsilon.$$

Next take $f = \mathbf{1}_A$ for a Borel set $A \subset [0, 1]$, and let $\varepsilon > 0$. By Definition 1.18, there is a countable family of open intervals $J_1, J_2, \ldots$ such that

$A \subset I = \bigcup_{k=1}^{\infty} J_k$ and

$$m(A) \leq m(I) \leq m(A) + \left(\frac{\varepsilon}{3}\right)^2,$$

hence

$$\left\|\mathbf{1}_A - \mathbf{1}_I\right\|_2^2 \leq m(I \setminus A) = m(I) - m(A) \leq \left(\frac{\varepsilon}{3}\right)^2.$$

We can take the J_k to be pairwise disjoint (otherwise any overlapping open intervals in this family can be joined together to form a new countable family of pairwise disjoint open intervals J_k' such that $I = \bigcup_{k=1}^{\infty} J_k'$). Let $I_K = \bigcup_{k=1}^{K} J_k$. Because the series $\sum_{k=1}^{\infty} m(J_k) = m(I) < \infty$ converges, there is a K such that

$$\left\|\mathbf{1}_I - \mathbf{1}_{I_K}\right\|_2^2 = m(I \setminus I_K) = \sum_{k=K+1}^{\infty} m(J_k) \leq \left(\frac{\varepsilon}{3}\right)^2.$$

We already know that for each $k = 1, 2, \ldots, K$ there is a non-negative continuous function g_k such that

$$\left\|\mathbf{1}_{J_k} - g_k\right\|_2 \leq \frac{\varepsilon}{3K}.$$

Putting $g = g_1 + \cdots + g_K$, we have

$$\left\|\mathbf{1}_{I_K} - g\right\|_2 \leq \left\|\mathbf{1}_{J_1} - g_1\right\|_2 + \cdots + \left\|\mathbf{1}_{J_K} - g_K\right\|_2 \leq \frac{\varepsilon}{3}.$$

It follows that

$$\left\|f - g\right\|_2 = \left\|(\mathbf{1}_A - \mathbf{1}_I) + (\mathbf{1}_I - \mathbf{1}_{I_K}) + (\mathbf{1}_{I_K} - g)\right\|_2$$
$$\leq \left\|\mathbf{1}_A - \mathbf{1}_I\right\|_2 + \left\|\mathbf{1}_I - \mathbf{1}_{I_K}\right\|_2 + \left\|\mathbf{1}_{I_K} - g\right\|_2 \leq \varepsilon.$$

Next take any non-negative square-integrable function f on $[0, 1]$. By Proposition 1.28 there is a non-decreasing sequence of non-negative simple functions s_n such that $\lim_{n \to \infty} s_n = f$. It follows that $\lim_{n \to \infty} (f - s_n)^2 = 0$ and $0 \leq f - s_n \leq f$, so by dominated convergence, see Theorem 1.43, we have

$$\|f - s_n\|_2^2 = \int_{[0,1]} (f - s_n)^2 \, dm \to 0 \quad \text{as } n \to \infty.$$

This shows that for any $\varepsilon > 0$ there is a non-negative simple function s such that

$$\|f - s\|_2 \leq \frac{\varepsilon}{2}.$$

Writing the simple function as $s = \sum_{n=1}^{N} a_n \mathbf{1}_{A_n}$ for some $a_n \geq 0$ and some

Borel sets $A_n \subset [0, 1]$, we know that for each $n = 1, 2, \ldots, N$ there is a non-negative continuous function g_n such that

$$\left\| 1_{A_n} - g_n \right\|_2 \leq \frac{\varepsilon}{2N a_n}.$$

Putting $g = g_1 + \cdots + g_N$, we get

$$\begin{aligned} \|s - g\|_2 &= \left\| a_1 \left(1_{A_1} - g_1 \right) + \cdots + a_N \left(1_{A_N} - g_N \right) \right\|_2 \\ &\leq a_1 \left\| \left(1_{A_1} - g_1 \right) \right\|_2 + \cdots + a_N \left\| \left(1_{A_N} - g_N \right) \right\|_2 \\ &\leq a_1 \frac{\varepsilon}{2N a_1} + \cdots + a_N \frac{\varepsilon}{2N a_N} = \frac{\varepsilon}{2}. \end{aligned}$$

It follows that

$$\|f - g\|_2 \leq \|f - s\|_2 + \|s - g\|_2 \leq \frac{\varepsilon}{2} + \frac{\varepsilon}{2} = \varepsilon.$$

Finally, for an arbitrary square-integrable function f on $[0, 1]$, we can write it as $f = f^+ - f^-$, where f^+, f^- are non-negative and square-integrable. Then for any $\varepsilon > 0$ there are non-negative continuous functions g^+, g^- such that

$$\left\| f^+ - g^+ \right\| \leq \frac{\varepsilon}{2}, \quad \left\| f^- - g^- \right\| \leq \frac{\varepsilon}{2},$$

and for $g = g^+ - g^-$ we have

$$\|f - g\|_2 \leq \left\| f^+ - g^+ \right\|_2 + \left\| f^- - g^- \right\|_2 \leq \frac{\varepsilon}{2} + \frac{\varepsilon}{2} = \varepsilon,$$

completing the proof. $\qquad\square$

The following exercise, which can be solved by applying Lemma 5.8, is used when constructing stochastic integrals in [SCF].

Exercise 5.3 Let $a < 0 < 1 < b$ and let f be a Borel measurable function on $[a, b]$ such that $\int_{[a,b]} f^2 \, dm < \infty$. Show that

$$\lim_{h \to 0} \int_{[0,1]} (f(x) - f(x + h))^2 \, dm(x) = 0.$$

Hint. Approximate f by continuous functions in L^2-norm and use the fact that every continuous function on a closed interval is uniformly continuous.

5.2 Modes of convergence for random variables

The partial sums of the Fourier representation of $X \in L^2(P)$ provide an example of a sequence converging to X in L^2-norm. We now explore how the notion of convergence familiar from Euclidean space $\mathbb{R}^n$ may be generalised to define several distinct modes of convergence for sequences of random variables defined on the same probability space. We will describe relationships between four distinct modes of convergence for random variables:

(i) convergence in L^2-norm;
(ii) convergence in L^1-norm;
(iii) convergence P-almost surely;
(iv) convergence in probability.

By way of contrast, for a sequence $x^{(1)}, x^{(2)}, \ldots \in \mathbb{R}^n$ the idea of convergence is quite unambiguous: $x^{(k)} = (x_1^{(k)}, x_2^{(k)}, \ldots, x_n^{(k)})$ converges to $x = (x_1, x_2, \ldots, x_n)$ as $k \to \infty$ if and only if $x_i^{(k)} \to x_i$ for each $i = 1, \ldots, n$; in other words, we have convergence for each coordinate. Convergence in $\mathbb{R}^n$ can also be captured in terms of the norm $\|x\|_2 = \sqrt{\sum_{i=1}^n x_i^2}$ or the norm $\|x\|_1 = \sum_{i=1}^n |x|$ defined for each $x \in \mathbb{R}^n$.

Exercise 5.4 Show that the following conditions are equivalent:

(1) $x_i^{(k)} \to x_i$ as $k \to \infty$ for each $i = 1, \ldots, n$;

(2) $\left\| x^{(k)} - x \right\|_2 = \sqrt{\sum_{i=1}^n (x_i^{(k)} - x_i)^2} \to 0$ as $k \to \infty$;

(3) $\left\| x^{(k)} - x \right\|_1 = \sum_{i=1}^n \left| x_i^{(k)} - x_i \right| \to 0$ as $k \to \infty$.

Since any $x = (x_1, \ldots, x_n) \in \mathbb{R}^n$ can be regarded as a function from $\{1, 2, \ldots, n\}$ to $\mathbb{R}$, assigning x_i to each $i = 1, \ldots, n$, the analogy between the above norms defined on $\mathbb{R}^n$ and the L^2-norm and L^1-norm considered in Chapter 4 is apparent. We now define convergence in these norms for sequences of random variables on a probability space $(\Omega, \mathcal{F}, P)$.

Definition 5.9

We say that X_n converges to X in L^2-**norm** and write $X_n \overset{L^2}{\to} X$ if

$$\|X_n - X\|_2^2 = \mathbb{E}\left((X_n - X)^2 \right) \to 0$$

as $n \to \infty$.

Remark 5.10

In Section 5.1 the sum of a series $\sum_{i=1}^{\infty} a_i E_i$ with $a_i \in \mathbb{E}$ and $E_i \in L^2(P)$ for $i = 1, 2, \ldots$ was defined as a random variable $Y \in L^2(P)$ such that (5.4) holds. It terms of convergence in L^2-norm this simply means that

$$\sum_{i=1}^{n} a_i E_i \xrightarrow{L^2} \sum_{i=1}^{\infty} a_i E_i.$$

Definition 5.11

We say that X_n converges to X in L^1-**norm** and write $X_n \xrightarrow{L^1} X$ if

$$\|X_n - X\|_1 = \mathbb{E}(|X_n - X|) \to 0$$

as $n \to \infty$.

Recall that for any $Z \in L^2(P)$ the Schwarz inequality (Lemma 3.49) implies $[\mathbb{E}(|1Z|)]^2 \le \mathbb{E}(Z^2)$ since $\mathbb{E}(1) = 1$. Hence we have the following inequality between the two norms:

$$\|Z\|_1 \le \|Z\|_2. \tag{5.8}$$

This means that if $\|X_n - X\|_2 \to 0$, then also $\|X_n - X\|_1 \to 0$ as $n \to \infty$, so convergence in L^2-norm implies convergence in L^1-norm. The converse is false in general, as the next example shows.

Example 5.12

For each $n = 1, 2, \ldots$ let $X_n = n \mathbf{1}_{A_n}$, where $P(A_n) = \frac{1}{n\sqrt{n}}$. Then $X_n \xrightarrow{L^1} 0$ since $\mathbb{E}(|X_n|) = nP(A_n) = \frac{1}{\sqrt{n}} \to 0$. But X_n does not converge to 0 in L^2-norm since $\mathbb{E}(X_n^2) = n^2 P(A_n) = \sqrt{n} \to \infty$ as $n \to \infty$.

In further contrast to the situation in $\mathbb{R}^n$, convergence in either of these norms is not the same as 'coordinatewise' convergence. For a sequence of random variables X_n the natural analogue of coordinatewise convergence to a random variable X is pointwise convergence, where $X = \lim_{n\to\infty} X_n$ means that, for every $\omega \in \Omega$, the real numbers $X_n(\omega)$ converge to the real number $X(\omega)$. Recall, however, that random variables are identified if they are equal to one another P-a.s. This leads to the following definition.

Definition 5.13

We say that X_n converges to X **almost surely** and write $X_n \xrightarrow{a.s.} X$ if there is an $A \in \mathcal{F}$ with $P(A) = 0$ such that $X_n(\omega) \to X(\omega)$ as $n \to \infty$ for all $\omega \in \Omega \setminus A$.

Example 5.14
Let $\Omega = [0,1]$ with Borel sets and Lebesgue measure. The sequence $X_n(\omega) = \omega^n$ converges to $X(\omega) = 0$ for all $\omega \in [0,1)$, but not for $\omega = 1$. Since the singleton $\{1\}$ has Lebesgue measure 0, it follows that $X_n \overset{a.s.}{\to} 0$.

One obvious question is whether convergence in L^1-norm or L^2-norm implies convergence almost surely. The following counterexample shows that we cannot always expect this.

Example 5.15
On $\Omega = [0,1]$ with Borel sets and Lebesgue measure, construct $X_1 = \mathbf{1}_{[0,1]}$, $X_2 = \mathbf{1}_{[0,\frac{1}{2})}$, $X_3 = \mathbf{1}_{[\frac{1}{2},1)}$, $X_4 = \mathbf{1}_{[0,\frac{1}{4})}$, $X_5 = \mathbf{1}_{[\frac{1}{4},\frac{1}{2})}$, $X_6 = \mathbf{1}_{[\frac{1}{2},\frac{3}{4})}$, $X_7 = \mathbf{1}_{[\frac{3}{4},1)}$, $X_8 = \mathbf{1}_{[0,\frac{1}{8})}$, and so on. We have $X_n \overset{L^1}{\to} 0$ and $X_n \overset{L^2}{\to} 0$ because $\|X_n\|_1 \leq \|X_n\|_2 \to 0$ since the lengths of the intervals tend to 0. However, for each $\omega \in [0,1)$ there are infinitely many n such that $X_n(\omega) = 1$, so $X_n(\omega)$ does not converge to 0 for any ω in $[0,1)$.

The next example shows that convergence almost surely does not necessarily imply convergence in either norm.

Example 5.16
A sequence converging almost surely but failing to converge in L^1-norm is built on $[0,1]$ with Borel sets and Lebesgue measure by setting $X_n(\omega) = n\mathbf{1}_{[0,\frac{1}{n}]}(\omega)$. Clearly $X_n(\omega) \to 0$ for each $\omega \in (0,1]$ since then $X_n(\omega) = 0$ if n is large enough. Hence $X_n \overset{a.s.}{\to} 0$. On the other hand, $\mathbb{E}(X_n) = 1$ for all n, so X_n fails to converge to 0 in L^1-norm and therefore also in L^2-norm.

We can, however, make progress by imposing additional conditions. For example, the dominated convergence theorem (Theorem 1.43) can now be stated as follows.

Theorem 5.17
If there is a random variable $Y \in L^1(P)$ such that $|X_n| \leq Y$ for all n, and $X_n \overset{a.s.}{\to} X$, then $X \in L^1(P)$ and $X_n \overset{L^1}{\to} X$.

We can characterise convergence almost surely by considering the set of all $\omega \in \Omega$ where, for infinitely many n, the values $X_n(\omega)$ and $X(\omega)$ differ by more than some given $\varepsilon > 0$. To make the notion that some phenomenon occurs infinitely often more precise, observe that Exercise 1.33 suggests an analogue for events of the lim inf of a sequence of real numbers. This motivates the following terminology.

Definition 5.18
Given a sequence $A_1, A_2, \ldots \in \mathcal{F}$ in some σ-field $\mathcal{F}$, define

$$\liminf_{n \to \infty} A_n = \bigcup_{n=1}^{\infty} \bigcap_{m=n}^{\infty} A_m,$$

$$\limsup_{n \to \infty} A_n = \bigcap_{n=1}^{\infty} \bigcup_{m=n}^{\infty} A_m.$$

Note that $\liminf_{n \to \infty} A_n$ and $\limsup_{n \to \infty} A_n$ both belong to $\mathcal{F}$.

We say that ω is in A_n **infinitely often** if $\omega \in \limsup_{n \to \infty} A_n$. For any such ω there are infinitely many n such that $\omega \in A_n$. Similarly, we say that ω is in A_n **eventually** if $\omega \in \liminf_{n \to \infty} A_n$. For any such ω we can find an integer k such that $\omega \in A_n$ for all $n \geq k$.

Our main interest is in $\limsup_{n \to \infty} A_n$. The next exercise applies the second Fatou lemma (Lemma 1.41 (ii)) to a sequence of indicator functions of sets (compare with Exercise 1.33).

Exercise 5.5 Show that for any sequence of events $A_1, A_2, \ldots \in \mathcal{F}$

$$P(\limsup_{n \to \infty} A_n) \geq \limsup_{n \to \infty} P(A_n).$$

Applying de Morgan's laws twice, we obtain

$$\Omega \setminus \left(\limsup_{n \to \infty} A_n \right) = \Omega \setminus \left(\bigcap_{n=1}^{\infty} \bigcup_{m=n}^{\infty} A_m \right)$$

$$= \bigcup_{n=1}^{\infty} \bigcap_{m=n}^{\infty} (\Omega \setminus A_m) = \liminf_{n \to \infty} (\Omega \setminus A_n). \qquad (5.9)$$

The following characterisation of convergence almost surely is a simple application of the definitions and (5.9).

Proposition 5.19

Given an $\varepsilon > 0$ and random variables $X_1, X_2, \ldots$ and X, write $A_{n,\varepsilon} = \{|X_n - X| > \varepsilon\}$ for each $n = 1, 2, \ldots$. Then the following conditions are equivalent:

  (i) $X_n \xrightarrow{a.s.} X$;

  (ii) $P(\limsup_{n \to \infty} A_{n,\varepsilon}) = 0$ *for every $\varepsilon > 0$.*

Proof Suppose (i) holds. Write $Y_n = |X_n - X|$. For each $\omega \in \Omega$ the statement $Y_n(\omega) \to 0$ means that for every $\varepsilon > 0$ we can find $n = n(\varepsilon, \omega)$ such that $|Y_k(\omega)| \leq \varepsilon$ for every $k \geq n$. If $Y_n \xrightarrow{a.s.} 0$, then such n can be found for each ω from a set of probability 1. Hence for any fixed $\varepsilon > 0$ we have $P(\bigcup_{n=1}^{\infty} \bigcap_{k=n}^{\infty} B_{k,\varepsilon}) = 1$, where $B_{k,\varepsilon} = \{|Y_k| \leq \varepsilon\}$. By definition, $\bigcup_{n=1}^{\infty} \bigcap_{k=n}^{\infty} B_{k,\varepsilon} = \liminf_{n \to \infty} B_{n,\varepsilon}$. But $B_{k,\varepsilon} = \Omega \setminus A_{k,\varepsilon}$, so by (5.9) we have $\Omega \setminus (\limsup_{n \to \infty} A_{n,\varepsilon}) = \liminf_{n \to \infty} B_{n,\varepsilon}$. Since $P(\liminf_{n \to \infty} B_{n,\varepsilon}) = 1$, we have $P(\limsup_{n \to \infty} A_{n,\varepsilon}) = 0$. As $\varepsilon > 0$ was arbitrary, (ii) is proved.

That (ii) implies (i) follows immediately by reversing the above steps. $\qquad\square$

In many applications, convergence almost surely of a given sequence of random variables is difficult to verify. However, observe that for fixed $\varepsilon > 0$ and with $A_{k,\varepsilon}$ as in Proposition 5.19, the sets $C_{n,\varepsilon} = \bigcup_{k=n}^{\infty} A_{k,\varepsilon}$ decrease as n increases. So if $X_n \xrightarrow{a.s.} X$, then for all $\varepsilon > 0$,

$$\lim_{n \to \infty} P\left(\bigcup_{k=n}^{\infty} A_{k,\varepsilon}\right) = \lim_{n \to \infty} P(C_{n,\varepsilon}) = P\left(\bigcap_{n=1}^{\infty} C_{n,\varepsilon}\right) = P\left(\limsup_{n \to \infty} A_{n,\varepsilon}\right) = 0.$$

Replacing $\bigcup_{k=n}^{\infty} A_{k,\varepsilon}$ by the smaller set $A_{n,\varepsilon}$ provides the following weaker mode of convergence, which is often easier to verify in practice.

Definition 5.20

We say that a sequence of random variables $X_1, X_2, \ldots$ **converges to X in probability**, and write $X_n \xrightarrow{P} X$, if for each $\varepsilon > 0$

$$P(|X_n - X| > \varepsilon) \to 0 \quad \text{as } n \to \infty.$$

Proposition 5.21

If $X_n \xrightarrow{a.s.} X$, then $X_n \xrightarrow{P} X$.

Proof It is evident that convergence in probability is weaker than convergence almost surely since $A_{n,\varepsilon} \subset \bigcup_{k=n}^{\infty} A_{k,\varepsilon}$. $\qquad\square$

Example 5.15 shows that it is strictly weaker because the X_n satisfy $P(|X_n| > 0) \to 0$ (hence $X_n \overset{P}{\to} 0$), but they fail to converge to 0 almost surely.

Comparison of convergence in probability with convergence in L^2-norm or L^1-norm is established in the next proposition.

Proposition 5.22

If $X_n \overset{L^1}{\to} X$ or $X_n \overset{L^2}{\to} X$, then $X_n \overset{P}{\to} X$.

Proof   Write $Y_n = |X_n - X|$. If $\mathbb{E}(Y_n) \to 0$, then $\varepsilon P(Y_n \geq \varepsilon) \leq \mathbb{E}(Y_n) \to 0$ as $n \to \infty$ for each fixed $\varepsilon > 0$. So convergence in L^1-norm implies that $X_n \overset{P}{\to} X$. Because convergence in L^2-norm implies convergence in L^1-norm, it therefore also implies convergence in probability.   □

The converse of Proposition 5.22 is false, in general. The sequence of random variables defined in Example 5.16 converges to 0 in probability since $P(X_n > 0) = \frac{1}{n}$, but we know that it does not converge to 0 in L^1-norm or in L^2-norm.

Borel–Cantelli lemmas

The following provides a simple method of checking when $\limsup_{n\to\infty} A_n$ is a set of P measure 0.

Lemma 5.23 (first Borel–Cantelli lemma)

If $\sum_{n=1}^{\infty} P(A_n) < \infty$, then

$$P\left(\limsup_{n\to\infty} A_n\right) = 0.$$

Proof   First note that $\limsup_{n\to\infty} A_n \subset \bigcup_{n=k}^{\infty} A_n$, hence for all k

$$P\left(\limsup_{n\to\infty} A_n\right) \leq P\left(\bigcup_{n=k}^{\infty} A_n\right).$$

By subadditivity we have $P\left(\bigcup_{n=k}^{\infty} A_n\right) \leq \sum_{n=k}^{\infty} P(A_n) \to 0$ as $k \to \infty$ since $\sum_{n=1}^{\infty} P(A_n) < \infty$. This completes the proof.   □

Our first application of this lemma gives a partial converse of Proposition 5.21.

Theorem 5.24

If $X_n \overset{P}{\to} X$, then there is a subsequence X_{k_n} such that $X_{k_n} \overset{a.s.}{\to} X$.

Proof We build a sequence A_n of sets encapsulating the undesirable be-haviour of X_n, which from the point of view of convergence occurs when $|X_n - X| > a$ for some real a. First take $a = 1$. Since convergence in proba-bility is given, $P(|X_n - X| > 1) \to 0$ provides k_1 such that for all $n \geq k_1$

$$P(|X_n - X| > 1) \leq 1.$$

Next for $a = \frac{1}{2}$ we find $k_2 > k_1$ such that for all $n \geq k_2$

$$P\left(|X_n - X| > \frac{1}{2}\right) \leq \frac{1}{4}.$$

We continue this process, obtaining an increasing sequence of integers k_n such that

$$P\left(|X_{k_n} - X| > \frac{1}{n}\right) \leq \frac{1}{n^2}.$$

Now put

$$A_n = \left\{|X_{k_n} - X| > \frac{1}{n}\right\}.$$

The series $\sum_{n=1}^{\infty} P(A_n)$ converges, being dominated by $\sum_{n=1}^{\infty} \frac{1}{n^2} < \infty$. So the first Borel–Cantelli lemma yields that $A = \limsup_{n \to \infty} A_n$ has probability zero. By Proposition 5.19 this means that $X_{k_n} \overset{a.s.}{\to} X$ almost surely, since for any given $\varepsilon > 0$ we can always find $n > \frac{1}{\varepsilon}$. □

It is natural to ask what the counterpart to the first Borel–Cantelli lemma should be when the series $\sum_{n=1}^{\infty} P(A_n)$ diverges. The result we now derive lies a little deeper, and requires the A_n to be **independent** events, whereas the first Borel–Cantelli lemma holds for any sequence of events, without restriction. Nonetheless, the two results together give us a typical **0–1 law,** which says that, for a sequence of independent random variables. the prob-ability of 'tail events' (those that involve infinitely many events in the se-quence) is either 0 or 1, but never inbetween.

Lemma 5.25 (second Borel–Cantelli lemma)
If $A_1, A_2, \ldots$ is a sequence of independent events and $\sum_{n=1}^{\infty} P(A_n) = \infty$, then $P(\limsup_{n \to \infty} A_n) = 1$.

Proof To prove that $P(\bigcap_{k=1}^{\infty} \bigcup_{n=k}^{\infty} A_n) = 1$ note that the events $\bigcup_{n=k}^{\infty} A_n$ decrease as k increases, hence

$$\lim_{k \to \infty} P\left(\bigcup_{n=k}^{\infty} A_n\right) = P\left(\bigcap_{k=1}^{\infty} \bigcup_{n=k}^{\infty} A_n\right).$$

Thus it is sufficient to show that $P(\bigcup_{n=k}^{\infty} A_n) = 1$ for each $k = 1, 2, \ldots$.

Now consider $\bigcap_{n=k}^{m}(\Omega \setminus A_n)$ for a fixed $m > k$. By de Morgan's laws we have $\Omega \setminus (\bigcup_{n=k}^{m} A_n) = \bigcap_{n=k}^{m}(\Omega \setminus A_n)$. The events $\Omega \setminus A_1, \Omega \setminus A_2, \ldots$ are also independent, so for $k = 1, 2, \ldots$

$$P\left(\bigcap_{n=k}^{m}(\Omega \setminus A_n)\right) = \prod_{n=k}^{m} P(\Omega \setminus A_n) = \prod_{n=k}^{m}[1 - P(A_n)].$$

For any $x \geq 0$ we know that $1 - x \leq e^{-x}$ (consider the derivative of $e^{-x} + x - 1$), so that

$$\prod_{n=k}^{m}[1 - P(A_n)] \leq \prod_{n=k}^{m} e^{-P(A_n)} = e^{-\sum_{n=k}^{m} P(A_n)}.$$

Now recall that we assume that the series $\sum_{n=1}^{\infty} P(A_n)$ diverges. Hence for any fixed k the partial sums $\sum_{n=k}^{m} P(A_n)$ diverge to ∞ as $m \to \infty$. Thus as $m \to \infty$ the right-hand side of the inequality becomes arbitrarily small.

This proves that

$$1 - P\left(\bigcup_{n=k}^{m} A_n\right) = P\left(\bigcap_{n=k}^{m}(\Omega \setminus A_n)\right) \to 0 \quad \text{as } m \to \infty.$$

Finally, write $B_m = \bigcup_{n=k}^{m} A_n$, which is an increasing sequence and its union is $\bigcup_{m=1}^{\infty} B_m = \bigcup_{n=k}^{\infty} A_n$. Hence

$$P\left(\bigcup_{n=k}^{\infty} A_n\right) = \lim_{m \to \infty} P(B_m) = 1.$$

$\square$

Example 5.26
The independence requirement limits applications of the second Borel–Cantelli lemma, but it cannot be dropped. Consider $A \in \mathcal{F}$ with $P(A) \in (0, 1)$, and let $A_n = A$ for all $n = 1, 2, \ldots$. Then $\sum_{n=1}^{\infty} P(A_n) = \infty$, but $P(\limsup_{n \to \infty} A_n) = P(A) < 1$.

Uniform integrability

We have shown that convergence in probability is strictly the weakest of the four modes of convergence we have studied. To study situations where the implications can be reversed we consider sequences of random variables with an additional property. The next exercise motivates this property.

Exercise 5.6 Let X be a random variable defined on a probability space $(\Omega, \mathcal{F}, P)$. Prove that $X \in L^1(P)$ if and only if for any given $\varepsilon > 0$ we can find a $K > 0$ such that $\int_{\{|X| > K\}} |X| \, dP < \varepsilon$.

We extend this condition from single random variables to families of random variables in $L^1(P)$.

Definition 5.27

$S \subset L^1(P)$ is a **uniformly integrable** family of random variables if for every $\varepsilon > 0$ there is a $K > 0$ such that $\int_{\{|X| > K\}} |X| \, dP < \varepsilon$ for each $X \in S$.

A uniformly integrable family S of random variables is bounded in L^1-norm since, taking $\varepsilon = 1$ in the definition, we can find $K > 0$ such that for all $X \in S$

$$\|X\|_1 = \int_{\{|X| \le K\}} |X| \, dP + \int_{\{|X| > K\}} |X| \, dP \le K + 1.$$

The sequence $X_n = n\mathbf{1}_{[0,\frac{1}{n}]}$ discussed in Example 5.16 is not uniformly integrable. For any $K > 0$ and $n > K$ we have $\int_{\{|X_n| > K\}} |X_n| \, dP = nP([0, \frac{1}{n}]) = 1$. On the other hand, $\|X_n\|_1 = 1$ for all n, so the sequence $X_1, X_2, \ldots$ is bounded in L^1-norm. This shows that boundedness in the L^1-norm does not imply uniform integrability of a family of random variables. However, the stronger condition of boundedness in L^2-norm is sufficient.

Proposition 5.28

If a family S of random variables is bounded in L^2-norm, then it is uniformly integrable.

Proof Given $y \ge K > 0$, we have $y \le \frac{y^2}{K}$. Use this with $y = |X(\omega)|$ for every ω such that $|X(\omega)| > K$. Then

$$\int_{\{|X| > K\}} |X| \, dP < \frac{1}{K} \int_{\{|X| > K\}} |X|^2 \, dP.$$

If there is $C > 0$ such that $\|X\|_2 \le C$ for all $X \in S$, we have $\int_{\{|X| > K\}} |X|^2 \, dP \le \|X\|_2^2 \le C^2$ for all $X \in S$, so the right-hand side above can be made smaller than any given $\varepsilon > 0$ by taking $K > \frac{C^2}{\varepsilon}$. $\qquad\square$

The next exercise exhibits a uniformly integrable sequence in $L^1(P)$ (compare this with the dominated convergence theorem).

Exercise 5.7 Show that if $X_1, X_2, \ldots$ is a sequence of random variables dominated by an integrable random variable $Y > 0$ (that is, $|X_n| \leq Y$, P-a.s. for all n), then the sequence is uniformly integrable.

A particularly useful uniformly integrable family in $L^1(P)$ is the following.

Example 5.29

Suppose that $X \in L^1(P)$ and that

$$S = \{\mathbb{E}(X \mid \mathcal{G}) : \mathcal{G} \subset \mathcal{F} \text{ is a } \sigma\text{-field}\}.$$

By Jensen's inequality with $\phi(x) = |x|$, we have $|\mathbb{E}(X \mid \mathcal{G})| \leq \mathbb{E}(|X| \mid \mathcal{G})$, so

$$
\begin{aligned}
KP(|\mathbb{E}(X \mid \mathcal{G})| > K) &\leq \int_{\{|\mathbb{E}(X \mid \mathcal{G})| > K\}} |\mathbb{E}(X \mid \mathcal{G})| \, dP \\
&\leq \int_{\{|\mathbb{E}(X \mid \mathcal{G})| > K\}} \mathbb{E}(|X| \mid \mathcal{G}) \, dP \\
&= \int_{\{|\mathbb{E}(X \mid \mathcal{G})| > K\}} |X| \, dP \leq \|X\|_1
\end{aligned}
$$

since $\{|\mathbb{E}(X \mid \mathcal{G})| > K\} \in \mathcal{G}$. It follows that

$$P(|\mathbb{E}(X \mid \mathcal{G})| > K) \leq \frac{\|X\|_1}{K}.$$

Moreover, to prove that S is uniformly integrable we only need to show that for every $\varepsilon > 0$ there is a $K > 0$ such that $\int_{\{|\mathbb{E}(X \mid \mathcal{G})| > K\}} |X| \, dP < \varepsilon$ for each σ-field $\mathcal{G} \subset \mathcal{F}$. Suppose that this is not the case. Then there would exist an $\varepsilon > 0$ such that for each $n = 1, 2, \ldots$ one could find a σ-field $\mathcal{G}_n \subset \mathcal{F}$ such that $\int_{A_n} |X| \, dP > \varepsilon$, where $A_n = \{|\mathbb{E}(X \mid \mathcal{G}_n)| > 2^n\}$. We know that $P(A_n) \leq 2^{-n} \|X\|_1$, so $\sum_{n=1}^{\infty} P(A_n) < \infty$. By the first Borel–Cantelli lemma, $P\left(\bigcap_{n=1}^{\infty} \bigcup_{m=n}^{\infty} A_n\right) = 0$. As a result, by the dominated convergence theorem,

$$0 < \varepsilon < \int_{A_n} |X| \, dP \leq \int_{\Omega} |X| \, \mathbf{1}_{\bigcup_{m=n}^{\infty} A_n} \, dP \to \int_{\Omega} |X| \, \mathbf{1}_{\bigcap_{n=1}^{\infty} \bigcup_{m=n}^{\infty} A_n} \, dP = 0,$$

which is a contradiction.

In particular, this shows that for an integrable random variable X and a sequence of σ-fields $\mathcal{F}_1, \mathcal{F}_2, \ldots \subset \mathcal{F}$, the sequence $X_n = \mathbb{E}(X \mid \mathcal{F}_n)$ is uniformly integrable.

For uniformly integrable sequences, convergence in probability implies convergence in L^1-norm.

Theorem 5.30
Let $Y_1, Y_2, \ldots$ be a uniformly integrable sequence such that $Y_n \xrightarrow{P} 0$. Then $\|Y_n\|_1 \to 0$ as $n \to \infty$.

Proof As the sequence is uniformly integrable, given $\varepsilon > 0$ we can find $K > \frac{\varepsilon}{3}$ such that $\int_{\{|Y_n| > K\}} |Y_n| \, dP < \frac{\varepsilon}{3}$. Also, $\lim_{n \to \infty} P(|Y_n| > \alpha) = 0$ for every $\alpha > 0$ since $Y_n \xrightarrow{P} 0$. So we can find $N > 0$ with $P(|Y_n| > \frac{\varepsilon}{3}) < \frac{\varepsilon}{3K}$ if $n \geq N$. For any $n = 1, 2, \ldots$ put

$$A_n = \{|Y_n| > K\}, \quad B_n = \{K \geq |Y_n| > \frac{\varepsilon}{3}\}, \quad C_n = \{|Y_n| \leq \frac{\varepsilon}{3}\}.$$

Then

$$\|Y_n\|_1 = \int_{A_n} |Y_n| \, dP + \int_{B_n} |Y_n| \, dP + \int_{C_n} |Y_n| \, dP$$

$$\leq \frac{\varepsilon}{3} + KP\left(|Y_n| > \frac{\varepsilon}{3}\right) + \frac{\varepsilon}{3} P\left(|Y_n| \leq \frac{\varepsilon}{3}\right)$$

$$\leq \varepsilon$$

for each $n \geq N$. Hence $\|Y_n\|_1 \to 0$ as $n \to \infty$. $\qquad \square$

We note an immediate consequence.

Corollary 5.31
If $X_1, X_2, \ldots$ is a uniformly integrable sequence and $X_n \xrightarrow{a.s.} X$, then $X_n \xrightarrow{L^1} X$.

Example 5.32
Suppose that X is square-integrable and $\mathcal{F}_1 \subset \mathcal{F}_2 \subset \cdots \subset \mathcal{F}$ is an increasing sequence of σ-fields contained in $\mathcal{F}$. Suppose further that $X_n \xrightarrow{a.s.} X$, where $X_n = \mathbb{E}(X \mid \mathcal{F}_n)$ for each $n = 1, 2, \ldots$. Then $X_n \xrightarrow{L^1} X$.

To see this, apply Jensen's inequality with $\phi(x) = x^2$, which shows that for each $n = 1, 2, \ldots$

$$X_n^2 = (\mathbb{E}(X|\mathcal{F}_n))^2 \le \mathbb{E}(X^2|\mathcal{F}_n), \; P\text{-a.s.},$$

so that

$$\mathbb{E}(X_n^2) \le \mathbb{E}(\mathbb{E}(X^2|\mathcal{F}_n)) = \mathbb{E}(X^2).$$

Hence $\|X_n\|_2 \le \|X\|_2$ for all $n = 1, 2, \ldots$, so that the sequence $X_1, X_2, \ldots$ is bounded in L^2-norm, hence it is uniformly integrable by Proposition 5.28. Corollary 5.31 now proves our claim.

5.3 Sequences of i.i.d. random variables

The limit behaviour of independent sequences is of particular interest when all the random variables in the sequence share the same distribution.

Definition 5.33
A sequence $X_1, X_2, \ldots$ of random variables on a probability space $(\Omega, \mathcal{F}, P)$ is **identically distributed** if $F_{X_n}(x) = F_{X_1}(x)$ (that is, $P(X_n \le x) = P(X_1 \le x)$) for all $n = 1, 2, \ldots$ and all $x \in \mathbb{R}$. If, in addition, the random variables are independent, we call it a sequence of **independent identically distributed (i.i.d.)** random variables.

Consider the arithmetic averages $\frac{1}{n} \sum_{i=1}^{n} X_i$ for a sequence of i.i.d. random variables as n tends to ∞. Since the X_i share the same distribution, their expectations are the same, as are their variances. Convergence of these averages in L^2-norm, and hence in probability, follows from the basic properties of expectation and variance.

Theorem 5.34 (weak law of large numbers)
Let $X_1, X_2, \ldots$ be a sequence of i.i.d. random variables with finite expectation m and variance σ^2. Then $\frac{1}{n} \sum_{i=1}^{n} X_i \xrightarrow{L^2} m$, and hence $\frac{1}{n} \sum_{i=1}^{n} X_i \xrightarrow{P} m$ as $n \to \infty$.

Proof Let $S_n = X_1 + \cdots + X_n$ for each $n = 1, 2, \ldots$. First note that $\mathbb{E}(S_n) = nm$ for each $n = 1, 2, \ldots$ by the linearity of expectation. Hence $\mathbb{E}\left(\frac{S_n}{n}\right) = m$ and, by the properties of variance for the sum of independent random variables,

$$\mathbb{E}\left(\left(\frac{S_n}{n} - m\right)^2\right) = \mathrm{Var}\left(\frac{S_n}{n}\right) = \frac{1}{n^2}\mathrm{Var}(S_n)$$

$$= \frac{1}{n^2}\sum_{i=1}^{n}\mathrm{Var}(X_i) = \frac{1}{n^2}\sum_{i=1}^{n}\sigma^2 = \frac{1}{n}\sigma^2 \to 0$$

as $n \to \infty$. This means that $\frac{1}{n}S_n \xrightarrow{L^2} m$. Convergence in probability follows from Proposition 5.22.   □

The law of large numbers provides a mathematical statement of our intuition that the average value over a large number of independent realizations of a random variable X is likely to be close to its expectation $\mathbb{E}(X)$.

Remark 5.35

The weak law of large numbers can be strengthened considerably. According to **Kolmogorov's strong law of large numbers**, for a sequence $X_1, X_2, \ldots$ of i.i.d. random variables the averages $\frac{1}{n}\sum_{i=1}^{n}X_i$ converge almost surely to m if the X_n are integrable. We shall not prove this here,[1] but will focus instead on the Central Limit Theorem.

Constructing an i.i.d. sequence with given distribution

Our aim is to construct i.i.d. sequences of random variables with a given distribution. In applications of probability theory one often pays little attention to the probability space on which such random variables are defined. The main interest is in the distribution of the random variables. In part, this also applies in financial modelling, but here the knowledge of a particular realisation of the sample space may in fact be useful for computer simulations. From this point of view the choice of $\Omega = [0, 1]$ with Borel sets and Lebesgue measure plays a special role since random sampling in this space is provided in many standard computer packages.

The simplest case, developed with binomial tree applications in mind, is a sequence of i.i.d. random variables X_n, each taking just two values, 1 or 0 with equal probabilities. The good news is such a such a sequence can be built with $\Omega = [0, 1]$ as the domain, so that $X_n : [0, 1] \to \mathbb{R}$ for each $n = 1, 2, \ldots$. To this end, for each $n = 1, 2, \ldots$ and for each $\omega \in [0, 1]$ we

---

[1] For details see M. Capiński and E. Kopp, *Measure, Integral and Probability*, 2nd edition, Springer-Verlag 2004.

put

$$X_n(\omega) = \begin{cases} 1 & \text{if } \omega \in \left[0, \frac{1}{2^n}\right) \cup \left[\frac{2}{2^n}, \frac{3}{2^n}\right) \cup \cdots \cup \left[\frac{2^n-2}{2^n}, \frac{2^n-1}{2^n}\right), \\ 0 & \text{otherwise.} \end{cases}$$

It is routine to check that these random variables are independent and have the desired distribution.

In the construction of the Wiener process in [SCF] we need a sequence of i.i.d. random variables uniformly distributed on $[0, 1]$ and defined on $\Omega = [0, 1]$ with Borel sets and Lebesgue measure. Such a sequence can be obtained as follows.

(i) Set up an infinite matrix of independent random variables X_{ij} on $[0, 1]$ so that $m(X_{ij} = 0) = m(X_{ij} = 1) = \frac{1}{2}$ by relabelling the sequence X_n constructed above in the following manner:

$$
\begin{array}{llll}
X_{11} & X_{12} & X_{13} & X_{14} & \cdots & & X_1 & X_2 & X_6 & X_7 & \downarrow \\
X_{21} & X_{22} & X_{23} & & \cdots & & X_3 & X_5 & \swarrow & \nearrow & \swarrow \\
X_{31} & X_{32} & & & \cdots & = & X_4 & \swarrow & \nearrow & & \cdot \\
X_{41} & & & & \cdots & & \downarrow & \nearrow & & & \cdot \\
& \cdots & & & & & \nearrow & & & & \cdot
\end{array}
$$

(ii) Define

$$Z_i = \sum_{j=1}^{\infty} \frac{X_{ij}}{2^j}$$

for each $i = 1, 2, \dots$. The series is convergent for each ω since

$$0 \le \sum_{j=1}^{\infty} \frac{X_{ij}}{2^j} \le \sum_{j=1}^{\infty} \frac{1}{2^j} = 1.$$

It turns out that Z_i is uniformly distributed on $[0, 1]$, that is, $F_{Z_i}(x) = x$ for each $x \in [0, 1]$. Indeed, for any n the sequence $X_{i1}, \dots, X_{in}$ is equal to a specific n-element sequence of 0s and 1s with probability $\frac{1}{2^n}$, so the sum $\sum_{j=1}^{n} \frac{X_{ij}}{2^j}$ is equal to $\frac{k}{2^n}$ with probability $\frac{1}{2^n}$ for each $k = 0, 1, \dots, 2^n - 1$. Given any $x \in [0, 1]$, there are $[2^n x] + 1$ numbers of the form $\frac{k}{2^n}$ in the interval $[0, x]$ (here $[a]$ denotes the integer part of a), so

$$m\left(\sum_{j=1}^{n} \frac{X_{ij}}{2^j} \le x\right) = \frac{[2^n x] + 1}{2^n} \to x \quad \text{as } n \to \infty.$$

Since $A_n = \left\{\sum_{j=1}^{n} \frac{X_{ij}}{2^j} \le x\right\}$ is a decreasing sequence of sets with $\bigcap_{n=1}^{\infty} A_n =$

$\{Z_i \leq x\}$, we therefore have

$$F_{Z_i}(x) = m(Z_i \leq x) = \lim_{n \to \infty} m(A_n) = x.$$

Moreover, the Z_i are independent. We verify that Z_1, Z_2 are independent. Once this is done, routine induction will extend this to the finite collection $Z_1, Z_2, \ldots, Z_N$ for any fixed N, which is all that we need. Note that $Z_{n1} = \sum_{j=1}^{n} \frac{X_{1j}}{2^j}$ and $Z_{n2} = \sum_{j=1}^{n} \frac{X_{2j}}{2^j}$ are independent because so are the random variables $X_{11}, \ldots, X_{1n}, X_{21}, \ldots, X_{2m}$. This implies that for any $A_1, A_2 \in \mathcal{B}(\mathbb{R})$

$$m(Z_{n1} \in A_1, Z_{n2} \in A_2) = m(Z_{n1} \in A_1) m(Z_{n2} \in A_2).$$

We can write the measure of each of these sets as an integral of the indicator function of that set. Now since $Z_{n1} \to Z_1$ and $Z_{n2} \to Z_2$ almost surely, we have $\mathbf{1}_{\{Z_{n1} \in A_1\}} \to \mathbf{1}_{\{Z_1 \in A_1\}}$ and $\mathbf{1}_{\{Z_{n2} \in A_2\}} \to \mathbf{1}_{\{Z_2 \in A_2\}}$ almost surely as $n \to \infty$. It follows by dominated convergence (all indicator functions being bounded by 1) that

$$
\begin{aligned}
m(Z_1 \in A_1, Z_2 \in A_2) &= \lim_{n \to \infty} m(Z_{n1} \in A_1, Z_{n2} \in A_2) \\
&= \lim_{n \to \infty} m(Z_{n1} \in A_1) m(Z_{n2} \in A_2) \\
&= m(Z_1 \in A_1) m(Z_2 \in A_2)
\end{aligned}
$$

for any $A_1, A_2 \in \mathcal{B}(\mathbb{R})$, proving that Z_1, Z_2 are independent.

Remark 5.36

It is possible to associate a sequence of i.i.d. random variables $Z_1, Z_2, \ldots$ defined on $[0, 1]$ with an i.i.d. sequence $Y_1, Y_2, \ldots$ defined on the space $\Omega = [0, 1]^{\mathbb{N}}$ consisting of all functions $\omega : \mathbb{N} \to [0, 1]$ so that the Y_n have the same distribution as the Z_n. To this end we consider $Z = (Z_1, Z_2, \ldots)$ as a function $Z : [0, 1] \to [0, 1]^{\mathbb{N}}$, and equip $[0, 1]^{\mathbb{N}}$ with the σ-field $\mathcal{F}$ consisting of all sets $A \subset [0, 1]^{\mathbb{N}}$ such that $\{Z \in A\} \in \mathcal{B}(\mathbb{R})$ and with probability measure $P : \mathcal{F} \to [0, 1]$ such that $P(A) = m(Z \in A)$. Then $Y_n(\omega) = \omega(n)$, mapping each $\omega \in [0, 1]^{\mathbb{N}}$ into $\omega(n)$, defines a sequence of i.i.d. random variables on $[0, 1]^{\mathbb{N}}$ such that $P_{Y_n} = P_{Z_n}$ for each $n \in \mathbb{N}$.

5.4   Convergence in distribution

Let $X_1, X_2, \ldots$ and X be random variables. We introduce a further notion of convergence concerned with their distributions.

Definition 5.37

A sequence of random variables $X_1, X_2, \ldots$ is said to converge **in distribution** (or **in law**) to a random variable X, written $X_n \Longrightarrow X$, if

$$\lim_{n \to \infty} F_{X_n}(x) = F_X(x)$$

at every **continuity point** x of F_X, that is, at every $x \in \mathbb{R}$ such that

$$\lim_{y \to x} F_X(y) = F_X(x).$$

Let us compare this mode of convergence with those developed earlier. In fact, convergence in distribution is the weakest (that is, easiest to achieve) convergence notion we have so far encountered.

Theorem 5.38

If $X_n \xrightarrow{P} X$, then $X_n \Longrightarrow X$.

Proof   For any $\varepsilon > 0$

$$\{X \le x - \varepsilon\} \subset \{X_n \le x\} \cup \{|X_n - X| > \varepsilon\},$$
$$\{X_n \le x\} \subset \{X \le x + \varepsilon\} \cup \{|X_n - X| > \varepsilon\},$$

so

$$F_X(x - \varepsilon) \le F_{X_n}(x) + P(|X_n - X| > \varepsilon),$$
$$F_{X_n}(x) \le F_X(x + \varepsilon) + P(|X_n - X| > \varepsilon).$$

If $X_n \xrightarrow{P} X$, then $P(|X_n - X| > \varepsilon) \to 0$ as $n \to \infty$. It follows that

$$F_X(x - \varepsilon) \le \liminf_{n \to \infty} F_{X_n}(x) \le \limsup_{n \to \infty} F_{X_n}(x) \le F_X(x + \varepsilon).$$

Suppose that $x \in \mathbb{R}$ is a continuity point of F_X. Then $F_X(x - \varepsilon) \to F_X(x)$ and $F_X(x + \varepsilon) \to F_X(x)$ as $\varepsilon \searrow 0$. As a result,

$$\lim_{n \to \infty} F_{X_n}(x) = F_X(x),$$

proving that $X_n \Longrightarrow X$.   □

The converse of Theorem 5.38 is not true. In fact, convergence in probability does not even make sense if X_n and X are defined on different probability spaces, which is possible since the definition of convergence in distribution makes no direct reference to the underlying probability space.

Example 5.39

Although $\lim_{n\to\infty} P(|X_n - X| > \varepsilon) = 0$ in general makes no sense unless X_n and X are defined on the same probability space, we can arrive at a converse of Theorem 5.38 in a very special (indeed, trivial) case. Suppose that X is constant, that is, $X(\omega) = c$ for all $\omega \in \Omega$. Its distribution function is

$$F_c(x) = \begin{cases} 0 & \text{for } x < c, \\ 1 & \text{for } x \geq c. \end{cases}$$

Now we can show that if $X_n \Longrightarrow c$ and all the X_n are defined on the same probability space, then $X_n \xrightarrow{P} c$.

To see this, fix $\varepsilon > 0$. We have

$$\begin{aligned} P(|X_n - c| > \varepsilon) &\leq P(X_n \leq c - \varepsilon) + P(X_n > c + \varepsilon) \\ &= F_{X_n}(c - \varepsilon) + 1 - F_{X_n}(c + \varepsilon) \\ &\to F_c(c - \varepsilon) + 1 - F_c(c + \varepsilon) = 0 \end{aligned}$$

as $n \to \infty$.

Exercise 5.8 Suppose that $|X_n - Y_n| \xrightarrow{P} 0$ and $Y_n \Longrightarrow Y$. Show that $X_n \Longrightarrow Y$.

Exercise 5.9 Show that if $X_n \Longrightarrow X$, then $-X_n \Longrightarrow -X$.

Exercise 5.10 Show that if $X_n \Longrightarrow X$ and $Y_n \xrightarrow{P} c$, where c is a constant, then $X_n + Y_n \Longrightarrow X + c$.

Since convergence in distribution is the weakest notion of convergence that we have defined, we may hope for convergence theorems that tell us much more about the distribution of the limit random variable than hitherto. The most important limit theorem in probability theory, the Central Limit Theorem (CLT), does this for sequences of independent random variables and highlights the importance of the normal distribution. This is very fortunate, since for normally distributed random variables we have a very simple test for independence: they are independent if and only if they are uncorrelated, see Exercise 3.38.

Example 5.40

We will be concerned solely with the CLT for i.i.d. sequences, although much more general results are known. The classical example of convergence in distribution describes how the distributions of a sequence of binomial random variables, suitably normalised, will approximate the standard normal distribution.

We phrase this in terms of tossing a fair coin arbitrarily many times. After n tosses there are 2^n possible outcomes, consisting of all possible n-tuples of H and T, where H stands 'heads' and T for 'tails'. We denote the set of all such outcomes by Ω_n. We assume that at each toss H and T are equally likely and that successive tosses are independent. By this we mean that the random variables $X_1, \ldots, X_n$ defined on n-tuples $\omega = (\omega_1, \omega_2, \ldots, \omega_n)$ in Ω_n by setting

$$X_i(\omega) = \begin{cases} 1 & \text{if } \omega_i = H, \\ 0 & \text{if } \omega_i = T, \end{cases} \quad \text{for } i = 1, 2, \ldots, n$$

are independent. Let P_n denote the counting measure on all subsets of Ω_n, that is, $P_n(A) = \frac{|A|}{2^n}$, where $|A|$ denotes the number of n-tuples belonging to $A \subset \Omega_n$. The sum $S_n = \sum_{i=1}^n X_i$ (which counts the number of 'heads' in n tosses) has the binomial distribution with parameters n and $p = \frac{1}{2}$; see Example 2.2.

We have $\mathbb{E}(X_i) = \frac{1}{2}$ and $\text{Var}(X_i) = \frac{1}{4}$ for all $i = 1, 2, \ldots, n$, which implies that the proportion of 'heads' $\frac{1}{n}S_n$ has expectation $\frac{1}{2}$ and variance $\frac{1}{4n}$. The weak law of large numbers (see Theorem 5.34) implies that $\frac{1}{n}S_n$ converges to $\frac{1}{2}$ in probability, i.e. for each $\varepsilon > 0$

$$\lim_{n \to \infty} P_n\left(\left|\frac{S_n}{n} - \frac{1}{2}\right| \le \varepsilon\right) = 1.$$

In other words, given $\varepsilon > 0$, the fraction of n-tuples for which the proportion of 'heads' in n tosses of a fair coin differs from $\frac{1}{2}$ by at most ε increases with n, reaching 1 in the limit as $n \to \infty$. This supports our belief that for large n, a sequence of n tosses of a fair coin will, in most instances, yield approximately $\frac{n}{2}$ 'heads'.

However, this leaves open the question of the limiting distribution of the number of 'heads'. The answer will be given by the simplest (and oldest) form of the CLT, known as the **de Moivre–Laplace** theorem, see Corollary 5.53 below.

5.5 Characteristic functions and inversion formula

We revisit characteristic functions, which were introduced in Section 2.4, as these provide the key to finding limit distributions. We begin with a result showing that the distribution of a random variable is determined by its characteristic function.

Theorem 5.41 (inversion formula)
If the distribution function F_X of a random variable X is continuous at $a, b \in \mathbb{R}$, then

$$F_X(b) - F_X(a) = \lim_{T \to \infty} \frac{1}{2\pi} \int_{[-T,T]} \frac{e^{-ita} - e^{-itb}}{it} \phi_X(t) \, dm(t). \qquad (5.10)$$

Random variables X and Y have the same distribution if and only if they have the same characteristic function.

Proof For any $a \le b$

$$\frac{1}{2\pi} \int_{[-T,T]} \frac{e^{-ita} - e^{-itb}}{it} \phi_X(t) \, dt$$

$$= \frac{1}{2\pi} \int_{[-T,T]} \frac{e^{-ita} - e^{-itb}}{it} \left(\int_{\mathbb{R}} e^{itx} \, dP_X(x) \right) dm(t).$$

Since

$$\left| \frac{e^{-ita} - e^{itb}}{it} e^{itx} \right| = \left| \int_a^b e^{itx} dx \right| \le b - a$$

is integrable over $\mathbb{R} \times [-T, T]$ with respect to the product measure $P_X \otimes m$, Fubini's theorem gives

$$\frac{1}{2\pi} \int_{[-T,T]} \frac{e^{-ita} - e^{-itb}}{it} \phi_X(t) \, dt = \frac{1}{2\pi} \int_{\mathbb{R}} \left(\int_{[-T,T]} \frac{e^{-ita} - e^{-itb}}{it} e^{itx} \, dm(t) \right) dP_X(x)$$

$$= \frac{1}{2\pi} \int_{\mathbb{R}} I(x, T) \, dP_X(x),$$

where

$$I(t, x) = \frac{1}{2\pi} \int_{[-T,T]} \frac{e^{-ita} - e^{-itb}}{it} e^{itx} \, dm(t)$$

$$= \frac{1}{2\pi} \int_{-T}^{T} \frac{\sin t(x - a) - \sin t(x - b)}{t} \, dt$$

$$+ \frac{1}{2\pi} \int_{-T}^{T} \frac{\cos t(x - a) - \cos t(x - b)}{it} \, dt.$$

The last integral is equal to 0 because the integrand is an odd function. Substituting $y = t(x - a)$ and $z = t(x - b)$, we obtain

$$I(x, T) = \frac{1}{2\pi} \int_{-T(x-a)}^{T(x-a)} \frac{\sin y}{y} \, dy - \frac{1}{2\pi} \int_{-T(x-b)}^{T(x-b)} \frac{\sin z}{z} \, dz.$$

It is shown in Exercise 5.11 below that

$$\int_{r}^{s} \frac{\sin y}{y} \, dy \to \pi$$

as $s \to \infty$ and $r \to -\infty$. Thus,

$$\lim_{T \to \infty} I(x, T) = \begin{cases} 0 & \text{if } x < a \text{ or } x > b, \\ 1 & \text{if } a < x < b. \end{cases}$$

By dominated convergence, see Exercise 1.36, we have

$$\lim_{T \to \infty} \frac{1}{2\pi} \int_{[-T,T]} \frac{e^{-ita} - e^{itb}}{it} \phi_X(t) \, dm(t) = \lim_{T \to \infty} \int_{\mathbb{R}} I(x, T) \, dP_X(x)$$

$$= \int_{\mathbb{R}} \mathbf{1}_{(a,b)}(x) \, dP_X(x)$$

$$= P_X((a, b))$$

$$= F_X(b) - F_X(a),$$

if a, b are continuity points of F_X, so that $P_X(\{a\}) = P_X(\{b\}) = 0$.

Finally, we show that (5.10) implies uniqueness. Suppose that X and Y have the same characteristic function, $\phi_X = \phi_Y$. If $a, b \in \mathbb{R}$ are continuity points of F_X, we have by (5.10)

$$F_X(b) - F_X(a) = F_Y(b) - F_Y(a).$$

It follows that the continuity points of F_X and of F_Y coincide, and by letting $a \to -\infty$ we obtain $F_X(b) = F_Y(b)$ at all continuity points b of F_X and F_Y. By right-continuity and the fact that the points where continuity fails form an at most countable set, we obtain $F_X = F_Y$. □

Exercise 5.11 Show that

$$\lim_{T \to \infty} \int_0^T \frac{\sin x}{x} dx = \frac{\pi}{2}.$$

Exercise 5.12 Show that if $\int_{\mathbb{R}} |\phi_X(t)| dt < \infty$, then X has a density given by

$$f_X(x) = \frac{1}{2\pi} \int_{\mathbb{R}} e^{-itx} \phi_X(t) \, dm(t).$$

Exercise 5.13 Suppose that X is an integer-valued random variable. Show that for each integer n

$$P(\{X = n\}) = \frac{1}{2\pi} \int_0^{2\pi} e^{-itn} \phi_X(t) dt.$$

5.6   Limit theorems for weak convergence

It is useful to consider convergence in distribution in terms of probability measures defined on the σ-field $\mathcal{B}(\mathbb{R})$ of Borel sets. We called such measures probability distributions in Definition 2.1. A probability distribution P uniquely determines a distribution function $F : \mathbb{R} \to [0, 1]$ by $F(x) = P((-\infty, x])$ for each $x \in \mathbb{R}$. Conversely, if two distribution functions agree, then the corresponding probability measures agree on the collection of all intervals of the form $(-\infty, x]$, where $x \in \mathbb{R}$, and this collection is closed under intersection and generates the σ-field $\mathcal{B}(\mathbb{R})$, so by Lemma 3.58 these measures agree on $\mathcal{B}(\mathbb{R})$. Thus there is a one-to-one correspondence between distribution functions and probability distributions.

Definition 5.42
Given probability measures P_n and P defined on $\mathcal{B}(\mathbb{R})$, we say that P_n **converge weakly** to P and write $P_n \Longrightarrow P$ if

$$\lim_{n \to \infty} P_n((-\infty, x]) = P((-\infty, x])$$

for each $x \in \mathbb{R}$ such that $P(\{x\}) = 0$.

Observe that if P_n and P are the probability distributions of some random variables X_n and X, then $P_n \Longrightarrow P$ is equivalent to $X_n \Longrightarrow X$. That is, in this case weak convergence is the same as convergence in distribution.

Theorem 5.43 (Skorohod representation)

Suppose that P_n and P are probability measures defined on $\mathcal{B}(\mathbb{R})$ such that $P_n \Longrightarrow P$. Then there are random variables X_n and X on the probability space $\Omega = (0, 1)$ (with Borel sets and Lebesgue measure) such that $P_{X_n} = P_n$, $P_X = P$ and $\lim_{n \to \infty} X_n(\omega) = X(\omega)$ for each $\omega \in (0, 1)$.

Proof Let $F(x) = P((-\infty, x])$ and $F_n(x) = P_n((-\infty, x])$ for each $x \in \mathbb{R}$. We put

$$Y(\omega) = \inf\{x \in \mathbb{R} : \omega \le F(x)\},$$
$$Y_n(\omega) = \inf\{x \in \mathbb{R} : \omega \le F_n(x)\}$$

for each $\omega \in (0, 1)$. It follows that

$$m(\{\omega \in (0, 1) : Y(\omega) \le x\}) = m(\{\omega \in (0, 1) : \omega \le F(x)\}) = F(x),$$

so F is the distribution function of Y. Moreover, F_n is the distribution function of Y_n by a similar argument.

Now take any $\omega \in (0, 1)$ and any $\varepsilon > 0$, $\eta > 0$. Let x, y be continuity points of F such that

$$Y(\omega) - \varepsilon < x < Y(\omega) < y < Y(\omega + \eta) + \varepsilon.$$

Then

$$F(x) < \omega < \omega + \eta \le F(y).$$

Since $\lim_{n \to \infty} F_n(x) = F(x)$ and $\lim_{n \to \infty} F_n(y) = F(y)$, we have $F_n(x) < \omega < F_n(y)$, so

$$Y(\omega) - \varepsilon < x < Y_n(\omega) \le y < Y(\omega + \eta) + \varepsilon$$

for any sufficiently large n. It follows that $\lim_{n \to \infty} Y_n(\omega) = Y(\omega)$ whenever Y is continuous at ω.

We put $X_n(\omega) = Y_n(\omega)$ and $X(\omega) = Y(\omega)$ at any continuity point ω of Y and $X_n(\omega) = X(\omega) = 0$ at any discontinuity point ω of Y. Then $\lim_{n \to \infty} X_n(\omega) = X(\omega)$ for every $\omega \in (0, 1)$. The distributions of X_n and X are the same as those of Y_n and Y, respectively, since the Xs differ from the corresponding Ys only on the set of discontinuity points of the non-decreasing function Y, which is at most countable and hence of Lebesgue measure 0. $\qquad\qquad\Box$

Corollary 5.44

*If P_{X_n} converges weakly to P_X, then the characteristic functions of X_n and X
satisfy $\lim_{n \to \infty} \phi_{X_n}(t) = \phi_X(t)$ for each t.*

Proof Take the Skorohod representation Y_n, Y of the measures P_{X_n}, P_X.
Pointwise convergence of Y_n to Y implies that $\phi_{Y_n}(t) = \mathbb{E}(e^{itY_n}) \to \phi_Y(t) = \mathbb{E}(e^{itY})$ as $n \to \infty$ by the dominated convergence theorem. But the distributions of X_n, X are the same as those of Y_n, Y, so the characteristic functions are the same.   □

The following result has many varied applications in analysis and probability.

Theorem 5.45 (Helly selection)

*Let $F_1, F_2, \ldots$ be a sequence of distribution functions of probability measures. Then there exists a subsequence $F_{n_1}, F_{n_2}, \ldots$ and a non-decreasing
right-continuous function F such that $\lim_{k \to \infty} F_{n_k}(x) = F(x)$ at each continuity point x of F.*

Proof Let $q_1, q_2, \ldots$ be a sequence consisting of all rational numbers.
Because the distribution functions have values in $[0, 1]$, there is a subsequence $n_1^1, n_2^1, \ldots$ of the sequence $1, 2, \ldots$ such that the limit
$\lim_{k \to \infty} F_{n_k^1}(q_1) = G(q_1)$ exists. Moreover, there is a subsequence $n_1^2, n_2^2, \ldots$
of the sequence $n_1^1, n_2^1, \ldots$ such that $\lim_{k \to \infty} F_{n_k^2}(q_2) = G(q_2)$ exists, and so
on. Taking $n_k = n_k^k$ for $k = 1, 2, \ldots$, we then have

$$\lim_{k \to \infty} F_{n_k}(q_i) = G(q_i)$$

for every $i = 1, 2, \ldots$. The functions G and

$$F(x) = \inf\{G(q) : x < q, q \in \mathbb{Q}\}$$

are non-decreasing since so are the F_n. For each $x \in \mathbb{R}$ and $\varepsilon > 0$ there
is a $q \in \mathbb{Q}$ such that $x < q$ and $G(q) < F(x) + \varepsilon$. If $x \leq y < q$, then
$F(y) \leq G(q) < F(x) + \varepsilon$. Hence F is right-continuous.

If F is continuous at x, we take $y < x$ such that $F(x) - \varepsilon < F(y)$. We
also take $q, r \in \mathbb{Q}$ such that $y < q < x < r$ and $G(r) < F(x) + \varepsilon$. Since
$F_n(q) \leq F_n(x) \leq F_n(r)$, it follows that

$$F(x) - \varepsilon < F(y) \leq G(q) = \lim_{k \to \infty} F_{n_k}(q) \leq \liminf_{k \to \infty} F_{n_k}(x)$$

$$\leq \limsup_{k \to \infty} F_{n_k}(x) \leq \lim_{k \to \infty} F_{n_k}(r) = G(r) < F(x) + \varepsilon.$$

Because this holds for any $\varepsilon > 0$, we can conclude that $\lim_{k \to \infty} F_{n_k}(x) = F(x)$.   □

Example 5.46

The F in Helly's theorem does not need to be a distribution function. For instance, if $F_n = \mathbf{1}_{[n,\infty)}$, then $\lim_{n\to\infty} F_n(x) = 0$ for each $x \in \mathbb{R}$.

In view of this example, we introduce a condition which ensures that a probability distribution is obtained in the limit.

Definition 5.47

A sequence of probability measures $P_1, P_2, \ldots$ defined on $\mathcal{B}(\mathbb{R})$ is said to be **tight** if for each $\varepsilon > 0$ there exists a finite interval $[-a, a]$ such that $P_n([-a, a]) > 1 - \varepsilon$ for all $n = 1, 2, \ldots$.

Example 5.48

If $P_n = \delta_n$ is the unit mass at $n = 1, 2, \ldots$, then $P_1, P_2, \ldots$ is not a tight sequence.

Theorem 5.49 (Prokhorov)

If a sequence $P_1, P_2, \ldots$ of probability measures on $\mathcal{B}(\mathbb{R})$ is tight, then it has a subsequence converging weakly to a probability measure P on $\mathcal{B}(\mathbb{R})$.

Proof Let $F_n(x) = P_n((-\infty, x])$ for each $x \in \mathbb{R}$. By Helly's theorem, there is a subsequence F_{n_k} converging to a non-decreasing right-continuous function F at each continuity point of F.

We claim that $\lim_{y\to\infty} F(y) = 1$. Take any $\varepsilon > 0$. Tightness ensures that there is an $a > 0$ such that $P([-a, a]) > 1 - \varepsilon$. Then for any continuity point y of F such that $y > a$ we have

$$F_n(y) = P_n((-\infty, y]) > 1 - \varepsilon \quad \text{for all } n = 1, 2, \ldots .$$

Hence, $F(y) = \lim_{k\to\infty} F_{n_k}(y) \geq 1 - \varepsilon$. Because $1 \geq F(y) > 1 - \varepsilon$ for each $\varepsilon > 0$, this proves that $\lim_{y\to\infty} F(y) = 1$. It follows that F is a distribution function, and the corresponding probability measure P on $\mathcal{B}(\mathbb{R})$ satisfies $P_n \Longrightarrow P$. $\qquad\square$

5.7 Central Limit Theorem

Characteristic functions provide a powerful means of studying the distributions of sums of independent random variables. Because of the following important theorem, characteristic functions can be used to study limit distributions.

Theorem 5.50 (continuity theorem)
Let $X_1, X_2, \ldots$ and X be random variables such that $\phi_{X_n}(t) \to \phi_X(t)$ for each $t \in \mathbb{R}$. Then $P_{X_n} \Longrightarrow P_X$.

Proof First we show that the sequence $P_{X_1}, P_{X_2}, \ldots$ is tight. For any $a > 0$

$$P_{X_n}([-2/a, 2/a]) = 1 - P_{X_n}(\{x \in \mathbb{R} : |x| > 2/a\})$$

$$\geq 1 - 2 \int_{\{x \in \mathbb{R}: |x| > 2/a\}} \left(1 - \frac{1}{a\,|x|}\right) dP_{X_n}(x)$$

$$\geq 1 - 2 \int_{\mathbb{R}} \left(1 - \frac{\sin(ax)}{ax}\right) dP_{X_n}(x)$$

$$= 2 \int_{\mathbb{R}} \frac{\sin(ax)}{ax} dP_{X_n}(x) - 1.$$

Using Fubini's theorem, we get

$$\int_{\mathbb{R}} \frac{\sin(ax)}{ax} dP_{X_n}(x) = \frac{1}{2a} \int_{\mathbb{R}} \left(\int_{[-a,a]} e^{itx}\, dm(t)\right) dP_{X_n}(x)$$

$$= \frac{1}{2a} \int_{[-a,a]} \left(\int_{\mathbb{R}} e^{itx}\, dP_{X_n}(x)\right) dm(t)$$

$$= \frac{1}{2a} \int_{[-a,a]} \phi_{X_n}(t)\, dm(t).$$

Since ϕ_X is continuous at 0 and $\phi_X(0) = 1$, for any $\varepsilon > 0$ there is an $a > 0$ such that

$$\left| \frac{1}{2a} \int_{[-a,a]} \phi_X(t)\, dm(t) - 1 \right| \leq \varepsilon.$$

Furthermore, since $\phi_{X_n}(t)$ converges to $\phi_X(t)$ for each t, the dominated convergence theorem (Theorem 1.43) implies that there exists an integer N such that

$$\left| \frac{1}{2a} \int_{[-a,a]} \phi_{X_n}(t)\, dm(t) - 1 \right| \leq 2\varepsilon$$

for all $n \geq N$. It follows that there is an $a > 0$ such that

$$P_{X_n}([-2/a, 2/a]) \geq \frac{1}{a} \int_{[-a,a]} \phi_{X_n}(t)\, dm(t) - 1 \geq 1 - 4\varepsilon$$

for each $n \geq N$. We can ensure by taking a smaller a that this inequality holds for each n, which proves that the sequence $P_{X_1}, P_{X_2}, \ldots$ is tight.

Now suppose that P_{X_n} does not converge weakly to P_X. It means that $F_{X_n}(x)$ does not converge to $F_X(x)$ at some continuity point $x \in \mathbb{R}$ of F_X. It follows that there exist an $\eta > 0$ and a subsequence $n_1, n_2, \ldots$ of the sequence $1, 2, \ldots$ such that

$$\left| F_{X_{n_k}}(x) - F_X(x) \right| > \eta \quad \text{for all } k = 1, 2, \ldots . \tag{5.11}$$

The subsequence $P_{X_{n_1}}, P_{X_{n_2}}, \ldots$ is tight because $P_{X_1}, P_{X_2}, \ldots$ is tight. According to Prokhorov's theorem, there is a subsequence $m_1, m_2, \ldots$ of the sequence $n_1, n_2, \ldots$ such that $P_{X_{m_k}}$ converges weakly to the probability distribution P_Y of some random variable Y. By Corollary 5.44, $\phi_{X_{m_k}}(t) \to \phi_Y(t)$. On the other hand, $\phi_{X_{m_k}}(t) \to \phi_X(t)$ for each $t \in \mathbb{R}$, so this implies $\phi_Y = \phi_X$. By Theorem 5.41, P_X and P_Y must coincide. This shows that $P_{X_{m_k}} \implies P_X$, contradicting (5.11). □

We conclude with a famous version of the Central Limit Theorem (CLT). We will concentrate on i.i.d. sequences, rather than seek to find the most general results. First we need some elementary inequalities.

Lemma 5.51
The following inequalities hold.
  (i) *For any complex numbers z, w such that $|z| \leq 1$ and $|w| \leq 1$ and for any $n = 1, 2, \ldots$*

$$|z^n - w^n| \leq n|z - w|.$$

  (ii) *For any $x \in \mathbb{R}$*

$$\left| e^{ix} - 1 - ix \right| \leq \frac{1}{2}|x|^2.$$

  (iii) *For any $x \in \mathbb{R}$*

$$\left| e^{ix} - 1 - ix - \frac{(ix)^2}{2} \right| \leq \min\left(|x|^2, \frac{1}{6}|x|^3\right).$$

Proof (i) Since

$$z^n - w^n = \left(z^{n-1} + z^{n-2}w + \cdots + zw^{n-2} + w^{n-1}\right)(z - w),$$

it follows that

$$|z^n - w^n| \le \left(|z|^{n-1} + |z|^{n-2}|w| + \cdots + |z||w|^{n-2} + |w|^{n-1}\right)|z - w|$$
$$\le n|z - w|.$$

(ii) We have

$$e^{ix} - 1 - ix = \int_0^x (s - x)e^{is}ds,$$

Estimating the integral gives

$$\left|e^{ix} - 1 - ix\right| = \left|\int_0^x (s - x)e^{is}ds\right| \le \frac{1}{2}|x|^2.$$

(iii) We have

$$e^{ix} - 1 - ix - \frac{(ix)^2}{2} = \frac{1}{2i}\int_0^x (s - x)^2 e^{is}ds.$$

Estimating the integral gives

$$\left|e^{ix} - 1 - ix - \frac{(ix)^2}{2}\right| = \left|\frac{1}{2i}\int_0^x (s - x)^2 e^{is}ds\right| \le \frac{1}{6}|x|^3.$$

Moreover, from (ii)

$$\left|e^{ix} - 1 - ix - \frac{(ix)^2}{2}\right| \le \left|e^{ix} - 1 - ix\right| + \left|\frac{(ix)^2}{2}\right| \le \frac{1}{2}|x^2| + \frac{1}{2}|x^2| = |x|^2,$$

which completes the proof. □

Take a sequence of i.i.d. random variables $X_1, X_2, \ldots$ with finite mean $m = \mathbb{E}(X_1)$ and variance $\sigma^2 = \mathrm{Var}(X_1)$. Let $S_n = X_1 + \cdots + X_n$ and write

$$T_n = \frac{S_n - mn}{\sigma\sqrt{n}}.$$

All T_n have expectation 0 and variance 1.

Theorem 5.52 (Central Limit Theorem)
Let X_n be independent identically distributed random variables with finite expectation and variance. Then $T_n \Longrightarrow T$, where T has the standard normal distribution $N(0, 1)$.

Proof Replacing X_k by $\frac{X_k - m}{\sigma}$ shows that there is no loss of generality in assuming $m = \mathbb{E}(X_k) = 0$ and $\sigma^2 = \mathrm{Var}(X_k) = 1$. Let ϕ denote the characteristic function of X_k (the same for each $k = 1, 2, \ldots$). By Lemma 5.51 (iii), for any $t \in \mathbb{R}$

$$\left| \phi(t) - \left(1 - \frac{t^2}{2} \right) \right| = \left| \mathbb{E} \left(e^{itX_1} - 1 - itX_1 - \frac{(itX_1)^2}{2} \right) \right|$$

$$\leq \mathbb{E} \left(\left| e^{itX_1} - 1 - itX_1 - \frac{(itX_1)^2}{2} \right| \right)$$

$$\leq \mathbb{E} \left(|tX_1|^2 \mathbf{1}_{\{|X_1|^3 > |t|^{-1/2}\}} \right) + \frac{1}{6} \mathbb{E} \left(|tX_1|^3 \mathbf{1}_{\{|X_1|^3 \leq |t|^{-1/2}\}} \right)$$

$$\leq t^2 \mathbb{E} \left(|X_1|^2 \mathbf{1}_{\{|X_1|^3 > |t|^{-1/2}\}} \right) + \frac{1}{6} |t|^{5/2} . \qquad (5.12)$$

Moreover, using Lemma 5.51 (ii) with $x = \frac{it^2}{2}$, we find that for any $t \in \mathbb{R}$

$$\left| e^{-\frac{t^2}{2}} - \left(1 - \frac{t^2}{2} \right) \right| = \left| e^{i\frac{it^2}{2}} - 1 - i\frac{it^2}{2} \right| \leq \frac{1}{2} \left| \frac{it^2}{2} \right|^2 = \frac{|t|^4}{8}. \qquad (5.13)$$

Since

$$\phi_{T_n}(t) = \phi^n \left(\frac{t}{\sqrt{n}} \right),$$

by Lemma 5.51 (i),

$$\left| \phi_{T_n}(t) - e^{-\frac{t^2}{2}} \right| = \left| \phi^n \left(\frac{t}{\sqrt{n}} \right) - \left(e^{-\frac{t^2}{2n}} \right)^n \right|$$

$$\leq n \left| \phi \left(\frac{t}{\sqrt{n}} \right) - e^{-\frac{t^2}{2n}} \right|$$

$$\leq n \left| \phi \left(\frac{t}{\sqrt{n}} \right) - \left(1 - \frac{t^2}{2n} \right) \right| + n \left| e^{-\frac{t^2}{2n}} - \left(1 - \frac{t^2}{2n} \right) \right|,$$

and from (5.12), (5.13) we get

$$n \left| \phi \left(\frac{t}{\sqrt{n}} \right) - \left(1 - \frac{t^2}{2n} \right) \right| \leq n \frac{t^2}{n} \mathbb{E} \left(|X_1|^2 \mathbf{1}_{\{|X_1|^4 > t^{-1/2} n^{1/4}\}} \right) + n \frac{1}{6} \left(\frac{t}{\sqrt{n}} \right)^{5/2}$$

$$= t^2 \mathbb{E} \left(|X_1|^2 \mathbf{1}_{\{|X_1|^6 > t^{-1/2} n^{1/4}\}} \right) + \frac{1}{6} \frac{t^{5/2}}{n^{1/4}}$$

$$\to 0 \quad \text{as } n \to \infty$$

and

$$n \left| e^{-\frac{t^2}{2n}} - \left(1 - \frac{t^2}{2n} \right) \right| \leq n \frac{1}{8} \left(\frac{t}{\sqrt{n}} \right)^4 = \frac{t^4}{8n} \to 0 \quad \text{as } n \to \infty.$$

This shows that $\lim_{n \to \infty} \phi_{T_n}(t) = e^{-\frac{t^2}{2}}$ for each $t \in \mathbb{R}$. By the continuity theorem this means that $T_n \Longrightarrow T$, where T has the standard normal distribution $N(0, 1)$.   □

The following result, which justifies our claims for the limiting behaviour of binomial distributions in Example 1.23 can be deduced from the Central Limit Theorem.

Corollary 5.53 (de Moivre–Laplace theorem)
Let $X_1, X_2, \ldots$ *be i.i.d. random variables with* $P(X_n = 1) = P(X_n = 0) = \frac{1}{2}$ *for each* $n = 1, 2, \ldots$. *Then for each* $a < b$

$$P\left(a < \frac{S_n - n/2}{\sqrt{n}/2} < b\right) \to \frac{1}{\sqrt{2\pi}} \int_a^b e^{-\frac{1}{2}x^2} \, dx \quad as \ n \to \infty.$$

Proof   Note that the expectation and variance of X_n are

$$\mathbb{E}(X_n) = \frac{1}{2}, \quad \mathrm{Var}(X_n) = \frac{1}{4}$$

and apply the Central Limit Theorem, observing that

$$T_n = \frac{S_n - n/2}{\sqrt{n}/2}.$$

□

Exercise 5.14   Use the de Moivre–Laplace theorem to estimate the probability that the number of 'heads' obtained in $n = 10\,000$ tosses of a fair coin lies in $(a, b) = (4900, 5100)$.

Example 5.54
In Example 1.6 stock prices were modelled by $n = 20$ equally likely additive up/down jumps of 0.50 from an initial price 10. This gives the price after n such jumps as

$$Y_n = 10 + 0.5 \sum_{i=1}^n (2X_i - 1) = 10 + S_n - \frac{n}{2} = 10 + \frac{\sqrt{n}}{2} T_n,$$

where $X_1, X_2, \ldots$ are i.i.d. random variables with $P(X_n = 1) = P(X_n = 0) = \frac{1}{2}$.

Since $\mathbb{E}(X_n) = \frac{1}{2}$ and $\mathrm{Var}(X_n) = \frac{1}{4}$, by the CLT we have $T_n \Longrightarrow T$, where T has the standard normal distribution $N(0, 1)$. It means that the distribution of Y_n can be approximated by the normal distribution $N(\mu, \sigma^2)$ with $\mu = 10$ and $\sigma = \frac{\sqrt{n}}{2} = 2.236$ when $n = 20$, as in Example 1.23.

Example 5.55
Consider a sequence of i.i.d. random variables $K_1, K_2, \ldots$ with distribution

$$P(K_n = u) = P(K_n = d) = \frac{1}{2} \quad \text{for } n = 1, 2, \ldots,$$

where $-1 < d < u$. In a binomial model with multiplicative jumps the stock prices at time step n are given by

$$S(n) = S(0)(1 + K_1) \times \cdots \times (1 + K_n)$$

with $S(0) > 0$ being the initial stock price (the spot price); see Example 1.7, where

$$u = 0.05, \quad d = -0.05, \quad S(0) = 10, \quad n = 20. \quad (5.14)$$

We want to understand the limiting distribution of S_n for large n. To this end, take

$$X_n = \ln(1 + K_n)$$

for $n = 1, 2, \ldots$, which form an i.i.d. sequence of random variables. This gives

$$S(n) = S(0)e^{\sum_{i=1}^{n} X_i}.$$

Suppose that

$$\mathbb{E}(X_n) = \frac{m}{n}, \quad \text{Var}(X_n) = \frac{\sigma^2}{n}$$

for some parameters m and $\sigma > 0$ (which can be expressed in terms of u, d). Then, according to the CLT, for

$$T_n = \frac{\sum_{i=1}^{n} X_i - m}{\sigma}$$

we have $T_n \Longrightarrow T$, where T has the standard normal distribution $N(0, 1)$. As a result, $\sum_{i=1}^{n} X_i \Longrightarrow X$, where X has the normal distribution $N(m, \sigma^2)$ with mean m and variance σ^2, and this implies that

$$S(n) \Longrightarrow S,$$

where $\ln S$ has the normal distribution $N(\mu, \sigma^2)$ with $\mu = \ln S(0) + m$.

In other words, the distribution of S is log-normal with parameters μ, σ, see Example 1.24. The numerical values $\mu = 2.2776$ and $\sigma = 0.2238$ in that example have been computed from $u, d, S(0), n$ in (5.14).

Index

Printed in the United States
By Bookmasters